AF606215

Acclaim for *God Above All*

"With profound insight and spiritual richness, this biography of Madre María Félix Torres beautifully captures her unwavering dedication to God's will. Her life of prayer, sacrifice, humility, and leadership in founding the Company of the Savior and Mater Salvatoris schools serves as a powerful testament to the transformative power of faith. Readers will find in Madre María Félix an inspiring model of virtue, apostolic zeal, and trust in God's Providence."

—***Most Reverend Frank J. Caggiano,*** Bishop of Bridgeport

"In reading the story of Madre Félix's life, I found a great spiritual model, mentor, and friend — a saint. God will be greatly glorified by this biography. Madre Félix, who loved consecrated religious life, will be a great intercessor and source of strength for religious sisters and superiors and a model for foundresses of religious communities yet to be given to the Church by God in the years to come."

—***Mother Agnes Mary Donovan, S.V.,*** Superior General, Sisters of Life

"Jesus told us that the greatest in His kingdom would be those who observe His commandments and teach others to do the same. Mother Félix spent her life saying yes to whatever God asked and helping generations of her religious sisters and students learn how to love God above all. This book is a compelling chronicle of her greatness, immersing us in her heroic faith, hope, and love. It is a classroom in which this humble master of the Christian life will mother you, too, on the road that leads to happiness, holiness, and Heaven."

—***Fr. Roger J. Landry,*** National Director,
The Pontifical Mission Societies, USA

PILAR ABRAIRA, C.S.

GOD ABOVE ALL

The Life of Venerable Mother María Félix

Translated by Patti Gutiérrez

SOPHIA INSTITUTE PRESS
Manchester, New Hampshire

First published in Spanish as *Dios sobre todo* by Ediciones Palabra,
Paseo de la Castellana, 210 28046 Madrid, Spain.

Cover supplied by *Ediciones Palabra*

Sophia Institute Press
Box 5284, Manchester, NH 03108
1-800-888-9344
www.SophiaInstitute.com

Sophia Institute Press is a registered trademark of Sophia Institute.

Hardcover ISBN 979-8-88911-480-2

ebook ISBN 979-8-88911-481-9

Library of Congress Control Number: 2024948650

SPA POD 2025

To all of you who,
like St. Ignatius and Madre Félix, ask God for
light to know His will and grace to fulfill it.

In conformity with the decrees of Pope Urban VIII,
we declare that there is no intention of anticipating
in any way the judgment of the Church.

Contents

PART THREE
"Hidden with Christ in God"

Foreword

POPE JOHN PAUL II, in his Letter to Women (1995), reflected on what he called the "feminine genius." This beautiful phrase describes the special capacity that women have to "see persons with their hearts," to place themselves at the service of others, and to recognize both the greatness and the vulnerabilities of each individual soul.

The Holy Father cited Our Lady and other saints as exemplars of the feminine genius. Perhaps, when coining this term, he also had in mind a contemporary woman who completely embodied this "genius": Venerable María Félix Torres (1907–2001). Several decades earlier, in 1952, she founded the Sisters of the Company of the Savior. She envisioned a religious congregation dedicated to educating girls and young women — empowering them to discover their God-given talents and unleash their potential to freely give of themselves for the greater glory of God.

This book will give you an understanding of Mother Félix and the religious congregation she founded. If you have children attending one of the Mater Salvatoris schools, as I do, you will gain a better understanding of the sisters who are forming your children.

The sisters' charism and their schools have been profoundly shaped by the life of Mother Félix. She was singularly devoted to discovering and serving the greater glory of God. The Lord had placed this strong desire in her heart from an early age, and this is key to understanding who she was. Her commitment to serving God drove her to establish her religious congregation and the Mater Salvatoris schools.

Mother Félix recognized the need to form the whole person — intellectually, morally, socially, and spiritually — and she believed this formation should begin at a young age. Her great desire was for girls and young women to become aware of their great dignity and thus realize their full potential to influence families, society, and the Church. She wanted her students to be immersed in truth, beauty, and goodness — the transcendentals that are at the heart of our Faith and are necessary for young people to develop a Catholic imagination. And she desired that her students encounter Christ and thus discover God's will in their lives, which she recognized as the true path to human flourishing. She once wrote, "To be what God wants you to be; this is what will give greater glory to God."

Considering herself to be a "mother of souls," Mother Félix prayed fervently that her students would one day take what they learned in school into the world. She loved them dearly and was overjoyed when they encountered Christ through spiritual formation, retreats, and recreation.

Mother Félix also saw herself as a daughter of the Church and a daughter of St. Ignatius of Loyola, and she founded her religious congregation "in the style of St. Ignatius." His Spiritual Exercises and Ignatian methods of discernment guided all her decisions — and they still guide the decisions of the Company of the Savior today. Her sisters were to be "contemplatives in action," bringing the fruits of their prayer and discernment into the daily lives of the girls entrusted to their care. And like the early Jesuits, she wanted her sisters, in the words of St. Ignatius, to "think with the Church" (*sentire cum Ecclesia*). She determined that her sisters, like the Jesuits, would take an additional vow of obedience to the pope.

Also like St. Ignatius, she showed great courage leading her new congregation. She made many difficult decisions and took many risks to expand their educational apostolate. Through it all, her primary concern was to surrender her will to what God wanted. This was the compass by which she navigated. She once wrote that she felt called to "move less and pray more, because Our Lord wants me to rely more on my knees than on my head." Her greatest fear was that she would not fully abandon herself to the will of God and what He might want for the Company of the Savior.

Relying on her journal entries, this book is a very personal account. What we learn is that Mother Félix did not lead a tranquil life. She experienced many joys, but she also encountered great struggles that came with leading a religious congregation through the turbulent years after the Second Vatican Council. She referred to those difficult moments as the "black pearls" of religious life, those inevitable times of suffering that can draw us closer to Christ if we allow them.

And yet, she also spoke of the "white pearls" — the many consolations that Our Lord gives to encourage us. It was important to her that her sisters live together in charity and truly love one another. In her personal journal, she wrote that she wanted her sisters to take a private vow of the virtue of joy — and that they should care for this vow with the same love that they give to their other vows. For parents and others who have spent time with the sisters, it's readily apparent that the sisters have embraced this virtue. Joy is one of the hallmarks of the Company of the Savior.

There was a vitality and a resilience in how Mother Félix led. She had a tender and motherly spirit toward her sisters, always concerned for their health and well-being. She had compassion for others and understood their fragility. But she was also demanding and set high expectations. In a letter to her sisters, she once wrote: "If we are not saints, we are nothing." We must be "saints of flesh and bone, not like those painted images on holy cards with beatific smiles, but like those that are full of energy, those who get up if they fall down and because of that fall tie themselves more tightly to the cross of Christ." This, she said, is what the Company of the Savior needs: "saints of this caliber, courageous and fervent, of an open and strong spirit, striving for the greater glory of God and for the salvation of souls."

The humility of Mother Félix was seen in her simplicity of spirit and the natural way she dealt with everyone. She once wrote in her journal that "there is nothing extraordinary in me, nothing supernatural." And yet those who knew her said that she possessed an "immense moral authority," not because of her position as a religious superior, but because "everything in her was love."

Throughout her life, Mother Félix surrendered the future of the Company of the Savior to the Lord. The result: both the congregation and the school expanded — first in Spain (Lleida and Madrid); then Venezuela (Caracas and Maracaibo); then San Juan, Puerto Rico; and Kalalé, Benin; and most recently in Stamford, Connecticut. Each of the seven schools is consecrated in a special way to Mary under her title Mater Salvatoris, the Mother of the Savior.

We can all be deeply grateful to God for the life of Mother Félix, a life that continues to bear fruit in the religious congregation she founded and in the tens of thousands of students who have been educated in the Mater Salvatoris schools. She is an example to all of us of what Our Lord can do if only we surrender to His will and pursue God above all.

Patrick E. Kelly
Supreme Knight
Knights of Columbus
October 7, 2024
Feast of Our Lady of the Rosary

Foreword (Spanish Edition)

Dios sobre todo. God above all. If the life of a human being can be summarized in three words, these are those of Mother María Félix. They are her words, genuinely hers, which she spoke in the face of great joys and also in anguish and setbacks. They are a variant of that motto, "to the greater glory of God," that she inherited from St. Ignatius of Loyola. Her words are a feminine, tender, and personal variation: God above everything, God always first.

This is, perhaps, the most surprising fact in the life of the founder of the Company of the Savior and of the Mater Salvatoris Colleges. Since she was fourteen, since that Holy Thursday when she met Jesus Christ who loved her, she put Him above all. She trusted that God took the reins of her life with His loving Providence, that everything was measured by His Fatherly love. She believed that beyond personal ups and downs, everything was fine if the Kingdom of God was advanced in souls. She knew how to put God and His interests above everything. This is how she was seen by those who came in contact with her, and this is how the Church, our Mother, saw her when declaring her venerable.

This first biography, published along with the declaration of her heroic virtues, seeks to demonstrate this fundamental idea: God above all. It seeks to reflect on how María Félix found in the path opened by St. Ignatius of Loyola her way of following Jesus Christ with totality of love and dedication. It seeks to show how this woman made God the center of her life and of those women who entrusted to her their spiritual journey. The objective of the book is to introduce you, dear reader, to the *leitmotif* of Mother Félix's life. It aims to promote a conversation with her that you can continue once you finish reading. She is open, spontaneous, expressive, and attractive in her simplicity; she lets herself be known. If a spiritual friendship arises from the reading of this book, it will have fulfilled its purpose.

I apologize in advance if at any time it becomes too obvious that the original language of the book is Spanish. It is not the fault of the translator, who has done a magnificent job, but of the fact that Mother Félix was a Spaniard, and her life must be viewed in that context. We wanted you to be able to immerse yourself in the religious and cultural environment that Mother Félix lived, with her own idioms, courtesy treatments, place names ... all in the service of a greater affinity with her: with her time and with her life and, above all, with her heart.

We entrust this desired fruit to the Holy Spirit. He is the one who creates harmony among the saints, who created it between Mother Félix and St. Ignatius and among those who later followed their path. May He grant us that affinity of heart into which we ask to be introduced on earth and which we hope to rejoice in definitively in Heaven.

Madrid, April 22, 2024
Regina Societatis Iesu

God Above All

Part One

Will I Always Be Yours?

CHAPTER 1

The Daughter of the "Boss"
1907–1921

A HAPPY FAMILY

IN 1907 THERE WERE no ultrasounds. In fact, electricity had just barely begun to illuminate towns such as Albelda, the hometown of María Félix Torres, located in the Pyrenees Mountains in the province of Huesca in northern Spain.

Her parents, Ramón and Florentina, could not see the child they were expecting even a month before her birth. They were both young, deeply in love, and had placed their many dreams, hopes, and trust in God. They had lost their first child at only four months of age. This new pregnancy was a cause for joy as well as concern for the whole family. That is why Florentina's mother, Mrs. Joaquina, quickly took action. She was not willing for her young, nineteen-year-old daughter to be alone to drink the bitter cup of this birth. The young couple was living in the town of Tamarite. She pleaded so much with her husband, "Bep" that he agreed to invite the young couple to Albelda to await their daughter's birth. That is why María was born there, where her maternal family had deep roots, and not in one of the many towns where her father Ramón was sent for work.

Ramón, an entrepreneur open to the idea of progress, was a man who deeply enjoyed his work. He began working early, while still a teenager, because he was the oldest boy in his family and he needed to contribute. He had gotten a position in a construction company in Barcelona, a large city on the northeastern coast of Spain. Soon his boss, Juan Estruch, sensed the boy's abilities. In addition to taking an interest in Ramón's studies, Juan began to entrust him with positions of responsibility. In fact, when Ramón was only twenty-three years old, Juan sent him as his right-hand man to the construction site of the El Musel Port, in Gijón in the Asturias Province in northwestern Spain. It was at that time that, on an excursion to Albelda for the feast day of St. Ramón, he met Florentina and proposed to her.

Flor, for her part, was the youngest daughter of the wealthy Torres family from Albelda. She was a responsible and sensitive girl, full of dreams, and very protected by her mother. It took a little while for Mrs. Joaquina to support Flor marrying this nameless boy, born in the nearby town of Alcampell. She thought, "It's anyone's guess what he did in the construction project in Gijón." She urged her future son-in-law to meet with their pastor, to take a catechism exam and to show that he loved her daughter well. Also, if he wanted to marry Flor, he would have to leave his job in the Asturias Province — which seemed as far away as America — and come to live near Albelda.

Ramón put first things first. Although it was difficult to say goodbye to his mentor, he soon obtained letters of recommendation from Mr. Estruch and started his own business as a contractor. This work, which involved several moves and some great disappointments, was not exactly Mrs. Joaquina's dream, but she had to recognize the boy's good will and the loyalty with which he worked to support his family. Ramón was putting together a modest fortune, had achieved company privileges that were rare in his time, and had not even touched the dowry provided by Flor. Little by little, his reputation as an upright man and his good manners were winning the esteem of the Torres family and the entire town.

When María was born, her parents got a surprise. They had unconsciously expected that the baby would be another boy, another "Ramón," as his father and as their deceased firstborn son were named. Nevertheless, that sharp little girl, with deep, lively eyes, became the center of the family without any difficulty. At fourteen months old she was already walking quite far, clinging to the backs of the chairs. The arrival of her brothers — Ramón (in 1909), José (in 1911), and Ángel (in 1914) — would help her to open up her heart little by little. She enjoyed accompanying her mother caring for the boys and, as they grew older, she began to enjoy even more being the captain of the tiny troop.

But what María really loved was hovering around her father. She followed him with her eyes and tried to imitate him in everything. That sometimes cost her dearly, as on one occasion when she was four years old. She burned her hands on the coal stove because she saw her father warm up next to the stovepipe and she did not want to be left out. "I'm like daddy!" she exclaimed as she put her hands on the stove. The cry of pain and shock was heard throughout the house. The best part of that battle scar was the outcome: Ramón was so affected that he spent weeks pampering her and carrying her everywhere.

Ramón Félix with his siblings visiting construction sites (Seira, 1917).

María grew up deeply loved and was well aware of it. She also loved her family, although sometimes her stubbornness or her far-fetched ideas caused them some displeasure. For instance, one time, like all children, she escaped her mom's vigilance, and Flor almost died of a fright when she found the girl with her cousins pretending to fly like planes on the window sill.

In 1912, when María was five years old, her father suffered one of the greatest setbacks of his life. Someone, out of envy, accused Ramón of altering the cement while working on La Peña reservoir. The state engineers came, took the necessary samples, and found that the accusation was a malicious lie.

That was to be expected. Ramón Félix was completely honest. However, he had suffered so much during that time that one morning he woke up practically bald, and the little hair he had left had turned white. From that point on, he made two changes in his life. He would no longer be in charge of the construction projects and, as if it were a sign of his resignation, he shaved his head completely.

The Daughter of the "Boss"

With his background and experience, Ramón did not have much trouble finding a new job. A few months later he was working for the company Catalana de Gas y Electricidad. He was the lead foreman in charge of the construction of the power station in Seira, a town in the northern part of the Huesca Province. It involved one of the great tasks of the century: channeling the energy from the waterfalls to the powerful Catalan textile industries and to the most remote corners of Spain. For Ramón, who had studied civil engineering through a correspondence course in the School of Engineers of Valencia, it was a great opportunity. In addition, that mountain town, which at the time was quite rural, promised to become a paradise for the children. It was six hours from Albelda by carriage through the canyon, or three hours by car. At that time it was a small village, with stone houses surrounded by towering cedars and luscious and steep meadows. The Catalana company had committed to building a whole new village for its workers, with white Swiss-style houses with wood finishing. It would have everything they would need: a school, a social club, a shrine dedicated to Our Lady of Mount Carmel, and, a few years later, it would even have a cinema and a library. There were more than two thousand workers, and there were plenty of kids. In this miniature society, the "Boss" — which was Ramón's nickname, alluding to his position — was an authority figure, and his eldest daughter was to become a similar figure among her and her brothers' little friends. Years later, remembering that time, María laughed and said that she had been a "big fish in a small pond."

The eldest of the Félix children was a natural leader. She was kind, active, full of creativity, with a strong and dominant temperament, but with delicate health. Before she was even ten years old, she had already had colic, measles, diphtheria, and rheumatic heart disease, which made her family think she would be forever crippled by illness. However, she recovered well from all her illnesses and was left with a greater desire to have fun with the other children of the village, running around as if nothing had happened.

She did not stand out as especially pious. Her mother and Mrs. Prima, her teacher, had taught her catechism and prayers, and she had some devotion to the Virgin Mary. Sometimes she would bring flowers to Our Lady in a burst of romanticism. However, as she would say later, she would do that rather carried away by her fantasy. She could just as easily have thrown them into the sea. She was confirmed at the age of eight and not very intentionally. Only at her First Communion did she get a glimpse for a moment of the mystical soul, deeply united to God, that she would one day become.

First Communion

She was prepared for the Sacrament by a priest who spent the summer as they did in the springs in the town of Camporrells, a town not too far north of Albelda. Since there was no parish in Seira and a priest only went there on holy days of obligation, María and her brother Ramón made their First

Parish Church of St. Vincent, Martyr, where María Félix was baptized and received her First Communion.

Communion in Albelda, where she had been baptized, on September 9, 1918. That same day thirteen years earlier, in the same church, with the same music and identical flowers, her parents had been married. Much later, María would consider that a little gift from the Lord, since on that day He would take possession of her soul forever.

Her disposition for this sacrament was indeed that of a fervent girl. She had promised not to look in the mirror so that she would only focus on receiving Jesus. However, as they were getting her ready, she opened her eyes to see if what she heard from her aunts was true: "She is so beautiful! What a nice dress!" What she saw was a disappointment: a white bundle of tulle and ribbon that was not worth giving in to vanity. Before the ceremony, she confessed her transgression, "remaining calm, happy, and eager to receive the Lord." This is how she described her first encounter with Jesus in the Blessed Sacrament:

> Music, flowers, lights, talks, family, everything remained in the background, half-vanished, without contours, confused. My whole soul, my whole being was absorbed in God. I was crying sweet tears. I felt as if I were another person. My parents, as they surrounded me, seemed strange to me, as if I had never seen them before. When I got home, I asked for permission to give the contents of my piggy bank to the poor. I gave it all away and still asked for two or three times more money from my parents. If they had not stopped me, there would have been no money left in the house that day.[1]

For the first time her heart had experienced the closeness of the living God and had trembled at His touch. However, this wave of fervor soon left her. Not until three years later would she be so moved again by the things of Heaven.

During the years she lived in Seira, María learned her first letters. The village teacher taught reading and writing and some geography, mathematics,

1 Autobiographical Writings, Notebook A (AGCS M 201,001). Note: All of the documents cited are unpublished manuscripts found in the General Archives of the Company of the Savior (AGCS) in Spanish. The quotes in this book are the translator's versions.

and science. In addition, from her mother she inherited a passion for reading. Secretly, she liked to read popular poems and perform plays for her family and friends. For his part, Ramón always thought that the best thing he could leave his children was a good education, and María was not going to be excluded from that important legacy. When her teacher let Ramón know that she had nothing more to teach this intelligent and precocious girl, who outperformed all of her classmates, he began to seriously consider the possibility of enrolling her in a boarding school in the city. He was also encouraged by a professor friend who tested María's knowledge and was pleasantly surprised. "Ramón, your daughter is outstanding," he said, "it wouldn't be good to waste her aptitude."

Of all the decisions they had made so far, this was one of the costliest for her young parents. Sooner or later, they knew that they would have to send the boys to study in Barbastro; but María, their little girl? In the end, her well-being won out over their preferences. They decided that in September 1921, she would begin her high-school studies in Lleida at La Enseñanza school, directed by the Sisters of the Company of Mary. For her, the happy time of intimate family life was ending, a time that had marked her for a lifetime. Remembering it, she would say of herself:

> I had an enormous capacity to love and to sacrifice myself for those I loved; a capacity that is not attributed to children and that, for their good, should be taken into account. When I loved, I asked nothing in return; I gave all of myself. This is the nature God gave me to force me to love Him more.

Chapter 2

"I Am Quite a Thinker"

1921–1922

The World of School

At the end of September came the long-awaited moment that everyone in the Félix home feared. María and her parents got into the Catalana company car and said goodbye to the boys, who stayed with their aunt and uncle for a few days. Their father would return soon. He was only going to accompany the travelers to Albelda because he did not think he had the strength to leave María at the boarding school.

They left Seira, passing through the towns of El Run, Castejón, El Pont de Suert, Buira, La Litera; they went through the detour of Alcampell and arrived in Albelda. In her parents' desire that María continue her education, she would leave behind the evenings spent as a family, the games and fights with her siblings, and all the times she and her father had dreamed about fabulous trips, studying the railway maps of Spain and Europe at Ramón's desk. Now a new world awaited María, and it would be several months before she would enjoy the warm security of those Sunday afternoons again.

María and her mother traveled to Lleida, the capital of the province of Lleida to the east of Huesca. Upon arrival in Lleida, she was welcomed by the Old Cathedral of St. Mary on the hillside, with its imposing profile, between Romanesque and Gothic styles. Later, once they were on the Rambla de Fernando Avenue, the modernist buildings invited more mundane thoughts. The Mangrané House, with its fairy-tale tower and tile mosaics, was a confirmation of what her parents had been warning María about for several months.

They had said some of the girls she was going to live with at school would be from noble families or the daughters of wealthy businessmen. Her teachers were going to be very well-educated religious sisters. Both groups would have exquisite manners. María, with the manners she had been taught at home, would have much to learn to keep up in such circumstances. It was part of the good that her parents sought for her.

Finally, they arrived at the Plaza de La Ereta and their destination: La Enseñanza school. The main façade, finished with three peaks and with an image of Our Lady of the Immaculate Conception on the gate, was that of the convent church. The entrance to the convent and school was on the side. Florentina and María approached the boarding school, called the gatekeeper, and immediately a sister appeared, who received them very kindly. She brought them to a room next to the hall, where the mother prefect came to meet them.

Mother Arnaldo, who emanated an innate authority, welcomed them with simplicity and kindness. To put María at ease, she briefly explained the daily schedule of the schoolgirls, which Florentina already knew from her previous investigations. There were two types of students in the school — those who studied for a high school diploma and those who only took the general education courses.

María Félix with her schoolmates (Lérida, 1922).

María, being one of the official students, would go to the public high school every day with the other residents, accompanied by a lay woman. Other than that, she would share the manner of life of the other resident students during the rest of the day: acts of piety, music, and embroidery classes, small household chores, recess, etc. Then, addressing María, she explained that there was a custom of assigning each new student an "angel": a more experienced classmate who would introduce her little by little to the customs and practices of the school.

María understood perfectly well that the time had come to separate from her mother. When she turned to her and saw her mother with tears in her eyes, María could no longer restrain herself. She hugged her and cried, but she parted quickly so as not to make everything harder. Finally, Florentina left, and María stayed with Mother Arnaldo, feeling terribly alone.

The nun, aware of the state of the new student, quickly called her angel, María Prim. She was the same age as María, very poised, with a spontaneous and pleasant character. Mother Arnaldo invited María Félix to accompany them for a moment to the chapel to greet the Lord and then to go up with María Prim to the resident students' room, where her luggage trunk was waiting for her. Afterwards, Mother Arnaldo left them, telling María Prim to show her new companion the school. They had a couple of hours at their disposal before the Rosary bell and dinner.

That first visit with her guide left María very surprised. María Prim explained everything related to school with an amazing naturalness — the schedule, the rules for visits, how to behave with the religious sisters, the way the laundry and the dining room worked, the life of piety, etc. A whole set of rules and customs that were nothing like her simple life in Seira. As the veteran rambled on, reeling off her litany of details, María was surprised to find it so different than she had expected. This school world was not, as had been imagined, a high-society hall or the Areopagus of Athens. Also, why such a strange life? Why did she feel so alone and so far removed from it all? Could she ever feel as comfortable as her guide through those high corridors, with large windows, which returned the echo of her footsteps?

After a while, María Prim, as if perceiving that her disciple was in another world, interrupted her thoughts with an invitation. Taking advantage of the margin of freedom they had been given, she proposed to the newcomer her first act of mischief: to enter the room of the mother prefect.

The prefect's cell! María did not even want to imagine a complaint arriving at her house, but neither did she intend to lose face with her first acquaintance, with whom she was getting along so well. She acted bravely and said she was willing.

As if they were going to pick up their aprons for dinner, the two girls went up to the resident students' room, crossed it until reaching the end of the beds, and finally reached Mother Arnaldo's door. María held her breath as she entered and had to hold it back even more to hide her amazement. She had hoped to find an elegant library, a four-poster bed, a fancy dressing table, or at least furniture as beautiful as that in her parents' room. She could never have imagined what she saw: a poor cot, a pinewood table, a common cattail chair, and an iron wash basin with its small porcelain jug. The crucifix that presided over the room seemed to smile at her astonishment. What could make women who had it all leave everything behind in order to dedicate themselves to these girls? She perceived, although she did not say anything to her companion, that there were many things to learn that awaited her in school. That night, in bed, she continued to mull over her surprise: how could such a cultured and virtuous person, of such a noble family, live there? God's answer did not delay. To a novice, toward the end of her life, she would confide: "God alone explained it to me. No one needed to tell me anything. The Lord made me understand it. It was a very great grace, very great." And she cried as she remembered it.

Hidden Reading

From the very start, she found the classes interesting and invigorating. At least this part met the expectations she had. Little by little, she began to feel herself again. She remembered her family, but without the separation from them overwhelming her with sorrow or lonesomeness. She enjoyed learning, being challenged by math problems, and explaining things that she grasped quickly to her schoolmates, who lagged behind. Since she was modest, her friends happily accepted her help. Academically, she felt very comfortable, and socially she had so many friends that it was as if she had been at the school for years. There was only one aspect of school life that she struggled with, and it upset her. She felt completely illiterate in matters of piety. Her schoolmates knew many prayers by heart, responded at Mass with ease, visited the Blessed Sacrament after class, and spoke knowingly about examples of the lives of saints that María had not even heard of. After a lot of embarrassment and asking for explanations, she decided to take extreme measures. She had to catch up as soon as possible. That is why, at the first chance, she swiped an extra book from the library, in addition to the one she was allowed to borrow, and hid it in her bed under her pillow. At night before the lights in the dormitory were turned off, she read as much as she could and fell asleep memorizing the Hail Mary, the Confiteor ("I confess . . ."), and so many other prayers that she had forgotten over the years.

She began with a devotional book but then continued with short biographies of saints, a commentary on the Gospels, treatises on the spiritual life, and so forth. In order not to accumulate a library in her bed, she kept secretly returning them and renewing her collection. In a couple of months, she had already gained a spiritual vocabulary and could defend herself in conversations about novenas, saints, and the titles of Our Lady with as much ease as when talking about cars, sports, or family plans. However, this reading not only provided her with the instruction she sought but with an unexpected discovery. Every time a book excited her — and this was becoming more and more frequent — its author had attached to his name two mysterious letters, whose meaning she did not understand: "S.J." She did not know what an "S.J." was, but she sensed that they were all wonderful beings, full of love for God and souls.

Too Fast

Ramón suffered from the absence of his daughter in the village almost more than Florentina. Therefore, as soon as he had to go down to Lleida for business, he asked the nuns for permission to visit María. The sisters agreed without question and led him to the parlor. When he arrived there and discovered that people visited the resident students separated by a grate, as if they were members of the community, he was very upset. He was not one to remain silent and go along with the "way things are done around here." So, he very politely but firmly asked the sisters to reconsider this shocking practice. They told him that they themselves were thinking about a change and that it was no problem for him to visit his daughter for now in a sitting room or take her on an outing. Ramón opted for the latter, and in that impromptu excursion he was able to verify María's academic progress and her inner transformation.

He took her by car to the Bank of Spain, where he had to meet with his agent. On the way he asked about her studies, about the school, and about her classmates. He could tell, and was pleased, that María had settled in and was learning a lot. Upon arriving at the bank, he allowed her to enter with him but told her to wait in the armchairs in the lobby, while he resolved the matter that had brought him to the city. María stayed there, looking curiously at the revolving doors of the branch and, above all, at the small lockers or metal file drawers that occupied a large part of the wall. She thought that perhaps the funds that moved the business world were kept there, well ordered. And, before she knew it, she began to pray. She asked God and His angels to make the fortunes on which the missions, the sick, the poor, the orphans, and the building of churches depended grow quickly. At the same time, she suffered thinking of the accounts that would finance vanities, dirty deals, quarrels, discord, greed, and pride. Thinking about this, she asked God to dry up these funds, to not allow the devil to sow sins with money.

Afterwards, as they were heading to a nearby bakery, Ramón asked María: "Have you been very bored?" And she answered him: "No *papá*, I've been thinking the whole time. You know, I'm quite a thinker." That remark was funny to Ramón, who asked her: "And what were you thinking about?" Once he knew her train of thought, Ramón did not say anything, but he was shaken up for a moment. His daughter was changing; for the better, but very fast. With these and other considerations, both of them got lost in their own thoughts until they arrived at the school. Once there, Ramón hugged his daughter and said goodbye until Christmas, which was not far off.

Christmas Vacation

On December 20th, while the Catalana coach was chugging up the Pyrenees, the telephone at the station was busier than in the entire previous month. At every moment it rang, and the same dialogue was repeated, with very small variations: "Don Ramón Félix?" "This is he," came the reply. "The coach has passed the Buira station." Ramón responded, "Thank you very much. The next station is El Pont de Suert, right?" "Yes, sir, it will take about half an hour," said the employee. "Very good. I will wait for your call."

The staff wondered if the Minister of Public Works or the general director of the Catalana company was coming to visit. In reality, María was coming back, totally oblivious to the commotion she was causing. On the way, she imagined how much her brother Ángel — who was almost eight years old — would have grown, the sled races they would have if it snowed a lot, and how she was going to arrange things so she could be faithful to the prayers she had begun to say every day in the school chapel.

The welcome at home was as warm as she expected. Her parents quickly involved her in the preparation of the Christmas Eve dinner and the Epiphany gifts. They showed her how the chickens and rabbits were doing in the farmyard. She was told about the plans for the coming days and was immersed in family life as if she had never left home. That year it snowed abundantly, and the sled races and evenings by the fireplace felt glorious to her. In addition, being close to her paternal aunts, uncles, and cousins — who also lived in Seira a little further down the river — made the family atmosphere truly endearing.

However, as the days went by, María began to notice that she was missing something. Her parents and brothers, as good as ever, did not share her interest in preparing spiritually for the birth of Jesus. Even her mother, who had taught her how to pray on her knees, thought her insistence on participating in Midnight Mass was a little exaggerated. She also told her a couple of times, somewhat annoyed, that María did not need to teach the children of Seira the entire catechism or all the pious songs she had learned in school. María, for her part, tried to convince her parents that nothing had changed in her; she simply lived more consciously the Christian faith that they had instilled in her. Otherwise, she kept quiet and suffered a little. Why couldn't her parents and siblings enjoy a friendship with the Lord as she did? That vacation left a bittersweet taste in her mouth. She loved her family more and more every day, but it hurt her that they did not know God better.

María Félix and her brothers, Ramón and José, with Antonia, their young aunt (Seira, 1921).

CHAPTER 3

Forever

1922–1923

HER FIRST SPIRITUAL EXERCISES

MARÍA BARELY HAD ANY trouble readjusting to school. She came back with a clear mind, ready to study and eager to see her friends. It was comforting to arrive at that old building and for the first time feel at home. She was also excited by the idea of having a tabernacle nearby again and the possibility of visiting it often without raising suspicions. She had a growing interest in everything related to God, and the school was the ideal place to get to know Him more. Years later she would say that by then she had already sensed her vocation, but that she lived it "her own way."

During these months her friendships were strengthened and, at the same time, they gave her a lot to think about. She saw how her schoolmates all had a best friend and a favorite religious sister. While María related very well with the other girls and encouraged any group of friends with her conversation, she didn't look for a "soul sister" to whom she could open her inner life. She felt that it was hidden from those around her.

That Lent was the first one she had observed with real interest. Now that she knew a little more about the love of Jesus Christ, she needed to prepare herself to experience His Passion, Death, and Resurrection by His side. Without the sisters knowing, she began to give her dessert to the poor on the way to the public high school, she prayed with her arms out in the form of a cross, and she sought discomfort in the way she slept. She also spent long periods of time in the gallery that overlooked the church. She would become so engrossed that she would not come when the bell rang. On one occasion she did not realize that they were calling down the hallway for her to go to the laundry room to pick up her clean laundry.

As her prayer life grew, she felt more vividly the desire to give something back to God. Some sins that she had committed during her childhood upset her. For example, the doves she had stolen when she found them abandoned, away from their lofts; the inappropriate conversations she had with some young girls of the village; the nonsense she had gotten herself into by having a boyfriend a few years earlier and the even more frivolous motives for which she had "dumped" him when she decided that she was only going to marry someone of nobility. Above all, however, it weighed on her conscience that she had taken Communion on a Sunday without keeping the eucharistic fast and had then kept silent about this fact in her subsequent confessions. She would have liked to be able to erase this sin with blood, and she took advantage of every opportunity that was offered to mortify herself in order to show God her repentance.

Shortly before Holy Week, the sisters announced a series of Spiritual Exercises. They put a sign on the boarding school bulletin board with the dates and the name of the director: Fr. Francisco Llorens, S.J. When one of her friends read the poster and said it was given by Fr. Francisco Llorens, a Jesuit, María had to hide her excitement. She finally knew what an "S.J." was! And she was even going to meet one in person!

She entered into those Spiritual Exercises as St. Ignatius asks, "with great courage and generosity," wishing to be converted and to let God work. She prepared diligently to make a general confession of her entire life, ready to undergo whatever penance was given to her. She was convinced that it would be something extraordinary, such as traveling to Rome on foot to ask the pope to forgive her sacrilege. The encounter of her expectations with the gratuitousness of the Lord's mercy moved her. She asked the priest for permission to spend entire nights in prayer and to fast "for real," but this time out of gratitude. The priest smiled and only allowed her to ask the mother prefect for permission to stay for a while praying before the Blessed Sacrament on the upcoming Holy Thursday.

Heavenly Fire

When this day arrived, April 13, 1922, María was on pins and needles. Inwardly she knew that it was not going to be like any other day. She thought to herself: "Today I'm going to tell Him yes." While one of the nuns fixed her chapel veil — which the girls wore with their uniform on solemnities — María asked the Virgin Mary to help her so that she would be in the presence of Mary's Son "to His liking."

María reached the kneeler and looked up at the altar. Only she is in a position to narrate what happened:

> I lifted my eyes to the altar and saw an immense flame burning with a clarity and softness that filled me with an ineffable sweetness. I opened my eyes wide, I wanted to be sure of what I saw, but that flame, shapeless, golden and luminous, motionless and penetrating my spirit, was not fire from the earth; it was heavenly fire that set my soul on fire. Completely aware, with an extraordinary understanding of what I was doing, irresistibly and sweetly drawn to the Lord, I offered myself to Him forever. Since that day I have been fully and consciously His; despite my infidelities, my great weaknesses, I am fully and consciously His forever.[2]

She was fourteen years old and was completely clear about what the main thing was in her life. She belonged to the Lord, and she was going to be His forever.

For a few weeks, she kept the discovery of her vocation completely secret. It was enough to make her immensely happy that she and God knew it. Before summer vacation, she spoke with the students' confessor and confided in him about her wish. This priest told her that she was still too young to discern whether what she felt was a true vocation and recommended that she say to the Lord repeatedly the lines from St. Teresa's poem: "I am Yours and born of You. What do You want of me, Lord?" That is what she did, faithfully, during that school year and the remaining two years of high school.

[2] Autobiographical Writings, Notebook A (AGCS M 201,001).

Moreover, since she was not content with this alone, she asked God for confirmation of her vocation, asking Him for simple but improbable signs. For example, when she was in the chapel, she said: "I will know that You want me to be a religious sister if she (the sacristan) extinguishes that candle last" (contrary to her usual order). When it happened as she had asked, she was very happy and considered it a gift from the Lord.

At that time, María read about the life of St. Thérèse of the Child Jesus and it excited her. She thought of being a Carmelite nun and was looking for the first possible chance to escape and pay a visit to the Carmelite convent on San Anastasio Street, which was three minutes from the school. The opportunity soon arrived. For the birthday of one of her teachers, she proposed buying a copy of the biography about the saint from Lisieux and offered to run the errand herself.

Through the gate, a nun greeted her with the traditional *"Ave María Purísima." ["Hail Mary Most Pure."] Sin pecado concebida ["Conceived without sin"],* María replied, quite embarrassed. "How can we help you?" answered the nun. Without realizing it, María found herself telling the sister about her concerns, her attraction to the Carmelite life, and her assurance that God was calling her to be entirely His. It was a delightful time and, before she knew it, it was time to run back to the school because recess had ended and she would be marked absent. Upon arrival she realized that she had not bought the book. Later, while the resident students prayed the Rosary, she started thinking about her carelessness. Her laughter gave away her joy, and she tried to hide it by closing her eyes and biting her lip.

High School Finishes

In the summer of 1923, María's family began to seriously worry. She would quarrel with her parents to let her receive Communion every Sunday — something unusual at the time and very striking in that small town — more than about anything else. She was no longer as interested in dresses and outings to the city. And, if that were not enough, she cut off her magnificent braids and donned a "boy" haircut, and not with the purpose of being fashionable. In addition, many days she taught catechism, poems, and songs to the children of the village. She also spent hours on her knees praying in her room. Ramón and Florentina tried to moderate those practices that seemed excessive to them. Since they hindered her devotions, María began to leave with a book under her arm to walk through the countryside. Her parents would have been even more mortified if they had known that, in those moments of solitude, she would kneel on the brambles and pray — for them even — with her arms raised in the form of a cross.

As September approached, tired of so much excessive piety, they told their daughter that they had decided to make a change. She was not going to return to school with the nuns but would finish high school in a boarding house for young ladies run by some of their acquaintances. This couple, the Azconas, were honest people but very indifferent in matters of religion. Since they had a daughter María's age, Enriqueta, she could make whatever plans their daughter made, but she was strictly forbidden to go back to school or be around church people.

At first María's heart sank, but once she was in Lleida, she saw that it was not going to be so bad. Enriqueta was not a ruthless guardian but rather a complacent young woman who lamented her mother's indifference and her father's anticlericalism. She did not dare to support María in the debates about religious subjects that usually formed at dinner, but she gladly prayed the Rosary with her in the storage room or read the magazine *Lluvia de Rosas (Showered with Roses)* that María brought from the Carmelites. Soon the residents' quarters became a little Upper Room because María dedicated herself to the apostolate with as much intensity as to studying.

Every morning she would tiptoe with her shoes in her hand to leave the house to go to the seven o'clock Mass, before the Azconas woke up. Afterwards, she had breakfast and went to school as if nothing had happened. However, things were happening. Those morning getaways were the center of her day where she gathered strength for the day. On one of those occasions, upon receiving Communion in St. Peter's Parish, she was so inundated with God's presence that she did not realize that the priest had already finished the whole line at the Communion rail and was approaching her again. She could barely tell him, by moving her head, not to give her Communion again, but she could not get up from her place. When, after a few minutes, she managed to return to her pew, she told herself that she would try to go to Mass in another church. She was embarrassed to think that the priest may have noticed what had just happened.

On Sundays she would have the pleasure of Enriqueta and another girl accompanying her on her adventure. That way they could quietly receive the Lord and, after breakfast, very well dressed, they could participate in the twelve o'clock Mass. The Azconas consented to them attending this High Mass, to which a good number of their acquaintances went, provided they did not receive Communion. Sometimes they went to the cinema and the theater, but María thought this was not suitable for a future religious sister and, taking the opportunity to offer a sacrifice, closed her eyes for a good part of the film. Given the eccentricities of their young guest, which were incomprehensible to them, the Azconas soon left her alone and refused to invite her to shows and other entertainment.

During this time, she continued to meet with the confessor of the school, who did not see very clearly María's vocation as a Carmelite. He advised her to pay attention to her lack of health and directed her toward some form of religious life in which she could put to use the studies she had carried out. However, María insisted that in order to die for the salvation of sinners she did not need much physical resistance; she also told him that her studies could be a grain of wheat buried in order to bear much fruit. Overcome by the stubbornness of his directee, the priest recommended her to the Carmelites as a possible postulant. They, in turn, invited her to meet with a priest of their order, who also did not clearly see a cloistered vocation. He suggested that she become a teaching Carmelite. María was a little disappointed. She did not think it was a good thing to have two spiritual directors and did not meet with him again. From that point on, she would continue to inquire where the Lord wanted her, but without seeking any advice other than that of her usual director.

Chapter 4

Student and Apostle
1924–1931

The Longest Degree

The summer of 1924 started off on a good foot. María came home having passed ethics and introduction to law, with three outstanding marks in science courses, and an extraordinary award in natural history. Her parents' satisfaction made them forget the battles of the previous vacation for a few days. Moreover, since they saw that her health was deteriorating and she was experiencing frequent dizziness, they feared that it was due to being upset about not being able to follow her devotions and gave her greater freedom. Inside, María knew that the discomfort was due to the chain cilice that she had been wearing all day long and wondered how and when she would tell her parents her plans to consecrate herself to God.

The occasion came earlier than she expected. One afternoon, while she was in her room, she overheard her parents talking about the financial struggle involved in keeping all the children in religious schools. In addition, they had to start thinking about María's university studies. It was clear that, for a while, they were going to have to do without the tailors and dressmakers of Huesca and the springs of Camporrells. As they ended the conversation with a kiss, María was plunged into a terrible struggle. How could she be silent about her determination to be a religious sister and postpone entry for several years if that meant a financial sacrifice for her beloved parents? It made no sense to make them pay for a degree that she didn't intend to use later at all. After a difficult night, she bombarded them the next morning before her father left on his way to the power station. She said: "*Papá, mamá* ... I don't want you to spend more money on my studies. It would be disloyal for me not to say so because I am not going to utilize them. I want to be a religious sister."

The announcement fell like a bombshell. Ramón responded, "Over my dead body," and Flor cried almost all morning. The boys, when they came home for lunch and learned what had happened, remained neutral. The tension could be cut with a knife. Since Ramón knew well that whoever is silent concedes, and even more so with a daughter like María, he did not delay in telling her that they had made a decision. As long as she was considered a minor — that is, until she was twenty-three years old — she was under their responsibility and would follow their house rules. For now, she would continue studying until she finished her degree and had a way to make a living. María understood well that those words contained all her father's love and pain and that an appeal was not possible. She complied without retort, but she asked him to allow her to get a teaching degree. Since she had completed high school, they would validate several courses, and she could finish in a couple of years.

Ramón said he would think about it, but the next morning he answered with a refusal. She would have to study something more in line with her skills and, since she was excellent in the field of science, the best option was medicine in Barcelona. Deep down, everyone knew that the reason for this was that there was no other degree that took longer.

Medical Student

The rules for her new student life were as strict as those imposed for the previous year. She would stay at the home of one of her professors, a friend of the family, and under no circumstances could she interact with Jesuits. Faced with this limitation, María was greatly surprised. How could her parents know about her desire to take advantage of her stay in Barcelona to meet the priests from the Society of Jesus? She had not told anyone and had only wanted it because she remembered how Jesuit spirituality had always helped her. In addition, she had the idea that they were experts in the discernment of spirits and vocational guidance. Her father thought something similar, although he did not see it as an advantage. A friend of his had told him that the Jesuits led all their directees to become nuns; hence his caution.

Upon arriving in Barcelona, María quickly became acquainted with the young adults of the Catholic Action for University Students and asked if she could help with anything. She also inquired if they knew any Jesuit priests who were dedicated to spiritual direction. Now a young woman, María felt, as a matter of conscience, that she was not obliged to obey her parents on this point. Thus, she began to meet with Fr. Ramón Orlandis, S.J., who, after several confessions, confirmed her in her religious vocation. He said, "Yes, the Lord wants you to be a religious sister. I tell you with full certainty, be very faithful." His words were like a powerful magnet that united her more closely with God. From then on, without having to make any effort, she lived the whole day in His presence. She began to form a habit of praying in such a way that she was completely lost in Him, without noticing anything that was happening around her.

The light of this certainty also illuminated her life as a student and her apostolate. She became friends with the most pious young women of her class, who also began to go to confession with Fr. Orlandis. She courageously engaged in a "war of words" with her atheist professor of biology. She would bring the priest the arguments of this professor that she could not answer. She accepted the position of first delegate of the Catholic Action group. Although her schoolmates would always tease her, asking her if she was studying to be a nun, she was quick to respond that it was her intention to become a better instrument of God in her apostolate. This had a lot of merit because she did not like medicine and was disgusted by the gruesome jokes that some of the students made about the corpses from the university morgue. Regarding her dealings with these young men, the priest advised her to consider herself like a lamb among wolves. María, apart from the bad jokes, did not feel uncomfortable among those "wolves," who were so friendly and respectful, but she recognized that what her director said to her was true. He said, "Give thanks to God because He has taken possession of your heart. If you loved some man, you would do crazy things. Not even the fear of God would stop you in your tracks."

It was true. The most powerful and most vulnerable part of María was her heart.

The Test of the Heart

María experienced this during her summer vacation in 1925. As soon as she returned home, María noticed that the atmosphere had changed. Now that she was working toward a degree, her parents were calm and loving. They practiced religion a little more, prompted by her example, and Ramón even made an agreement with the bishop that the parish priest could reside in the town so that María could receive Communion several days during the week. The only condition he placed on her was that, in return, she should not receive Communion every Sunday at the High Mass because it was torture for him to hear the comments of his colleagues and subordinates about his daughter's pious passions. María was delighted to accept. If the priest was in town not only a few days but every day of the week, she could receive Communion early in the morning, and so she did.

But what truly reassured her parents was the frequency with which the young notary, Ignacio Lafuente, began to come from the nearby town of Benasque to visit the Félix home. He was a very good young man, from the city of Zamora in northwestern Spain. He lived with his mother and sister. It was apparent that he enjoyed being with María very much. They had interesting conversations about their common interests of art, culture, and piety. The boy was a member of the Marian Congregation and was a catechist, just as María was. He told Mr. and Mrs. Félix about the pious practices and activities of the Marian Congregation and those carried out by his sister with her friends in Benasque. María told him every day about how her parents had been giving her permission for more of these activities thanks to his conversations. Their friendship grew very quickly, and one day when her wonderful ally did not come down to Seira, María felt she was missing something. However, she did not perceive that slowly something was changing within her until a friend jokingly told her: "The other day I saw you with Ignacio, the notary. You were so lovey-dovey!"

She and Ignacio? Lovey-dovey? What about her religious vocation? María felt as if she had been rammed in the chest. As soon as she could, she slipped away from her friend's company and ran to her house in a stupor. She got down on her knees beside her bed, opened the Bible at random, trying to seek clarity about what was going on, and the first word on which her eyes rested was: "adulteress." Adulteress. There was the answer from Heaven, more blinding than lightning. She had been unfaithful to the Lord, letting another love take the place that belonged to Jesus Christ. She promised God that she would do whatever it took to become His own, and at the first chance she got, she told Ignacio that she planned on being a religious sister. He had intended to marry her and did not understand such a sudden change. Suffering because of her decision, he tried a couple of times to persuade her to change her mind. María also suffered when she saw the damage she had caused to her friend through her lack of prudence, but the anchor had already been dropped. Both of them already knew what María's vocation was, and neither one of them was going to go against God.

The Archangel and Luzbel

Before her parents knew that all hope of an engagement had been broken, María approached them to clarify the topic of her studies. She felt that to continue studying medicine, she needed to have the vocation of a doctor, and she was certain enough that she did not have that calling. She asked for permission to transfer to chemistry, which could be studied with magnificent professors in Zaragoza, a city only a few hours southwest of Seira. Her parents agreed to the request, even though they were disappointed since their son Ramón was going to start his studies in Barcelona that year, and now the siblings would not be together. They arranged lodging for her at the house of the chief of the Zaragoza post office, a relative of their friend Petra Chesa.

From her first moment in Zaragoza, she felt at ease. Her new hosts had a serene home full of respectful people. In addition, they lived only fifteen minutes from the school and a four-minute walk from the church of the Sacred Heart, which was run by the Jesuits. There María met Fr. Luis Pujadas, S.J., who would be her spiritual director for the next four years.

This fervent and somewhat gruff priest was very enthusiastic about Ignatian spirituality and began a formation with María like that of the Jesuit novices. He taught her to do an examination of conscience twice a day, to grasp the movements of God and to respond better to them. He encouraged her in her life as an apostle and in her studies. He taught her how to conduct herself in spiritual direction and encouraged her to be completely sincere so that she could be better directed. He also helped her to recognize the loving hand of the Father in everything that surrounded her. This enhanced something that was already happening in María's soul. For her, everything served as a springboard for her spiritual relationship with God.

This priest and his teachings were a blessing to her, even though she did not think to tell him about the most extraordinary graces she received. It seemed to her that they were normal things that happened to everyone. Therefore, when the Jesuit asked her what had happened to her on this or that occasion when he had seen her totally absorbed during Eucharistic adoration, he only received this as an answer: "I don't know, *Padre*. Sometimes the Blessed Sacrament makes me feel a lot of devotion."

What she did speak of were her plans to become a religious sister as soon as possible. She also confessed — once she had rejected the idea — that she had planned to run away to serve God in the leprosy hospital in Fontilles if her parents were still determined to deny her the necessary permission. When the priest expressed his surprise and asked her why she had not told him anything about this unusual plan, María replied: "But *Padre*! How was I going to put you in such a compromising position? If my parents had come to Zaragoza to look for me, anyone could have told them that I go to confession with you, and what would you have done, knowing my secret?"

Another topic that María talked about with her director, as she had done in Barcelona, was that of her apostolate among her classmates. In her class there were about twenty people, of whom only three were women: Irene Suñer, Matilde Sevilla, and her. Everyone got along well. They attended the symphonic orchestra every month because some of the men had surprised María and her friends with a membership. They stayed on the weekends to attend the bull fights and soccer games. Several of them, who were members of the Marian Congregation, accompanied the girls to visit the Blessed Sacrament in the nearby church of the Handmaids of the Sacred Heart of Jesus.

Her classmates truly appreciated María. They enjoyed the friendly debates she had with an atheist student who would approach her during laboratory practices to raise his objections against the Faith. As soon as everyone heard: "María, María..."—which was his way of starting the conversation—they would all gather around the opponents to witness the entertaining debates that they called "Luzbel's battles against the Archangel." María welcomed her classmate warmly but did not allow him to go too far. Instead, she led the conversation with charity and firmness. Thus, she started to become, without intending to, a point of reference among her fellow classmates. When they accompanied her to the church of the Handmaids, they said half-jokingly: "We are going to burn down the convent, so we can get rid of the nuns who are our competition." She answered them in the same tone: "All right, but let me know first so that I may enter and die in the fire, making reparation for all of you! I love you all very much and it's important to me that you're all saved."

On Sundays, she went with Matilde to a school in the Las Delicias neighborhood to teach math, reading, and religion classes to girls in the gypsy community who did not attend school. Her heart would buzz with enthusiasm when she heard them talking about the advances they were making in science and in the Christian life. She saw more and more clearly the importance of women's education and was happy to think about the influence these girls could have on their environment. That is why she did not miss any classes and, if a student was missing one Sunday, she asked about her. If it was due to illness, she would visit her home and ask about her needs and those of her family. She spent almost all the money that her parents sent each month for her expenses on them. But what really moved her was to find out how the love that flooded her was penetrating some of the girls. One of them, who began with a total ignorance of the things of God, ended up leading the Daughters of Mary club as president. And, despite the opposition of her father, who threatened and insulted her when he saw her get up early to go to the parish, this girl participated in Holy Mass every day.

María Félix's love for Jesus in the Blessed Sacrament was contagious because it was becoming more and more the center of her life. Some mornings, after receiving Communion at St. Paul's church, instead of spending a long time in thanksgiving at the end of Mass, she liked to leave the church early and wander through the neighboring streets. Since she had just received Communion, she felt like a living tabernacle. It made her happy to think that, walking around while she embraced Christ and told Him that she loved Him with all her soul, the Lord could bless the people who lived in that area. In order for the Lord to be loved everywhere, she thought, she would even go to Hell itself to tell Him that she loved Him.

As for her friends — those from the university and those from the residence of the Teresian Sisters, where she stayed for her second year —, several joined the Catholic Action group for women that María inaugurated with the help of Fr. Pujadas. They would also turn to her when they had doubts about their conscience. One of them, in fact, asked María to help her escape the most serious mistake of her life. She was about to run off with a professor, a married man and father. With others who had fewer difficulties, the help that María could provide was of a different nature. She would have wished for all of them to be religious sisters, but God was revealing what He wanted for each one of them regardless of human plans and expectations.

One Holy Thursday, praying before the altar in the residence of the Teresian Sisters, she felt the Lord saying to her: "Ask me for the vocation of Asunción and that of Milagros." "But the former is going to get married, and the latter is as wrapped up in the world as possible!" she retorted. The Lord answered, "It doesn't matter, ask me for those vocations." "Okay, Lord, I ask You for a vocation for Asunción and for Milagros," María responded. The Lord said, "I will grant you these vocations: tell both of them that they will be religious sisters."

Amazed, the next day, she took advantage of a study time in the residence to communicate to her friends the heavenly message. The laughter with which they received the news puzzled her even more. The situation was now as ridiculous as the experience of the previous night was undeniable in her conscience. However, a few days later, while praying in the convent of the Handmaids, Asunción took off the pearls that she never took off day or night and put them in her bag. María knew, once again, that the Lord does what He wants. Before a year had passed, Milagros had left behind the newest fashions and cheering on the most famous *pelota* players in order to enter the novitiate of the Society of St. Teresa of Jesus. Asunción, on the other hand, upset the Teresian Sisters. After writing to her boyfriend to say goodbye, she entered the novitiate — assisted by María Félix — as a Handmaid of the Sacred Heart of Jesus in the city of Gandia on the eastern coast of Spain.

The one who was always left behind was María herself, who was only waiting to finish her degree quickly so she could take the final step and be able to consecrate herself to God.

In the Lion's Mouth

Between her second and third year, at the end of the summer, she tested her parents about her vocation. She asked them for permission to enter the Handmaids, convinced that this time they would let her, but the result was quite the opposite of what she expected. Not only did they send her back to Zaragoza but her father went into a strange depression that worried the whole family greatly.

María went to see him, but when he saw her, he did not recognize her and barely knew of her arrival. It seemed as if he was out of touch with reality. This went on for several months, until one morning he realized how strange it was that María was by his side and told her not to stay for him, that she had to resume her studies. He himself did not realize it, but it was the sign that he was beginning to recover. However, by the time María returned to the city, she had lost the right to take the final exam for several courses, and this would prolong her degree for another year.

Toward the end of 1928, however, her parents began to accept that they were not going to be able to entice María to marry willingly. During Holy Week, when they tried to arrange a marriage for her with the son of some friends, it failed completely. There was great disinterest on both sides and especially from María, who had spent all the extra money that they had sent to her to make new dresses on the poor. With pain, but with a sincere desire to seek her happiness, Ramón and Florentina gave her permission to enter the Handmaids.

That is when her most difficult battle began. Until now, the difficulties had been external, and the joy and the strength to overcome them flowed irresistibly from within her. Suddenly, she found herself in a completely different situation: at last, her parents had given her permission, the sisters looked kindly upon her, and her director approved it. However, she began to experience a reluctance that she had never felt. It seemed to her that, for some incomprehensible reason, the Lord did not want her to be a Handmaid. Fr. Pujadas, puzzled, told her that this was an obvious temptation, that she was just homesick. However, he affirmed, as St. Ignatius recommends, that this period of desolation was not the time in which to make a change.

In these circumstances, which were terribly painful for her, she learned that there was a Protestant pastor in the city with a reputation as a spiritual and impartial man who was very knowledgeable about people. She wondered whether he could help her clarify her situation. Moreover, she knew that in the evangelical communities, there were people who were very dedicated to the apostolate but without the need to take religious vows or to leave their family. Without knowing very well what to say to him, she wrote a letter to the pastor, presenting her difficulties. If she could continue to believe in the Blessed Virgin and all her privileges and in the Real Presence of Jesus Christ in the Eucharist, María would embrace Protestantism. She sealed the envelope very carefully and left in a hurry with the intention of throwing it into the mailbox. The central post office on Independencia Avenue was a block and a half from the residence. Upon arriving, she stood before the mouth of the bronze lion that opened his jaws for the national mail and mustered: "For the greater glory of God." It was her usual ejaculatory prayer whenever she put letters to her family and friends into the mailbox. That was the manner in which she always entrusted to God the fruit her words would bear in others. She had said it hundreds of times. Except this time, it sounded different. For the greater glory of God? Could that step she was taking be for the greater glory of God? To flee from her vocation and even from the bosom of the Church? A torrent of light tore through the dense, suffocating darkness into which she had moved the previous few months. She tore up the letter right then and there. She felt both shame and liberation. The next morning, she went to confession with Fr. Pujadas, and a few days later she wrote to the provincial superior of the Handmaids, in Gandia, requesting entry into their institute. She was accepted, and they chose her date of admission as June 7, 1929, the Solemnity of the Sacred Heart.

Her conscience should have been calm, and yet she could not find peace. She prayed for days in anguish, asking the Lord for a sign of His will, and it seemed as if He had granted it in a providential event. When the calendar of examinations was published, they did not finish, as in other years, at the end of May, but began precisely on the day of the Sacred Heart of Jesus. Happy with that coincidence, which seemed to be a wink from God, she went to see Fr. Pujadas. He told her that God has no deadlines and insisted that she could enter another day. She obeyed and proposed to enter as soon as her degree was finished and continued to prepare for her exams.

Other mishaps were still going to happen to her that would delay her entry further. She spent the entire night before the organic chemistry exam studying for it, without even going to bed. Around four or five in the morning she went down to the chapel to pray for a while and from there she left for the university, convinced that she was magnificently prepared on the subject. It was an oral, public exam and, shortly before she went on stage, she commented to her classmates: "If they ask me about aldehydes, I'll nail it."

The examiner said, "Miss María Félix, would you be so kind as to explain to us the physical properties of aldehydes?" María was so lucky! As admiration buzzed through the room, María, with a lost gaze, stood before the examiner without saying a word. Her face was as blank as her mind. She did not remember anything she had reviewed the night before. The professor, who considered her a brilliant student, tried to reassure her and told her not to worry, that he understood that she was unwell and that she would appear in the record as absent. What did God want with that incomprehensible failure? She had a sense, but she no longer dared to take anything for granted.

After this, the last exam she had left was German, an elective course. She spent the morning at the door of the exam room and, as the last student left, she asked discreetly why she had not been called. They replied that she was not on their list. It turned out that the assistant who was supposed to register her in September had forgotten to do it. She would have another chance after the summer.

In September, she took the organic chemistry exam and passed, but this time she failed German. She went with haste to tell Fr. Pujadas and to share her perplexity with him. She could not ask her parents to pay for her to stay another year in Zaragoza for an elective course. It did not seem appropriate to enter the Handmaids in this manner, without finishing her degree and still feeling an atrocious repugnance, believing that it was not of God. On the other hand, she didn't want to go home because she felt as if it would be a step backwards in her desire to consecrate herself to God. What could she do now? The priest, distant and stern, replied: "I don't know. I think you will wander astray and condemn yourself in the end." And, without saying another word, he left the reception room. María, with a heavy heart, returned to her residence, thinking about which path she should take.

At Home Again

To get out of that impasse, she wrote to Mr. Fons, her former professor at the public high school in Lleida, asking him to hire her as an assistant. She would stay at the Working Women's House, a residence she could afford with her modest income. Thus, with the excuse that her studies were going to get rusty in the village, she avoided returning to her parents' house. She knew that they would no longer try to hold her back, but she wanted to be safe from her own fragility in seeking God's will. That is how she ended up spending the remaining months until returning to Zaragoza in January and passing the German exam.

She finally had a degree in chemistry, but she still didn't know clearly what God wanted from her. How many tears María would still have to shed before the tabernacle of the chapel of her residence back in Lleida! But on the outside, no one could have seen the inner battle she was fighting. She had gotten very involved with the apostolate with other young people in the city, such as Paquita Rovira. She prepared her classes thoroughly, and her students admired her clarity and enthusiasm. She also sought out a Jesuit spiritual director, Fr. Juan Serrat, S.J. With his help, she began to find peace, especially after Fr. Pujadas told her — when she had met with him in January in Zaragoza — that it seemed logical to him that she not enter if she felt so badly about it.

María about to complete her degree in chemistry (Zaragoza, 1929).

With the arrival of summer, a new setback arose for her plans, which were too undefined. Mr. and Mrs. Félix decided to move to Barcelona to reunite in a single city their young children — resident students until now in Barbastro and Zaragoza — with their older brother, who continued studying for his degree. There María could work as much as she wanted and would not lose any of the studies she had completed. How could she tell her parents that she would not return because being in their house was a constant temptation for her? Since she did not know anything else that God wanted, she gave in and followed them, and she doubled down on begging God to clarify her path.

In Barcelona, in their apartment on Almogávares Street next to the headquarters of the Catalana de Gas y Electricidad Company, she went through a time of fervor and spiritual combat. Her parents and siblings went out of their way to make her feel at home, pampered her with devotion, and made it very painful for her to think about a separation. She loved and admired her father more every day. Now that her grandmother Joaquina, a widow for fourteen years, had become crippled, Ramón had invented his own wheelchair and cared for the comfort of his mother-in-law like the most tender of children. And, as for María, he cared for her as he did before her departure, as the apple of his eye. In the mornings, he was the one who would wake her up before going to work. María, who had never been a morning person and usually stayed up late reading, was very grateful for this affectionate gesture. One of those days, her father, touching the bed, was taken aback. He had noticed under the sheet a wooden board, and María had a very hard time explaining to her father her desires for penance! Poor Ramón, bewildered, accepted the explanation of his beloved daughter, understanding that there was a mystery between God and her that clearly escaped him. Since he was a man of conviction, his acceptance reflected the integrity of his character. From then on, when one of the boys dared to question María about her austerities, it was the accuser who got reprimanded. María thought about how this put her at ease and was moved. How could she cause sorrow to such a good father, who only deserved gratitude? However, she felt God very close, and His presence filled her with great desires for the apostolate, for holiness, but also for definitive dedication and consecration to Him.

She returned to Catholic Action, in which she worked literally day and night. At night, in order not to disturb anyone at home, she worked by the light of an oil lamp — with which she almost caught her hair on fire several times! During the day, so that her parents would not suspect anything, she would say she was going to the dentist. Then she would continue her apostolic journeys without giving further explanations. She ended up making them think that she was either falling in love with a dentist or had considerable dental problems. She read and studied, participated in all the activities of the association, and helped the poor. She would also give classes in order to have more resources with which to remedy so many miseries. However, that life of dedication did not fulfill her. She dreamed of being a religious sister in order to definitively embrace the chastity and poverty she had promised God in the depths of her heart. She was living her obedience in private, as obedience to the guidance of the Catholic Action chaplain, but she wanted to have the guarantee of the Church that this was God's will for her. In addition, she felt that she needed to live that ideal with other sisters in community.

God's hand in her life, as at so many other times, was to come unexpectedly and in a way that was difficult to interpret.

Chapter 5

"He Wanted Us to Be His Own; He Wanted Us to Be Ignatians." 1931–1939

"Do Something for Our Lord"

On April 14, 1931, the Second Spanish Republic was proclaimed.[3] The atmosphere in the city of Barcelona was one of enormous agitation. In La Plaza de San Jaime, Francesc Macià's statements were enthusiastically received by the defenders of the federal state, while supporters of the monarchy trembled at the consequences that this change could have in the very near future. María was also worried, although for very different reasons.

Her brothers, especially Ramón, the eldest, were well known in traditionalist circles. Moreover, because of their temperament and age — they were twenty-two, twenty, and seventeen years old — she knew well that they were not going to sit and wait for things to happen. The fear of what they might say or do and the consequences of their actions alternated with the satisfaction of

[3] On April 14, 1931, given the result of the municipal elections, which showed very little support for the monarchy in the main cities, King Alfonso XIII left Spain. Immediately afterwards, a revolutionary committee formed itself as a provisional government and proclaimed the Second Spanish Republic. The position of the Church was very precarious. The extremists considered the Church to be an ally of the monarchy and capitalism and began their attacks. From May 11th to 13th, numerous convents and religious schools suffered fires and looting in Madrid, Valencia, Alicante, Murcia, Seville, Málaga, and Cádiz due to the passivity of the law enforcement authorities. The new republican authorities, imbued with secularism, were also interested in ending the social influence of the Church.

seeing them so brave, defending their patriotic ideals and selflessly disregarding their own safety. For her part, María trembled with rage when she walked the streets among the crowds that swarmed shouting, "Long Live the Republic," and she would hear mockery and threats against Jesus Christ and the Church. Now, in order to counteract the anticlerical environment of atheistic propaganda, she had to work body and soul for the Christianization of society.

However, soon her wings were clipped. In May, as soon as news of the burning of churches and convents began to arrive, her brothers Ramón and "Pepe" (José) took to the street as improvised public speakers, denouncing the abuses and the apathy of the public law enforcement. Florentina, terrified, telephoned her husband, and he gave strict orders for the whole family to go back to the village. In her last years of life, Florentina still remembered how she sent three of her children to Seira, while she waited with one of them in the city for the laundry to dry in order to properly pack up the suitcases and close up the house.

In the village, the atmosphere was nothing like Barcelona. There the air of revolution did not arrive except through allusions in the newspapers. The gatherings at the social club revolved around bullfighting and soccer, while literary gatherings were the entertainment of the most cultured young people. María's walks from the library to the outlook and from the outlook to a friend's house made her feel imprisoned in a golden cage or held as a prisoner on probation. She needed to get out. So, when she heard that Ángel was working on enrolling in the university for the next academic year, she immediately offered to do the paperwork in the city. Florentina suspected something and she refused to let María go alone. She gave her the exact amount of money for the trip there and back and forbade her from taking a small bag of clothes just in case. If she was going there and back in one day, she didn't need anything.

With or without clothes, María left home forever. Once she finished Ángel's paperwork, she accompanied him to the coach line and, with immense affection, said goodbye to him from the door of the coach. Ángel was confused. Wasn't she coming back with him? Their mother had been very clear. María was too. She stayed in Lleida "to do something for our Lord."

Somewhat disoriented, because she had only five *pesetas* in her pocket, she went to the Casa de Familia to ask for lodging on credit from the nuns. She hoped to get hired as an assistant at the public high school for now and would pay it back with her wages. She knew she was starting a new life. Whatever it was, it was going to be entirely for God. Family life was very sweet to her, but it was not for her.

After a few weeks, she learned that in the Normal School for Teaching there was an atheist professor who did a lot of harm to the students. Not knowing why, María felt that with that news came an invitation from God. Why couldn't she use the same means for Jesus Christ that this teacher used for her purposes? In addition, it was said that the government was planning to suppress religious schools. Speaking with her spiritual director, Fr. Serrat, María decided to set up an educational center in which the unity of science and faith would be preserved intact, an academy in which to educate young women who would like to complete high school, which was necessary for a teaching degree and for higher studies.

The academy was opened, under the name of Academia Nueva, and it was truly something new. Until that point, most of the girls went to La Enseñanza or to the schools of the Dominicans or of the Sisters of the Holy Family to attend primary school or to acquire a general education. Only the wealthiest families sent their daughters for a time to Tarragona, to the school run by the Religious of Jesus and Mary, with the same intention. If they wanted to finish high school as students of any of these schools, they had to study at the public high school, as María Félix had done. Now, about twenty young women from wealthy families began their high-school studies at the Academia Nueva, calling attention to the issue of women's education in the city.

The teaching staff was composed of María Navés, a very pious nationally accredited teacher; Manuel Portugués, professor of geography and history from the public high school, and María Félix herself: director, science professor, and soul of the institution. The academic level was high. María did not want to jeopardize the girls, who had to take their exams in the public high school, so she tried to prepare them with knowledge superior to that which was required. The small number of students and the personal contact with each of them allowed a higher level of education and fostered an environment of serious intellectual work. In addition, the Academy became a center of religious and spiritual formation. Fr. Serrat gladly agreed to give weekly apologetics lessons for the older students as well as many of their mothers and relatives. These meetings made the Academia Nueva a topic of frequent conversation among the pious women of the city.

Over the months, María had to change the location of the Academy several times. She had to leave the first place she rented after a few weeks due to financial difficulties. Then, everything went from good to great. Although they were always nearly under water financially, she felt the need to trust God completely. She later said, "I felt that if I reserved something for the summers or for difficult times, it was like stealing from God. Our Lord always provided as a Father." The fact that God blessed María's blind trust and her way of using money, always for the good of the students, is evidenced by the increase in the number of girls. That was the reason she had to change locations three times between 1931 and 1934, in addition to an event that she always considered to be a tender gift of Providence:

> When the Academy was first opened, before starting classes, a bill arrived from the electrician for the amount of fifty *pesetas*. That was a large amount for me, who had not had a single cent for a long time. Nevertheless, at that time, I had never seen a bill returned without paying the full amount, and it did not even cross my mind to beg them to postpone the deadline. I took the bill and told the worker to wait a moment. I took the bill and went to kneel before the Christ that hung over the visiting room and said to the Lord: "You pay for it, since I cannot." And immediately there was another knock on the door. It was the daughter of Mrs. Mangrané, who had come to register her daughter Pilar. She brought me the amount of the monthly tuition in an envelope. Exactly fifty *pesetas*. I gave them to the worker and went to kiss Christ.[4]

Thus, through intimacy with Jesus, she resolved her spiritual and material difficulties.

4 Autobiographical Writings, Notebook B (AGCS M 201,002).

"A Society of Jesus for Women"

In those years in Lleida, María had a similar experience to that of St. Ignatius of Loyola in the cave of Manresa, although updated to the twentieth century. Since she spent many hours alone in the Academy, her mornings looked like those of an austere hermit, mostly devoted to prayer and penance. In love with Christ crucified and encouraged by the examples of the holy Jesuits, to her nothing seemed enough in order to seek union with God and to pray for the salvation of souls. On several occasions, Fr. Serrat had to ask her for an account of what she was doing in regard to penances, because he saw her emaciated. He would even greet her, as a reprimand, saying: "When are they burying you?"

In the end, he chose to tell her that she could not live alone in the Academy unless María Navés lived with her, and that she should submit to her companion regarding anything that would affect her health. She did so willingly, but then she chose to mortify herself with some internal penance, the only sacrifice that no one had forbidden her. Since she enjoyed studying very much, she decided not to prepare her classes as well so as not to seek her personal satisfaction. She would later repent of this mistake and say that not preparing classes is an injustice to the students and that the work that God entrusts to us must be done with all our heart.

This twenty-three-year-old teacher was extremely thin, cheerful, and passionate about education and studying. She had no money for her own things but managed to move forward everything she considered to be for the greater glory of God. Other young women who had spiritual direction with the Jesuits became interested in joining her. The first was Carmen Aige, a "good girl" from the high society of Lleida who was pondering what God wanted from her. Fr. Serrat had strongly advised her to meet with María.

"She is very worthy, you could be very good friends," he said to María when he introduced them. María understood perfectly. Carmen, although more austere and rigid in her manners, had a passionate heart that beat strongly with her same ideals. With her astute perception of people, María got an idea of the incalculable value of the woman that would be her first companion:

> She was a diamond in the rough set in a worldly pendant: serious, dignified, strict to the point of ferocity; settled on firm rock with sharp principles of moral rectitude; tenderly pious, vehement and passionate under cold, rigid manners, sustained by innate pride; made for commanding and dominance; and preferring to break rather than bend. On the outside, she was polished, elegant, helpful, confident in being distinguished through artistic temperament and personal dignity; and she maintained her social status and social benefits because of both her prudence and education. As soon as I met her, I opened my arms and heart to her, and I realized that she was a precious stone that was too hard to be polished by mankind. She could only be carved by God.[5]

Then others would come: Montserrat Amigó, a brave teacher who dreamed of being a Jesuit and who asked María for math classes but warned that "she was not going to be caught"; Carmen Badía, also a nationally accredited teacher, whose humility impressed María in a series of Spiritual Exercises at the Old Seminary of Lleida; Inés Tarragona and Inés Linés, cousins of Carmen Aige, who at the time were fifteen years old but already sensed that they would consecrate themselves to God; and Victorina Jené, niece of a common friend of Carmen and María. The thing they all had in common was their Ignatian nature and fervor.

This interest in everything Ignatian — which attracted many young women to María Félix — was a call from God that María clearly recognized on July 31, 1932. Six months before, the government had decreed the dissolution of the Society of Jesus in Spanish territory. Most had gone into exile, but some Jesuits, such as Fr. Serrat, remained in Spain with the permission of their superiors to give Spiritual Exercises and retreats for small groups. María attended one of these retreats that he preached at the Sagrada Familia School on St. Ignatius's Feast Day. After the priest's talk, which excited her, she went ahead to pray a while longer and then meet up with her friends. Years later she would recall:

5 Autobiographical Writings, Notebook C (AGCS M 201,003).

> When I was there, next to the tabernacle, I felt as if I had been transported, as if I were immersed in the abyss of the Divine Presence. As if I had been transferred from this world to another. I felt God, and I felt inundated with light and joy. Then this was impressed upon my soul: that I would also live the Rules and Constitutions of St. Ignatius in the manner of the Society of Jesus and that there would be many young women who would embrace that way of life. The Lord assured me, promised me, and infused in me a full certainty of that, greater than that resulting from the evidence. I did not see anything, nor did I hear anything with my physical senses. It was a truth that went into my soul without entering through the doors of the senses and that seized it, subjecting all its powers with complete domination, without any struggle or repugnance. I left the chapel with great peace, with great serenity, and what amazes me the most is that I did not feel amazed. It seemed to me the most natural thing in the world, the most obvious, the easiest — a Society of Jesus for women. As if my entire life I had thought the same thing, as if it were a universal conviction. However, from those feelings about my vocation on the feast day of St. Ignatius, I did not deduce that I had to found a religious congregation, nor did I deduce anything specific. It was enough for me to be certain that this vocation would come about, and I was not worried about how or when. Nor did I say anything at the moment to the priest. Perhaps because it seemed to me that the vocation was evident to everyone and seemed to me the most natural thing in the world.[6]

For the first time, she was clear about her vocation. She was to belong to a *Society of Jesus for women*. How or when, only the Lord knew. From then on, María's demeanor became even more intimate, brighter, and attractive. She became, if possible, an even better apostle, and encouraged others to be so as well. Without knowing very well how, she managed to get Carmen to overcome her family prejudices against studying. She not only agreed to teach at the Academy, but also to finish high school and study for a university

[6] Ibid.

degree in order to be able to teach. Carmen's other minor renunciations, such as evenings at the theater with her friends or painting her nails, came little by little, as logical consequences of her particular vocation.

For her part, María was happy. This grace from St. Ignatius's feast day sustained her inwardly. She needed the strength of this certainty for the difficult test that was about to arrive suddenly. For the academic year 1932–1933, her father Ramón announced that he had gotten her a position in the public high school in Manresa. It seemed to him that María was embarking on a "crazy adventure" and, on top of that, she was dragging others with her, and he wanted to stop it in time. María thought she could combine the position with her work at the Academy, so she was hopeful. However, when she found out that the schedules were incompatible, she told him that she would not accept it. She expressed her enormous gratitude, but the Academy was her priority. Her father was so upset that he told her that this was his last goodbye. This hardship lasted several months, but in the end his love for his only daughter won out and there was reconciliation, although not agreement. María would not work for that school.

In addition, in that school year María became ill with acute endocarditis, but she didn't pay special attention to it. The day after receiving the diagnosis, Fr. Serrat went to see her. "What are you thinking of doing?" he asked. María replied, "To get up and resume my ordinary life." "What about treatment? I don't think the best rest therapy for your endocardium is giving science classes to teenagers," he retorted. She answered, "*Padre,* let me get out of bed. I am certain that my life is God's and that human predictions will always fail."

Fr. Serrat perceived something of supernatural prudence because he did not use his moral authority to keep her in bed but rather he let María continue her active life. It seemed that during this time God bore her up on eagle's wings.

On Eagle's Wings

Of course, María was progressing in great strides. At that time, she experienced confusion that helps us to understand how God worked in her soul. She began to read St. Teresa of Jesus. She liked her firm and strong spirituality, which at the same time was tenderly delicate in her love of Jesus Christ. However, María was troubled to recognize that some of the things that the saint described in the highest states of prayer happened to her as well. That could not be. María did not feel like a saint, but saw herself as full of imperfections. These must have been psychological suggestions or phenomena that she needed to clarify. She began to read psychology books and to enter into a small labyrinth that she ended up cutting short. She decided that this self-analysis was stealing time from God that she owed to Him. She chose to overcome her embarrassment and tell the priest everything. Whatever he said, she would do it. Fr. Serrat, upon hearing her report, reassured her completely. He told her to no longer resist that prayer in which God went in and out of her soul as if it were His own home.

In addition, during that school year, the bishop granted her permission to have a semipublic chapel in the Academia Nueva with the Blessed Sacrament reserved. Many years later, she still remembered how "the first day that the Blessed Sacrament was there I was beside myself." She had probably experienced what she would write in 1940, when she obtained the same permission for the residence in Barcelona: "Jesus is home! Our tabernacle is very poor, but it contains the One who is the whole Treasure of Heaven and earth. May He be blessed a thousand and one times."

That presence of Jesus at home and Carmen's courageous decision to stay at the Academy in the summer, instead of going to the farmhouse with her relatives, were two of the great joys of this crucial year. They dedicated the entire month of July to St. Ignatius with great intensity. They read his biography and cultivated their devotion to him. They both felt the desire to make a vow of consecration to God that bound them forever to His exclusive service. They spoke to Fr. Serrat, and he approved it very happily. They set the date of August 15th, the Solemnity of the Assumption. That day, at the Mass celebrated by Fr. Serrat, before receiving Communion, María and Carmen consecrated themselves silently to the Lord forever, for whatever He wanted, although at that time they did not know very well what they were offering themselves for specifically. It was a day of much spiritual comfort, of which María later said:

> Our consecration had no external ceremony, not even a formula that gave some external formality to that act. Nonetheless, that day the Lord put a seal on our souls, on our hearts, and on our whole being. We were already fully and completely His. It would be a sacrilege to use even one breath of our life in profane pursuits.[7]

A few days later, with great joy, they realized that August 15, 1934, was the five hundredth anniversary of the vow made by Ignatius of Loyola and his first companions in Montmartre.

Madrid: The Unfinished Doctorate

Finally, everything was moving forward smoothly. María already had a companion who would be with her through thick and thin, and the Academy was running wonderfully. For the next school year, they only had to make plans, organize the schedule, think about Carmen's studies, and so forth. However, in the midst of these deliberations, a question would resonate in María's heart that would end up launching her so many times into new and generous commitments: "What about the glory of God?" It would be so great if Carmen had a formation similar to her own in order to be a better instrument in the apostolate! And for this, wouldn't the best thing be for her to study at a top-notch university? With the extensive general education that she already had, she could study philosophy and literature and gain a lot.

The Universidad Central had just moved the Philosophy Department to a new location. It was now in the Ciudad Universitaria neighborhood in Madrid, the largest city and capital of Spain, located in the center of the country. The Philosophy Department had a good reputation because of its professors: Ramón Menéndez Pidal, José Ortega y Gasset, Manuel García-Morente, and Xavier Zubiri, among others. In addition, if Carmen moved to Madrid, María could accompany her and study for her doctorate. What about the Academy? Since the religious schools were not closed at the moment, it was not really necessary for it to continue functioning. What they offered to the girls could continue to be offered by the public high school, academically, and, in terms

[7] Ibid.

of religion, by the different apostolic movements of the city. With enormous detachment, which always characterized her, María convinced Carmen, who in turn did the same with her mother. They packed their bags and left for Madrid. In their luggage there were no great treasures, but there was one curious thing: María refused to leave behind the huge pots she had bought for the Academy's kitchen, convinced that the small group of Ignatians would grow.

Arriving in the capital, they fell in love with the atmosphere of the university and religious life. They got in touch with Fr. Enrique Herrera Oria, S.J., who introduced them to the Marian Congregation of the Handmaids and to the educational weeks of the Federación de Amigos de la Enseñanza (FAE) [Federation of the Friends of Education]. (Just one year later, María would be appointed as president of that congregation.) They also became involved in study circles and taught catechism. Carmen's classes, which were very interesting, also had hands-on sessions at the Prado Museum, and María asked permission to accompany the group. They allowed her and, between these cultural outings and those of the apostolate, she realized that she was not paying much attention to her doctoral courses. In reality, although she did not realize it, she was looking more for a place to fulfill her vocation than achieving *summa cum laude*. Later she would say with some sorrow that she regretted how scattered she was during her years in Madrid.

They stayed in several different places. They started out in the residence of the Teresian Sisters. They had to leave before long because of an incident that was unpleasant at the time. However, it shows us that María, without fully realizing it, was still searching for her religious vocation.

The Teresian Sisters had treated María very well. They had provided her with private students so that she could pay for her lodging. Carmen paid for her lodging with what her family had offered to contribute — despite being very upset by her departure. The financial aid from Mr. and Mrs. Félix was spent completely on Carmen's and María's studies and other needs. However, in the residence, María soon began to feel like an uncomfortable guest. In her zeal for religious life and for the Handmaids of the Sacred Heart of Jesus in particular, she began to lead some of the residents to that congregation. As if that were not enough, one day something went missing in the room of one of the young women. The Teresian Sisters demanded that María show them what she had in the trunks that she kept in the storage room. María refused to open her belongings because that is where she kept the pots she brought from Lleida. How was she going to explain the purpose of the pots, which she herself did not fully understand? She defended herself as well as she could, and she ended up being asked to leave. The Teresian Sisters let her know that she would have to look for a different lodging for the next school year. It was the second time this had happened to her. She had already been expelled by the Teresian Sisters in Zaragoza because her friend Asunción entered another convent. María remembered how Fr. Pujadas had teased her at that time: "You are not worthy to suffer persecution for Jesus Christ, so you suffer it for the Handmaids." In any case, from this incident she learned two things: first, that she would never force a young woman to violate her privacy by showing her belongings; and second, that it is important to respect the field of apostolate of each movement or congregation. Without resistance or rigidities, recognizing and respecting the vocation of each one, she would teach her companions to avoid all proselytism in a field already cultivated by others.

Under Attack

During the 1935–1936 school year, the streets of Madrid became more and more tense. In addition to the political instability and insecurity, there was also an increase in anticlericalism and religious persecution. It got to the point that María and Carmen had to go to Mass with their veils hidden in their bag to avoid insults and humiliations on the way to the church.

In June, Carmen returned to Lleida with her family. Given their privileged social situation, Mr. and Mrs. Aige were very worried. María was still in Madrid. She had just registered for the exam to become a professor at a public high school. Then, warned by Fr. Herrera of the imminence of an armed uprising, she left on July 12th to Barcelona to be with her family.

Settled once again in the apartment on Almogávares Street, María put all her energies at the service of the Church. The Church was living through a terrible persecution, particularly in Barcelona. Although in theory the Second Spanish Republic governed that area, the real power was exercised by the committees of the revolution. There were extremists who were determined to put an end to the "fascist enemy." They made no distinctions between political activists and devout Catholics, all of whom they considered to be nationalists. One could be killed both for wearing a tie or a religious habit, carrying political propaganda against communism or devotional pamphlets. Just in the city of Barcelona, a month after the war began, more than two hundred and fifty priests and religious had been killed. María finally saw clearly what God wanted from her. She would risk her life working for the Lord in this immense vineyard.

She joined the National Confederation of Labor (CNT by its initials in Spanish) in order to obtain a position as a professor at the Maragall Institute and managed to get Carmen admitted to the one in Tarrassa, although she had not finished her degree. Carmen, threatened in Lleida by the defection of her brother Luis, had moved with her mother and sister to the house of some friends in Barcelona. Her mother's serious illness — which would lead to her death — and the economic situation of her family, accustomed to living comfortably, were a cause of suffering beyond the pain of war. That is why it was a great joy for María to provide Carmen with a job, in addition to using her own salary to help with other hardships. With what María earned, she tried to help her own parents. Her brothers Ramón and Ángel had been conscripted by the Republic, and their father Ramón was in poor health. She sent Carmen, without Carmen's knowledge, part of her monthly allowance, and what was left was devoted to others in need since she always had plenty left over.

In the institute where María worked, the teachers were polite to each other, but there was a general sense of suspicion. That is why Mr. Fons, her former professor, introduced her to some fellow professors as an "expert in Latin," which was the code phrase for Catholics to make themselves known. Soon her intellectual capacity also made a place for her among the atheist professors. María felt comforted by Mr. Fons, who encouraged her to continue fostering devotion to the Sacred Heart of Jesus by asking her if she had "picked up her rations on the first Friday." She also felt supported by the other faculty members, including the director, who admired María despite being a fervent socialist.

As for her interior life, her spirit was lifted again. In communication with the Jesuits, she kept sacred vessels, books, and ornaments on the terrace of her house, and soon afterwards she obtained an even more valuable treasure. They entrusted her with the distribution of Communion to some of the faithful and the pyx with the Blessed Sacrament, which she reserved in a jewelry box. The presence of the Lord in the Blessed Sacrament filled her with courage. One day, in the middle of an air raid, she escaped from the Arco de Triunfo underground metro station, to which her family had almost dragged her, in order to run home to get the reserved Eucharist. With the jewelry box hugged to her chest, she walked back to the shelter

> along the same abandoned street, among the same deafening booms, with a reverence and with an infinite joy. It was not that I thought He would deliver me from death, nor was it even the feeling that I was not afraid of death with Him. My joy was to save my Blessed Lord from the fire, from the rubble, from irreverence.[8]

She did not reflect on it, but her fundamental concern was more and more Jesus Christ and less herself: "Many times when I was in bed, I had to get up to sit with the Blessed Sacrament because it seemed an atrocity for me to rest and for Him to be so persecuted." She went to confession while walking along Las Ramblas; she took Communion, from the hands of a priest friend, in a private room of a bar, keeping two glasses of *horchata* in front of them to avoid raising suspicion; she wrote encrypted letters to her companions to keep their vocation and their hope alive; she renewed her vow of consecration to God every August 15th with whomever could meet her in Barcelona; and she even posed as the girlfriend of Pedro Miró de Mesa, a Jesuit, to save his life in an interrogation. The latter was futile. The priest had been carefully investigated, and María's frivolous and forced acting did not convince the militiamen.

She desired to be a martyr and to share in the suffering of others because of her fidelity to God and to the Church. For this reason, she was delighted when Fr. Alfonso María Thió, S.J. — recently released from the

[8] Ibid.

Modelo Prison — invited her to participate in a unique project in September 1937. He asked María and Carmen if they would teach at the academy that his sister, María Jesús, a Religious of Jesus and Mary, was planning to open for students from the religious schools that had been closed during the war. The faculty would be composed of, apart from himself, religious sisters from various congregations that were scattered throughout the city and some secular university professors who had been dismissed for their political ideas or for their declared Catholicism. The curriculum would be as complete as the one that characterized the formation of the Society of Jesus. The idea was to provide a solid academic formation — for boys and girls, as expected from a secular academy — as well as to be a center of religious dissemination to their families. The Lauria Academy, as the institution was named, would have oral examinations before rigorous magistrates, theatrical performances that would lift the spirit. Several times *El Divino Impaciente* (*A Saint in a Hurry*, a dramatization of the life of St. Francis Xavier by Pemán, was performed), days of formation for families, confessors available in the evenings, and even an office for the falsification of documents to help priests, religious, and committed lay people flee persecution. María did not make him beg. They could count on her and certainly also some other young women from her closest circle. The danger did not matter, even though the chosen location was above a naturalist-anarchist federation that depended on the Iberian Anarchist Federation (FAI). Just as they say, "the closer to the danger the further away from harm." God would not fail them.

This is how she spent the war: classes, clandestine Masses, searches, bombings, endless lines to get medicine for her father who was sick with asthma, and above all, with the ever-growing conviction — stronger every year — that God wanted something from that small group of young women. Once again on August 15th, they gathered to make their vow to the Lord: to be entirely His in the style of St. Ignatius.

Part Two

Leading the Company

Chapter 6

Feeling Her Way Along

1939–1944

Gathering the Dispersed Women

At the end of the war, María found herself in a strange and disturbing situation. Her brothers Ramón and Ángel were imprisoned in concentration camps for having been officers of the Republican army; her vocation companions were spread out over different Spanish cities, each with her own family; and she herself was living again in her parents' house. Everything was so different from what she thought it would be! To top it all off, her brothers were imprisoned on charges contrary to their political ideals. Ramón had been surprised by the military uprising while working in the town of Berja in the province of Almería in southern Spain. He was an engineer and had not fought for the nationalists in order to avoid reprisals against his family. Ángel, for his part, had volunteered to serve in the army to take the place of their sick father when he was drafted. The two, especially Ángel, had fought in the "fifth column" as infiltrators in favor of the nationalists, and now it was the nationalists who had them held in concentration camps. María and her other brother, Pepe, had to look for evidence of their true political affiliation in order to free them. Thanks be to God, that last part was easy. As for María's vocation, after so many efforts to leave her parents' house, it now seemed further away than ever. She was again among her own family, and each of the "Ignatian" women who shared her desire to consecrate themselves to God seemed indispensable in her own family during this difficult time of reconstruction.

But this did not darken her mood. One would have had to live through the horrors of war to understand the sense of liberation she experienced during that time and the spirit with which she set out to get her brothers out of prison and gather the dispersed women. She wrote letters to Ángel — "Angelitín" or "Lalito," as she affectionately called him — full of tenderness and tenacity, in which she told him about what she had been doing in Barcelona and Bilbao to get him out of the prison in Deusto where he was being held. She traveled alone to the capital of Biscay, through a still turbulent Spain, to save her parents from the anxiety of such exhausting errands. She spent a month in the city, writing to him almost daily and giving an account of her efforts in favor of him and their cousin Antonio, who was also imprisoned. During Holy Week, on April 5, 1939, she wrote:

> Do you pray the novena of trust in the Sacred Heart? Do it every day. Be men of faith and piety. Celebrate these days of Holy Week as well as you can. Remember as Christians the mysteries of our redemption and consider that the greatest Goodness and Innocence suffered before we did. Rejoice in the Resurrection, and if you can, take Communion and rise again to grace, and that you may rejoice more, I will send you cakes. [...] Ask me for whatever you need. Don't let your facial hair grow, and comb your hair well. Always present yourselves as clean and dignified and do not let yourselves go. Today in the corridor of the court I was asked if I was there for any of my children. Judging from my appearance, I can advise you, love you, and embrace you as your little mother.[9]

Ángel, once released, left for Almería to do the same for Ramón. Almost a year later, due to the lack of results from his efforts, María would take care of getting Ramón out of jail.

As for her companions, she wrote to some of them and was glad to see that, although physically separated, they continued to support each other in spirit and their vocation had not waned. She wrote to Carmen Aige and

[9] Letter to Ángel Félix, March 30, 1939 (AGCS M 604.01.A,162).

Montserrat Amigó, who were in Lleida, telling them about her plans to open an educational center similar to the Academia Nueva, where they could all get together and start their life together. She also made them aware of the difficulties she was encountering. After acknowledging receipt of the sad news about Victorina, who had taken the vow with them in 1938 but was now dealing with her family's opposition, María wrote them in that same letter:

> You can live in spiritual community and encourage each other in divine service with frequent and mutual edification. One more incentive to respond with greater fidelity to the divine call. Let us not lose sight of the fact that our vocation is the greater glory of God always and everywhere. For the greater glory of God! For us it is not a mere slogan or a cliché. It is something essential to our life, the target of our love, the strength of our activity, the reason for our sacrifice, and it is the beginning of our transformation into *alter Christus* because the greater glory of God and none other was the vocation of Jesus Christ, the Model and Captain given to us by our Heavenly Father and whom we necessarily find by following the footsteps of our holy Father Ignatius.

And so that they did not rest on their laurels until the time came to start being religious sisters, she encouraged them, writing:

> Our vocation does not have a tomorrow for its realization, as that of missions, hospitals, teaching, etc.; it only has the present moment. It is to glorify God, for His greater glory, in our own sanctification and in that apostolate that is most necessary and within the reach of our means. This can and should always be done. You have a good vineyard in which to work and an excellent director — Father Serrat. Work with faith. Seek new vocation companions and the Lord will reward us by giving us the opportunity to be religious sisters if He so wishes. Pray for that to happen.
>
> Your poor sister in Jesus and Mary,
> María.

Finally, in the postscript, she provided them with a way to bring life to these holy desires: "Try to celebrate the month of St. Ignatius and read his biography written by Father Casanovas. Tell me if you do not have a copy."[10]

Although she wanted to live in community so that the example of the good women would encourage her, she also knew well that she had an important influence over all of them and felt responsible for their spiritual progress.

For this reason, she insisted that they meet in Barcelona to renew the vow they had been making on August 15th each year. This year there were more of them than ever. At the Mass celebrated by a Jesuit in the chapel of the Sisters of Mary Reparatrix on Caspe Street, Montserrat Amigó, Inés Tarragona, and María Amor Sarret all professed for the first time. María Amor was a student of philosophy, the only daughter of the tailor of the Jesuits, who would joyfully have entered the Society of Jesus had she been born a man. Those who renewed their vows were María Félix, Carmen Aige, and Victorina Jené. They were accompanied by another young woman who did not make her vow at that time because her spiritual director advised against it. The similarity of their vow with that of the first Jesuits in Montmartre did not escape them. Commenting on it while they had breakfast in the Horchatería Valenciana, they decided to celebrate in the nearby Manresa. They went there in the afternoon, full of joy, "to expound on our fervors, to renew our promises of fidelity, and to ask for the grace to remain firm in our vocation for the greater glory of God in that place where our holy Father Ignatius received so many graces."[11]

But after this exceptional moment of joy, they returned to daily life. María was worried that they were still separated and did not have the money to start a school or live in community. The means to initiate this apostolate and to strive to help each other was again given by the Jesuits. Fr. Thió told María that, having missed some schooling during the war, the older girls from the Lauria Academy were going to be a little behind if they returned to the religious schools. Perhaps she and one of her companions could

10 Letter to Carmen Aige and Montserrat Amigó, June 15, 1939 (AGCS E 20,002).

11 Community Notes from Barcelona, Summer 1939–May 1940 (AGCS D 102.11.A,001).

continue their education and prepare them on their own for official exams. The idea seemed providential to her. María Félix and María Amor would be the first teachers of the school, which they called Re-Vir-Cien (composed of the beginning of the words religion, virtue, and science in Spanish). Two other young women came to collaborate at the beginning through the efforts of Fr. Fayos, their spiritual director. They had an interest in teaching but did not feel a religious vocation. Soon María clarified her intentions with them, and they separated from the endeavor. In mid-August, some private classes began to be given, and on October 1st the academic year 1939–1940 began.

Meanwhile, the Ignatian women in Lleida came and went as they were able, and small steps were taken: Carmen enrolled in the Teaching School to be trained as a teacher; Montserrat, who did not yet have a leave of absence, worked on being able to leave her position as a nationally accredited teacher in a town near Lleida; Victorina was looking for a job for her sister so that her family would not depend on her teacher's fees for their support. As for Carmen's studies, about which she knew well, María was touched and wrote:

María Félix with her brother, Ángel, with pupils in Re-Vir-Cien (Barcelona, 1939).

Current façade of Re-Vir-Cien, Barcelona.

> I have said nothing to her, but I have admired the pearl that is set in the crown of her merits. A single indication has been enough for her to register in the Teaching School, and I know positively that it has always disgusted her greatly. Blessed are you a thousand times, my sweet Lord.[12]

María really allowed herself to be edified and carried away by her desires for the other women's holiness.

Poor and Happy

During Christmas vacation, María Félix traveled with María Amor to Madrid to participate in the VIII Educational Week of the FAE. Fr. Enrique Heras, S.J., a fervent missionary, was there and spoke to them at length and with enthusiasm about the mission in India. She was taken with the thought of starting the female university apostolate in that country! At the same time, Fr. Herrera recommended that they establish a novitiate in Salamanca due to the academic character of this city, and also to give a more universal dimension to the work they wanted to undertake. They visited Salamanca on the Epiphany and were received by the superior of the Jesuits with apprehension. He was a venerable but older religious who was not fond of novelties. This experience plunged María into a sea of doubt. What did God want from them? The return trip, more sad than the trip there, she spent uttering a never-ending rosary of "*Fiat, fiat*! . . ."

The following month, although the path was still unclear, she had a joy that softened all her sorrows. On the occasion of the students' Spiritual Exercises, in the diocese of Barcelona, they were granted permission for the reservation of the Blessed Sacrament in the chapel of Re-Vir-Cien. That building at 627 José Antonio Avenue — today the Gran Via de les Corts Catalanes — became her heaven. A very small community began to be formed, which from its very first moment was centered on Jesus in the Eucharist. María began to live at the school so as not to leave the Blessed Sacrament alone. María Amor told her parents that she also had to stay to accompany

[12] Autobiographical Writings, Notebook D (AGCS M 201,004).

María because Montserrat had to go to Barcelona for her studies. Poor Ramón's objections were useless. He responded to his daughter's phone call with: "The Lord will have such brave defenders in you women!" He knew perfectly well who defended whom and that María and her companions needed to be close to Jesus in the Eucharist.

After the Spiritual Exercises of the younger students came the series for the older students; later their teachers would need to make them. There were also the Masses and the acts of the Marian Congregation, which began almost at the same time as the founding of the school. In this way, they were given permission by the diocese to have the Blessed Sacrament indefinitely, and their way of life, little by little, was gaining stability.

Stability yes, but not comfort. Although the building in which they were staying was large, it was not enough to house a school with students from six different grades and serve as a residence for several of their teachers. "God above all," María would say. In the absence of suitable spaces, they slept in the classrooms on cots that they would put up when the girls left. They reorganized the classrooms and stretched them to unimagined limits, but that could not last forever. In addition, the weight of the financial troubles was a major burden. María continued to be — in her own words — a spendthrift as always, but they experienced real difficulty in continuing to pay the bills. Even so, for the following school year, she dreamed of opening a residential college and starting the apostolate to which all the women felt especially called. That is why the possibility of renting a second floor of the house was considered. That would also facilitate the official recognition of the school, which would no longer be a simple academy located in a little apartment.

The doubts of some of her companions in the face of these projects, for which they had no means, hurt her soul. Was not the lack of trust in God far more dangerous than the lack of means? She wrote to Fr. Serrat about these plans, in case he could shed light on them for her with his prudence and discretion. She needed to clarify those motives that drove her to embark on what seemed to be crazy:

> I don't know how a financial question can weigh into what seems to us to be for God's greater glory. I am sure that poverty has a great love for us and that it will never leave us. It seems to me that more than an obstacle to our plans, it must be their salvation. Without poverty, we would not have to make any act of faith or trust to such an extent as with it. Nor would the struggle be so hard, nor would victory be so difficult. Perhaps our apostolate would become a form of entertainment and the life of perfection that we strive for would become a kind of honest way of life. It is not crazy to trust God, but it is very crazy to teach the Provider how to provide.[13]

With the threat of an eviction hovering over the school, María wrote in the annals of the house:

> Thanks be to God, material poverty falls at our feet as if we were preparing ourselves for that spiritual poverty so deeply felt by our Father St. Ignatius and so vividly reflected in the Constitutions of the Society. According to them, it must constitute the strongest wall of defense of the religious life that we wish to profess. However, thanks also to God, we do not lack joy and good spirits: *Pobrets i alegrets* (poor and happy), as they say where we are from. May everything be *ad maiorem Dei gloriam*.[14]

In April, she traveled with Carmen to Palma on the island of Mallorca in the Mediterranean Sea. There were some young women there that Fr. Heras had told them about who wanted to be missionaries in the style of St. Ignatius. The trip was exciting. First, because of their motive: the possibility of finding new Ignatian companions and giving a boost to what they sensed would be the foundation of a religious order. Secondly, because they traveled by plane, a feat for someone in Spain in 1940. Lastly, because of the scene of their conversation with the three young Mallorcan women. They were taken on a boat, with lighted candles, and they entered a stalactite cave owned by one

[13] Letter to Fr. Juan Serrat Matabosch, S.J., January 28, 1940 (AGCS E 48,192).

[14] Community Notes from Barcelona, 1940–1941 (AGCS D 102.11.A,001).

of their fathers to speak to them alone inside. The impressive beauty of the grotto, the ideals they shared, the strength of their young lives, eager to build something great, inspired them to praise God and to greater generosity. However, despite the good will of all, they realized that their vocations did not coincide. Those women wanted to be missionaries above all, even if they had to sacrifice the Ignatian spirit. For María, Carmen, and all their companions, the essential thing was to follow Christ, in the style of St. Ignatius, in His mission to give the Father the greater glory. Within this decidedly Ignatian vocation, they could take on any type of apostolate.

Upon returning from Palma, María, a little ashamed, informed Fr. Serrat of the failure of the expedition. He took pity on them and, perhaps because he himself was bewildered, he put the whole matter into the hands of Fr. Alfredo Mondría, the superior of the Jesuit province of Aragon, which covered that territory. The priest asked them to come almost a month later, on May 14th, and assured them that they were most welcome. He happily listened to their explanation of the path they had traveled, and he promised them a Jesuit priest to lead the monthly Spiritual Exercises they wanted to carry out. He agreed to help them with their formation as Jesuits. And he also told them about a French institute that had existed for more than a hundred and fifty years, the Society of the Sacred Heart of Jesus. He suggested that they see if they felt that their vocation could fit there.

The latter gave a bittersweet tone to the interview because it seemed like another step backwards. After leaving the women in Palma, she and Carmen had felt reaffirmed that their vocation was something new that needed to take shape. However, María only wanted to know the will of God and, until now, it had been shown to her through venerable Jesuit priests. Could not this also be a sign of the divine will, since the proposal was coming from the father provincial himself? This was how she received it internally when the priest gave her an informational booklet from the French institute to take to her "sisters."

During the second half of June, and until July 1st, the feast of the Most Precious Blood, they resolved to deliberate on this subject in the presence of God, with more prayer and penance and without talking to each other, so as not to influence each other. With an impressive spiritual finesse, because it called into question the greatest dream of her life, María wrote to them all:

> We must consider in His Divine Presence whether it will be His will that the first common act of our vocation be to renounce it out of our love for our Lord Jesus Christ represented in the superiors of the Society of Jesus. It could well be God's plan that He gave us our entire vocation so that in one act we would give Him all the glory He has the right to expect from it. That in the very instant of birth, He would sacrifice her to His glory. Having achieved the greater glory of God, what more do we want? What else do we seek?[15]

July 1st arrived and, one by one, they all said they felt they should continue along the path they had begun. All but one. María, as she had planned to do from the beginning, said that during the time of deliberation she had been overworked — this was true — and that she had no time to reach a conclusion. She would lean on whatever side the majority had chosen. As for the letters that came from Lleida, they said the same as those from Barcelona. Unanimously, all the Ignatian women wanted to move forward with *their vocation.*

The Spiritual Exercises of 1940

This joy of the unanimity of opinions was quickly quelled by Fr. Mondría's response. The provincial superior insisted that the matter should not be settled until after the Spiritual Exercises they were going to do in August. For these he had appointed Fr. José Sola as director, who would not preach them for an entire month but only for ten days, since María, worried about supporting the series financially, did not dare to prolong them.

Those ten days were for María a time of intense inner struggle. Fr. Sola made her suffer a lot. He was insistent that she reveal to him the supernatural phenomena that she experienced in prayer, and this caused her great confusion. It seemed to her that it was like asking a savage to scientifically catalog and classify a pile of shiny stones. How could she know what was a precious

[15] Autobiographical Writings, Notebook D (AGCS M 201,004).

stone and what was a common crystal? In the end the only answer she could give was: "Look, *Padre,* there is nothing extraordinary, nothing supernatural in me. I am a sinner." That answer was not enough to convince him but rather stoked his interest. He wanted at all costs to know her well in order to have more insight about her path. In addition, he asked her to write a summary of how they wanted to live, like an outline of their Constitutions. However, María was a chemist, not a canonist. When the Lord had promised her that she would live the rules of St. Ignatius, He had not explained all the details to her and, of course, had not instructed her on how to make these Constitutions of the holy founder concrete in the life of her community.

She began what she could and wrote, full of embarrassment, a summary of the origin of her vocation so that Fr. Sola could give it to the provincial. The third of her tortures — as she called them — came from the temptations of some of her companions against their Ignatian vocation. She felt clearly that the Lord asked her for an extraordinary penance for the sake of those who were tempted. She did it, offering it for them, and soon they came to tell her that their doubts had been cleared up. A fourth source of suffering came directly from God. She felt that the Lord invited her to bind herself more closely to Him through a vow of perfection. He asked her to open her conscience more to the director of the Spiritual Exercises and to speak to him more precisely about that feeling she had about her vocation in 1932, as if the approval or disapproval of the superiors of the Society of Jesus depended on it. María, at the time, felt she did not have the strength for so many things.

She finished the Spiritual Exercises exhausted and grateful because, despite everything, the Lord had blessed her very much. Of the ten women who had gathered at Re-Vir-Cien for the Spiritual Exercises, nine came out determined to carry out that Ignatian vocation and renewed or made their annual vow on August 15th. Those who made it for the first time were Carmen Badía, Inés Linés, and Amparo Font.

Toward the Constitution of the Company

In October, convinced by her perseverance, Fr. Mondría gave the green light for the Ignatian women's intention and put them in contact with the apostolic administrator of Barcelona. They could finally entrust their vocation to the hierarchy of the Church! On the 11th of that month, María went to the archbishop's palace, accompanied by María Amor and Montserrat. Bishop Miguel de los Santos Díaz Gómara received them paternally and granted them permission to live as a religious community. He also explained to them that, in order to move toward the foundation of an institute, they had to give him a report twice a year about their life, observance, and activities. Finally, he made them one final recommendation that was quite unusual. He didn't want them to get tuberculosis from being cooped up in such small quarters, nor did he want them roaming the streets. He said, "If you stay in an apartment, you will easily lean toward one or the other; so as soon as possible try to find a house with a yard."

That was a challenge with their very limited resources, but they needed to try. How good it would be if Carmen were with them to start this search! That would be impossible until mid-October because that month her sister María Josefa was getting married in Lleida. On the 17th, Carmen finally managed to move to Barcelona, and María was immensely happy. She had been her first vocation companion; but, in addition, her practical sense and her qualities as an excellent homemaker made her a great counselor for the choice of a residence. They liked a mansion at 59 Ganduxer Street, on the corner of Via Augusta. It was expensive because it was large and had a magnificent yard, but the owner, a very polite older man, was inclined to make things easier for them. They asked Fr. Castro to celebrate the Mass of the Holy Spirit and decided to rent it, despite the difficulties.

On the 29th, in anticipation of their imminent move to the new residence, the four who lived in common met to elect a superior. The vote was secret, but it was easy to guess which was María's vote: there was only one that was not for her, and it was blank. Her disappointment was profound. She had been preparing the ground for weeks for Carmen to be chosen because she hoped Carmen would know how to give religious form to the life of the group and because she wanted to obey, not to give the orders. But in the end, God above all and above everyone; there was no time for tantrums. They had a move in the making to start a new life. She only allowed herself to vent before the tabernacle and in the annals of the house, in which she noted: "In the first vote there was one blank vote. The vote was repeated and one of us was chosen. It was a cunning act and without positive results."[16] Thank God, the letter makes it clear to posterity who was the author of the writing.

The first act of government of the new superior was to appoint Carmen as the director of the university student residence and the move of the community — as well as the two young women from Manresa who wanted to accompany them as residents — to the Ganduxer mansion. They took with them the only four pieces of furniture that were not essential for the classes. Blankets were scarce resources, reserved for the residents or for someone who was sick. They only had a few more chairs than inhabitants so they did not stay for long in any room but had to be carried back and forth. They jokingly said that they were all going from here to there like a snail with its shell. The front door did not close well; it was braced with a chair and that was good enough. What was going to attract a thief in that residence? As usual, poverty welcomed them into their new home and the Lord made up for everything. From the very first night, He stayed among them, sharing their austerity in a poor wooden tabernacle. María felt overwhelmed and at

Boarding students of the Ganduxer Residence Hall (Barcelona, 1940).

[16] Community Notes from Barcelona, 1940–1941 (AGCS D 102.11.A,001).

the same time exultant with gratitude to God. She thought what she would repeat so many times in word and in writing: that nothing is poor if Christ is present.

From then on, María and those who were still teachers at Re-Vir-Cien had to get up a little earlier to travel to the school without cutting short their time for prayer, Mass, and breakfast that preceded the classes. Carmen would remain in the residence to attend to the resident students and to initiate a certain set of rules for a novitiate with the young aspirants, who were multiplying and would be incorporated little by little. "Wouldn't it have been great if I could have been a real novice!" María thought. That is why she was talking with Carmen about the style of the formation of the novitiate in their future congregation. In the meantime, what María could do in the evenings was to care for the quality of the community acts of the few young women who made up the group and cultivate with care the young residents that God had entrusted to her. Only God knew what He wanted from each one of them, but if any of them did have an "Ignatian" vocation, it did not mean they should squander their university studies. For María,

María Félix with exercisers of Re-Vir-Cien and Ganduxer (Barcelona, 1943).

the formation of her companions and the spiritual relationship with the residents were a duty of justice that she felt as intimately as the preparation of her classes. That is why, the week after the move to Bonanova — which is what the residence was called because of the neighborhood in which it was located — she organized a series of Spiritual Exercises for the residents directed by Fr. Pradas, S.J. Putting young women in direct contact with Jesus Christ was the only necessary thing. Then the Lord would speak to the heart of each one, inviting her to the path of holiness He had for her. She also dreamed of bringing together university students in the Marian Congregation or in another zealous institution that could most support evangelization and the Church.

María did not lack ideals, but she also knew how to keep her feet on the ground, taking the necessary steps for strengthening their endeavors. In December, on the feast day of St. Francis Xavier, she gathered together the eight women who were living in Barcelona at the time to choose a name for their institute. It had to be something that reflected their love for Jesus Christ but also their Ignatian style of discipleship. The name with the most votes was Company of Christ the King, followed by Company of St. Ignatius. Others, such as Sodalitium of Jesus, Society of the Sacred Heart, and so on, also displayed significant features of the love that pervaded these women. The election, which took place in front of the tabernacle of the chapel of the Blessed Sacrament of the Jesuits of Caspe, was followed by an hour of silent prayer for everyone to express their gratitude.

However, this solemnly chosen name was not going to last. Two years later, on Pentecost, they would vote again, and the name chosen would be Company of the Savior. What was the reason for this change? When they were asked many years later, none of the first sisters could remember the reason. Perhaps because in 1939 a Company of Christ the King had been approved in Cádiz? Perhaps because some of the Ignatian women were not completely convinced from the beginning? In the semiannual reports to the bishop of Barcelona, after 1940 the name "Company of Christ the King" did not appear again, but the small community appears unnamed. Only in the document from October 1942, in which María gave an account of the last election, did she state that, until that time, for various reasons they had not come to an agreement on the name they should bear. In any case, the change was what God wanted, and María, full of consolation, on May 24, 1942, was able to write:

> Pentecost. In the morning, we prayed for the gifts and fruits of the Holy Spirit for everyone and asked for the name of the Company. In the afternoon, we sought again the name for the Company. We chose the Company of the Savior with great devotion and consolation. During the last hour, we felt intense joy to have a name and to be called the Company of the Savior. Prostrate before the tabernacle, I gave infinite thanks and offered myself. It is a name of light and sweetness; it contains all the mysteries of God's love; all the plans of our divine Captain; symbol of the divine ideal, and will never end. Thank You, Jesus, my Savior.[17]

Returning to the end of 1940, the year was almost over, and the Company of the Savior needed some Constitutions. Aware of her ignorance in these matters, María again requested the help of the father provincial. How could she turn her sisters into a Society of Jesus for women if she herself was not a Jesuit? She asked if the Jesuits could help her write the Constitutions since they had been living the Rules and Constitutions of St. Ignatius for centuries. Fr. Mondría promised to write to Fr. Cándido Mazón, a promising canonist from the Pontifical Gregorian University, who had just received a doctorate with a thesis on the rules of men and women religious and by some miracle had not been hired by the Catholic University of Chile. He was coming to Barcelona to teach canon law and liturgy in the Faculty of Theology and, without a doubt, he was the ideal man to help them.

In December, Fr. Mazón arrived in Barcelona and stopped by the residence to make himself available to the aspiring religious sisters. At that time the priest was forty years old. He had been a diocesan priest and then, at twenty-six years old, he had entered the Society of Jesus, determined to

[17] Spiritual Writings, 1942–1944 (AGCS M 202.06,001).

identify himself with Christ and all that came with this. He was a renowned theologian, a good teacher, a born organizer, a conscientious and tireless worker, a dear brother to all, as well as somewhat harsh, and quite a joker. Fr. Mazón was distinguished above all by his piety and by his qualities as a spiritual director. He knew how to admirably combine firmness and understanding, to welcome people, and to tell them unambiguously what he saw was wrong or clearly awry. Of course, he did it with an unmistakable love and with a relentless sense of humor, which did not take away from the seriousness with which he strove for holiness. For María and her companions he was not only the canonist advisor they expected but became a true father appointed by Providence to teach them to be authentic religious sisters and daughters of St. Ignatius. For his part, the priest also grew fond of them very quickly. He was impressed by the sincere dedication of these women who, even flying blind, were able to hit the mark and live as authentic Jesuits. In July he led their Spiritual Exercises, and after that he would always be with them. In person, while he could, or from his later assignments through letters, he would collaborate with them until the end of his days.

Like Gold in a Furnace

Fr. Mazón's help fueled María's confidence. Is the time of their conversion already coming? She sincerely wanted it. She also wanted to offer to the Lord that vow of perfection that she had been delaying since the Spiritual Exercises of 1940. She could not get it out of her head because she was convinced that God was asking for it. However, until now she had not had a stable spiritual director with whom she had enough confidence to talk about this subject. She would have spoken to Fr. Serrat, but he was in Lleida and only came every once in a while. She did not dare talk to Fr. Thió, her regular confessor, because this Jesuit already had his reservations about the vocation of the Company of the Savior, and this could contribute to his distrust. For María, who was very actively aware of her sins and weaknesses, to speak of a "vow of perfection" sounded like an attempt to make herself interesting, and she was disgusted by the thought of bringing it up to another person. In addition, she sensed that getting so close to the fire of God's love was not child's play. She thought:

> I must be holy. Holy!... Jesus makes me feel clearly what it means to be holy. I feel a horrible fear of launching myself down this path. I don't think I would have a hard time dying torn apart by beasts, nor shot by a firing squad. But to fight with myself one day after another ... to fall and get back up again and again, to start again every day without ever reaching the goal.... To be holy is to fully realize God's plans for the Company and for my very poor soul. To be holy to me is the same as living crucified. How horrible! What has become of my vow of perfection? Many years ago, Jesus asked me for great holiness, and I have not taken a single step. If [Fr. Mazón] knew me well, he would not allow me to live here as a religious sister and much less as a superior. I lack generosity, a lot of generosity. Jesus keeps calling and I resist. Writing about it has gotten me even more entangled.[18]

As she would later write:

> To say yes to God, to everything that He would like, and always, out of pure love, because it is His will; to be completely God's, without reserving anything, forever, only so that He may be pleased.... This is what being holy meant to me. This is what I desired with all my soul, and how my desire grew, knowing that it was possible because God wanted it![19]

Fr. Mazón knew María well and therefore, when she finally dared to bring up her internal struggle, during the Spiritual Exercises of 1941, he only answered with a no. A dry no. And María breathed a sigh of relief. She had the excuse that her director would not allow her to take the vow. Nevertheless, mysteriously, she felt less faithful to God. This was how it continued throughout the retreat. But then, on the last day, when the priest commented on Jesus' apparitions to Mary Magdalene and St. Peter, everything changed:

[18] Spiritual Writings, April 1941 (AGCS M 202.02,001).
[19] Autobiographical Writings, Notebook A (AGCS M 201,001).

> I was the object of divine mercies. With the eyes of my soul, I saw Jesus before me, with more certainty and greater effects than if I saw Him with my physical sight. I saw He was stern because I avoided the vow of perfection. "But is it necessary for me?" I asked Him. Then He, with a lot of love, asked me: "María, do you love Me?" I broke into tears pierced with pain and confusion. I would ask the priest again and as many times as necessary. Yes, He knew that I loved Him, but not with my love but with His love because He gave me that intense love that flooded me.[20]

She asked Fr. Mazón again but without mentioning, out of embarrassment, the grace of that morning: "*Padre,* I have to ask you for something: to allow me to make the vow of perfection. I am convinced that the Lord our God wants it." He replied, "Sincerely, María, I don't think you are cut out for that." "You're right, *Padre,*" she answered, "I'm not. However, if the Lord asks for it, He will give me the grace, won't He?" Fr. Mazón said, "That's what we have to see, if the Lord asks ... do nothing for now. Be very faithful to what you feel God is inspiring you to do, as if you have already done it. Later on, we will see."

That is how he kept her for several months, during which time María cried every time she remembered that question: "Do you love Me?" With the delays, her love for Jesus grew and with her love, her martyrdom. Finally, on March 25, 1942, before the Blessed Sacrament exposed, she felt again that special presence of Jesus Christ and the Virgin, who asked her: "We fulfilled the will of the Heavenly Father, and will you not make the vow of perfection?" María answered, "If you want it, then make the priest tell me yes."

The time had almost come. That same day she asked Fr. Mazón, who asked her to write down what she understood by a vow of perfection. María wrote in an outline:

> I understand that the vow of perfection obliges me, when it comes to God, to do all things for His greater glory. As for the Rules, to fulfill them all with loving fidelity. Regarding my behavior, to

[20] Autobiographical Writings, Notebook D (AGCS M 201,004).

> choose the most universal good, the greater glory of God. Faced with virtue and my obligations, not to adopt a dualistic position ("yes but no").
>
> By the vow of perfection, I must strive: To feel a more tender and intense love for Jesus Christ and the Blessed Virgin. To be more diligent and faithful in the Spiritual Exercises and in observance of the religious life. To be impartial. To spiritual, constant, and diligent cultivation of the souls that the Lord has entrusted to me in a certain way.
>
> By the vow of perfection, I hope that the Lord will grant me: That He will triumph in me and I will disappear in Him. An increase of grace to serve Him more perfectly. That the acts I perform by virtue of the vow be meritorious (I would like to be able to offer merits to the Lord so that He may be greatly glorified and save many souls). A profound humility, a large heart, and a great charity to deal with souls.
>
> By the vow of perfection, I lose all rights and ownership of myself. I will no longer be mine, and Jesus will take me as completely His (I have trembled at the thought of this). If I now live on the Cross, the vow of perfection will affix me to it. The vow of perfection will be the fire that will consume me on the altar of the greater glory of God.[21]

A few days later, Fr. Mazón returned the note and asked when she wanted to make the vow. They agreed that she would do it on Holy Thursday during Communion. It was not in vain that she had given herself to the Lord, completely and forever, on that same day when she was fourteen years old. Now she could ratify that surrender, giving Him what He asked for. So they agreed, and on Holy Thursday, April 2, 1942, in the Maximum College of Sarriá, the priest gave her Holy Communion, and she offered her vow to God, offering herself to Him for the crucifixion. "Since then," she would write, "in my body and in my soul, I have experienced many times that my vow was accepted. Long live Jesus!"[22]

[21] Note to Fr. Mazón, March 25, 1942 (AGCS M 205.01.A,001).

[22] Autobiographical Writings, Notebook D (AGCS M 201,004).

That same year, marked by this grace of union with the Lord, was also a year of strong purification. It seemed as if God had placed her in a furnace so as not to leave in her any trace of imperfections but only love for Him and His plans for the Company of the Savior. In a few months she was going to lose her father, her spiritual director, who was assigned to Bilbao, and the bishop who had welcomed them in Barcelona, because a new prelate was appointed for the diocese. All this in a year in which they also had to remove a fibroma and papilloma from her uterus, and she would again suffer a spell of endocarditis that would continue relapsing until 1948. It was as if God left her without human support to reinforce her heart in total trust in Him.

During the week after Easter Sunday, her father Ramón's health worsened. Ever since the war, he had been struggling with a lingering asthmatic bronchitis. He seemed to have a stronger cold than normal, but he continued alternating work with moments of rest, hoping to improve. On the night of April 18th into the 19th, the disease showed itself in all its harshness. After a few hours of struggling to breathe, with little relief provided by medication, he gave his soul to God. María, warned by her brothers in the morning, had arrived at her parents' house when Ramón was already unconscious. As he died, Florentina and her children prayed fervently, kneeling beside the bed. Then the siblings, one by one, before the corpse of their father promised to imitate his virtues and never abandon their mother. That afternoon, when she arrived home exhausted, María wrote in her journal:

> Holding vigil with the corpse of my father; real and absolute effective offering to God of the person who has loved me the most on earth and whom I have loved the most. Persistent and overwhelming sentiment of feeling detached from everything and belonging solely to God.[23]

Her will was strong, but this did not spare her from grief and the feeling of emptiness and loneliness. During the following week, grief was making its way

[23] Personal Journal, April 18, 1942–April 15, 1944 (AGCS M 202.06,001).

into her soul, and the shock was giving way to a painful lucidity. When she did an examination of conscience, she saw:

> Gradually the pain of separation from my father has increased. The feeling of loneliness and emptiness has also increased. Jesus has hidden Himself and even in prayer I feel more alone and forsaken. I believe that my moral state, in part, is a repercussion of physical exhaustion and that it will pass and that I have to be patient. Fr. Mazón comforts me and sustains me in a special way. Thanks to the reflections he gives me, I do not escape into loneliness, and I contain all signs of the absolute disinterest I feel for everything around me. In the midst of everything, I feel humbled about this state, and I ask forgiveness from God our Lord and beg Him to give me strength to get out of it.[24]

Caring for her community, cultivating the young women with vocational doubts and drafting the Constitutions — whose first draft was a continuous headache — were both a burden and a counterweight to her pain. As for the help from Fr. Mazón, who sustained her so much, it would not be her main source of support for much longer. In December, shortly before the feast of the Immaculate Conception, the priest warned some young women who were about to enter the Company of the Savior that they would either enter on the feast of the Virgin, or they would not see him anymore. Since this taunting tone was typical of how he treated them, María did not take him seriously. She thought it was a loving push or a way of scolding the three dawdling aspirants. It was neither the one nor the other. On the day of the solemnity, in the morning, Fr. Mazón celebrated Mass for the community and exposed the Blessed Sacrament. In the afternoon, when someone came to reserve the Blessed Sacrament, it was not he who appeared but another Jesuit. When asked about the change, he informed them of what had happened. Fr. Mazón's appointment as provincial superior of Aragon had just been announced in the residence. María, who a week before had written, "I have never felt supported by a more secure hand, nor has anyone led me more

[24] Ibid.

firmly and gently to the fulfillment of God's will,"[25] understood perfectly. In a few weeks he would leave for Bilbao, the seat of the government of the province. She was alone again, or rather alone in the arms of God. Therefore, in early January, when she heard the news that the Holy See had just appointed a bishop for Barcelona, Bishop Gregorio Modrego Casáus, it hardly surprised her. Bishop Miguel Díaz Gómara was leaving, and she would have to put their vocation in the hands of a new shepherd whom they did not know. What did it matter? She would renew once again her surrender and her "I trust in You." God was determined to take the reins of all their lives.

However, over time she was beginning to see the details of God's plans. Fr. Mazón, sincerely interested in the good of his favorite daughters, was not going to leave them altogether. Once a month, taking advantage of his visits to Barcelona, he would visit the residence to attend to the community and, on more than one occasion, to the aspirants and young women of the Marian Congregation. All of them — the community, the residents, and the former students of the school — had immense fondness for him. As for the new bishop of Barcelona, Bishop Modrego, he turned out to be a good friend of Fr. Mazón and a determined protector of the nascent Company of the Savior. In any case, these and other difficulties of those years served to forge the Lord's path in María's heart. Through them she learned to survive the ups and downs, relying solely on her trust in the love of Jesus Christ. Even in the midst of the darkness into which problems sometimes plunged her, she again uttered her typical "God above all" and remembered: "By the vow of perfection I was attached to the Cross. In the present trials I realize that the will of Jesus is not a formula; it is a tangible reality. Look, Jesus, I want to love You. To everything You do I will always tell You Amen. I want to love You and nothing more."[26]

Stations of the Cross Made of Xs

These years of trials and internal growth were also years of external growth for the Company of the Savior. Guided by the spiritual direction of some Jesuits, more postulants had entered. This was a great joy for María, who would have

[25] Autobiographical Writings, Notebook D (AGCS M 201,004).

[26] Personal Journal, April 18, 1942–April 15, 1944 (AGCS M 202.06,001).

gladly been vaporized so that from every one of the atoms scattered throughout the world, thousands of Ignatian vocations would be born who would work for the Church and give themselves to the greater glory of God. In addition, the way of life of the Ignatian women had become increasingly religious under the tutelage of Fr. Mazón. Half-jokingly, half-seriously, they all recognized him as their novice master. He provided them with the schedules of the Jesuit novitiates (which they followed almost exactly) the community prayers for the religious in formation, the rules for the students, and those for different functions, and he guided them in applying all of these things to a female community.

In the meantime, María struggled with the text of the Constitutions, broadening the first formula given to the apostolic administrator of Barcelona to a more complete and appropriate constitutional text. It was not enough to indicate their desire to be a Society of Jesus for women and to explain the origin of this desire in an inspiration from God. She had to explain the nature and purpose of the institute, its activities, the sources of its spirituality, its process of formation and incorporation of its members, the concrete way in which they embraced the evangelical counsels of chastity, poverty, and obedience, the Spiritual Exercises prescribed for all members, the structure of governance, the manner of administration of goods and the erection of new houses, and also, at that time, hundreds of minute details, such as the stipulation of the dowry of the candidates or the way of proceeding with ordinary and extraordinary confessors. It was a considerable mess in which the rookie superior general found herself more than lost. In December 1940, she made a very brief draft of the Constitutions, which the bishop returned to her in January 1941 with the annotations from Fr. Cagigós, visitor of religious sisters, on all the points that had to be revised to adapt them to canon law. María, with many difficulties, made the corrections, and she breathed a little sigh of relief when Fr. Mazón, in mid-1942, began to collaborate actively through notes that he proposed for her consideration. However, the responsibility, in the end, fell on her.

This Fr. Cagigós — a faithful priest who was zealous about his mission but abrupt in his manners — was quite a hard nut to crack at first. He did not like new inventions and had no qualms about letting María and her vocation sisters know. If they wanted to be religious sisters, there were already many female congregations to copy as a model. Why create "an institute similar in everything to the Society of Jesus"? Why take on a fourth vow of obedience to the pope when this loyal adherence was already logically implied in every vow of obedience? Why these novelties of being able to go with or without a habit depending on whether it was appropriate for the apostolate? In an almost merciless way — or so it felt to María — he marked the points on the Constitutions that had to be modified and the others that he would eliminate. So, he made them go back and forth from the bishop's office on several occasions for objections, "buts," and amendments.

Without a doubt, a key turning point in his dealings with the Company was the surprise visit he made to the community in September 1943. On the 15th of that month, in the afternoon, he appeared without warning at the mansion on Ganduxer Street to examine the house and lifestyle of those that had gathered there. Guided by one of them, he toured everything: the common areas of the residents; the rooms in the attic reserved for the community; the dining room, which was in the basement where he saw an austere supper prepared; and the garden. Then he gathered the community in the library to talk with them, and spent quite a while with them. At the end of the meeting, his expressions were quite different, and his tone manifested an evident satisfaction. As if he were a school principal proud of a student's performance, he told them that he would call Fr. Mazón to tell him about his visit and that he was pleasantly impressed. They could count on him to help them in whatever they needed.

From that time, he tried to keep his word. Although he was never too permissive, he was extremely available. He asked María to come several times to continue working on the Constitutions, especially in 1944, when they had already been under the responsibility of the ecclesiastical hierarchy for more than three years and could soon be approved as a pious union. In April of that year, on the 13th, he summoned her again to his office. He was perplexed. Some of the points of the Constitutions that María proposed were so broad in their form that it would be advisable to be constituted as a secular institute. If they still wanted to be religious sisters, they had to change them, more because the norms in Rome were definitive, and they ran the risk of not being approved. He showed María the corrected draft. It was full of Xs written in pencil. María counted so many "stations of the Cross made of Xs" and began to tremble. A few days earlier, entrusting this meeting to the Lord, she had clearly felt that changing something of the substance in the Constitutions was like scourging Jesus again. She told Fr. Cagigós so, without euphemisms. The heart of the rigorous canonist must have been moved by María's firmness, her pleading but serene eyes, and her final comment: "But, if it cannot be, we will not be founded. We will do whatever the Church tells us." He told her to come back the next day, but to his home, and that he would see what could be done. María went, accompanied by Carmen, with three copies of the Constitutions, one for him, another for her, and the third for Carmen, who read one by one the paragraphs marked with a cross. As Carmen read, María would pray silently, "Sacred Heart of Jesus, I trust in You," and at each ejaculatory prayer Fr. Cagigós, just like that, would tell them a possible way to save the original text. Returning home, she wrote: "Thanks be to God, for now the issue of the Constitutions has been resolved without having to remove the points that we considered to be the main ones. Blessed be God for everything."[27]

Thus, with a "Blessed be God," the first stage was closed, because a month later Bishop Modrego approved these Constitutions *ad experimentum* and canonically erected the Pious Union of the Company of the Savior.

[27] Community Notes from Barcelona, April 14, 1944 (AGCS D 102.11.A,002).

Chapter 7

"All in God's Time"
1944–1952

Madrid: The First Foundation

Along with the joy of already being something legitimately constituted in the Church, the last school quarter of 1944 brought an important concern for María. The owner of the building the school rented wanted to evict them and make renovations and was not open to dialogue. For two months, she and her companions toured Barcelona, talked to one person after another, asked educational and government institutions for a place for their purpose, proposed merging with another school in the area, and so forth. All for nothing. Toward the end of June, with great sorrow, they began to accept that the school was going to close.

Again, God was going to provide in an unexpected way. The Jesuits, who had been informed of their distress, offered them a field of apostolate. They had a school in a working-class neighborhood that until the war had been run by the Augustinian sisters. After the bombings, with the reconstruction, they had taken it over but only in the field of ministry. As for the rest, some young women from Catholic Action were running it as best they could. They would be grateful for a religious congregation to get behind the school and shape it. María saw in this the open window that God was offering them. She had asked God for a long time for an opportunity to help young women whose families were of modest means, and this work they were proposing bore the genuine seal of God. It did not solve the financial problem of not having a stable source of income — the schools were free — but it made possible the apostolate that was closed to them in Re-Vir-Cien. In September, they began the school year with a primary school program in the morning and, in the evenings, a school of business, tailoring, folk art, and general education for workers. They would also offer some free basic classes and catechism for the community on Sundays.

The Escuelas del Sagrado Corazón (Schools of the Sacred Heart), as they called them, became the apple of the sisters' eyes. How precious it was to be able to prepare the students for First Communion or to help them gather Christmas gifts for children who were even more poor than they were. Most of the students were themselves in need and orphans of war. With God's help, a lot of good was done. Some marriages were convalidated, several vocations emerged, and the families of the girls grew very fond of the young women. They encouraged these young women to call themselves *Madres* because, even though they dressed as lay women, were they not all religious sisters? They did so, and with great joy they realized that this also contributed to giving a religious tone to their life and to the way they treated each other in the community. Madre Félix, Madre Aige, Madre Sarret, Hermana Badía, and the rest. To María those names sounded glorious, as if the Heart of God had always destined them to be called this way. Fr. Mazón was very pleased to learn of this change and, in his letters to her during this time, with affectionate sarcasm, he called María "Most Reverend Mother Superior General of the S.S.," alluding to the Latin name of the Company, *Societas Salvatoris*. He also referred to the hard work that the translation of the Constitutions involved so that they could be sent to Rome.

The opening of the Schools of the Sacred Heart in the Gracia neighborhood meant once again splitting the community into two different houses. The three women assigned to the schools settled as best they could in the former quarters of the school caretaker. Madre Félix, as superior general, visited them frequently but remained in the house on Ganduxer Street. They also had their difficulties at their residence hall. More than once she had to sleep on the floor when she returned from a trip because new residents had joined and there were no beds left. Of course, there was no way she was going to let any of her sisters give her the one in her room. It was her privilege to be able to offer something to the Lord for these girls and their families. Also, the way she saw it, wasn't it a blessing from God to have the house so full? She had to do something to reciprocate the divine generosity that continued to send forth residents on a daily basis.

However, Madre Félix was neither naïve nor insensitive. It weighed on her that the others shared her troubles, and she wished "that I alone would suffer all the anguish of economic hardship and that my sisters, free from all material concerns, could devote themselves more freely to spiritual things."[28] But she also felt carried away with joy when she sensed that as their needs increased, so did God's tenderness. She wrote, "I feel so united with God and so loved by Him as I begin the year in debt, not knowing whom to turn to, without strength, without relying on myself for anything! Everything will be His, and if everything is His, everything will be perfect and to His liking."[29]

This is the same way that she faced the illness that afflicted everyone in the house for a few weeks. It caused quite a fright because for a few days they thought that they had typhus. This was even more so the case with the holy death of the first of her sisters to go to Heaven: The angelic Sister Carmen Badía, a victim of sepsis, died on October 17, 1945, visibly aided by the maternal presence of the Virgin Mary.

As if Carmen had gone to Heaven in order to intercede for the Company of the Savior and its apostolate, shortly after she died the possibility arose of turning the residence on Ganduxer Street into a residential college. It would be the first female college in the city and would be affiliated with the University of Barcelona. The Company was not going to give academic degrees or officially recognized credits, but it did commit itself to offer the students cultural and formative activities that would complement their degrees. What would they call the new college? They called it Mater Salvatoris (Mother of the Savior), in order to put it explicitly under the protection of the Virgin Mary.

Since Madre Félix was always thinking big, the summer after the first year as a college they celebrated with a magnificent excursion to "discover Spain." The objective of the trip was twofold: to help the university women become more cultured and to find a possible location for a foundation by looking

28 Spiritual Writings, April 22, 1944 (AGCS, M 202.10,001).

29 Letter to M. Carmen Aige, December 31, 1974 (AGCS E 20,074).

around different cities of Spain. For this apostolic-cultural journey, she organized a complete itinerary, just as she used to do with her father. They went from central Spain to the north, passing through the towns of Toledo, Madrid, Salamanca, Valladolid, Burgos, San Sebastian, Bilbao, and, of course, through Loyola, the small hometown of St. Ignatius. There she renewed her gratitude for their Ignatian vocation and the desire to found colleges in many other cities. Upon their return, she wrote to Fr. Mazón saying, "When Your Reverence comes, we will talk about this and about laying a foundation in Madrid."[30]

In fact, she did go to Madrid in August 1946, accompanied by Madre Aige, with letters of recommendation for some gentlemen of the Complutense University and the Ministry of Education. They wanted to open a Mater Salvatoris residential college in the Parque Metropolitano in the Ciudad Universitaria neighborhood, and soon found a suitable house at 5 Sierra Street. When she returned to Barcelona, she had to think about who could go to Madrid to start the foundation. With much sacrifice on her part, Madre Félix supported what she perceived to be God's will: the time had come to let go of Carmen Aige. She was her *alter ego*; she fully shared her opinions in all matters; she was prudent, confident; she would govern that community far better than herself. Madre Montserrat Amigó could accompany her as director of the residence, and Madre Victorina Jené would also be a lot of help in dealing with the university students. With Madre Gazo, a junior sister, who at the time was nineteen years old and eager to study, and the fervent Laureana Miguel as coadjutor sister, the community was sufficiently equipped. Only the most important thing was missing: to seek permission from the bishop's office to have the Blessed Sacrament in the residence as soon as possible. Madre Félix wrote, "The day that this happens, I will feel the greatest joy of the foundation, and until that day I consider them to be soldiers in the field without a tent to cover themselves."[31] That is why she recommended them to "entrust this matter to the patron saints chosen by Madre Carmen for the foundation in Madrid and to place all their trust in the Blessed Virgin. She will give them Jesus."[32]

[30] Letter to Fr. Mazón, July 5, 1946 (AGCS M 301.46,001).

[31] Letter to M. Carmen Aige, October 3, 1946 (AGCS E 20,011).

[32] Ibid.

Holding Pattern

While these pioneers settled in Madrid, Madre Félix moved heaven and earth to accelerate the approval of the Company of the Savior as a religious congregation. Fr. Mazón was in Rome for the General Congregation of the Jesuits, and it would be wonderful if he presented their files to the Sacred Congregation for Religious. With the help of the diocesan chancellor, Madre María Amor Sarret, and Madre Inés Tarragona, Madre Félix corrected and copied the new Latin text as many times as requested, as well as the other documents. With much haste, in the petition that accompanied the file, she filled in the section corresponding to the founder. What could she put? She came up with the best answer she could:

> In the presence of God, I have judged that I should either put all of the women or I should only put those from August 15, 1934. The latter seemed more honest to me, and I have written both of their names. One of the women, the one making this declaration, is the most unworthy, the most wretched and greatest sinner among all who are or ever will be part of the Company of the Savior.[33]

From then on it would always be the same. If someone asked her about the foundation, she would speak of a group of Ignatian women, or of Carmen Aige, or of Bishop Modrego, or even Fr. Mazón. Anyone but herself, the "greatest sinner among all who are or ever will be part of the Company of the Savior."

While waiting for the answer from Rome, there was much to do. Ever since the Spiritual Exercises in August 1946, the question of a habit had been pending, and it was time to get down to work. From the beginning, she had thought of the Company of the Savior as an apostolic body, in which everything — including their clothing — should be ordered to the greatest good of souls. She understood that it was best to leave it up to the major superiors who would wear a habit, and in what circumstances. Ordinarily at home they all wished to wear it as an unmistakable sign of their consecration to God. After much prayer, and looking at drawings proposed by the sisters, an initial

33 Letter to M. Carmen Aige, September 27, 1946 (AGCS E 20,008).

pattern took shape: a black wool tunic down to their ankles, with wide sleeves, black band cincture, white coif, and a long black veil, which was white for the novices. Would this be the habit that the Virgin Mary wanted for them? The only sure thing was that the Virgin expected their characteristic dress to be modest. Madre Félix dreamed that the "Little Company" would receive the same glory as the sons of St. Ignatius: that among other people, with or without a habit, they could be distinguished as Ignatians through their outward appearance, which would show the serene joy of God.

The happy occasion of receiving the habit took place in Barcelona on January 1, 1947. A month later, on February 9th, they had their vesting ceremony and a celebration of vows at the house in Madrid. It was worth waiting for Fr. Mazón to be present, taking advantage of his time in the capital on his way to India. Madre Félix was also present for both celebrations. She entertained herself thinking how God had always foreseen this habit but had reserved it until now while He prepared them internally to wear it worthily. At the same time, was it not a wink of approval that in the bishop's office they were allowed to dress also as lay people? Like the brave people who fight for Christ in the trenches of the world? She expressed this in a very long circular letter at the end of that year.

Along with the habit, in 1946 Madre Félix also designed the medal that would serve as their insignia. There was not much to think about. They were all very clear what their emblem had to look like. Madre Félix went to see a very well-known silversmith from Barcelona, Capdevila, and asked him for round silver pieces, with the anagram of the name of Jesus framed by the rays of the sun, just like the emblem of the Jesuits. The Company of the Savior was nothing more than a small boat that followed in the wake created by the Society of Jesus. That is why she was so comforted to have the same shield as them. Those first letters of the Greek name of Jesus, which she wanted to bear engraved on her soul; the nails, which reminded them of the three vows by which they were united to Christ crucified; the rays, some straight and precise, like the unfailing substantial glory of God, and others wavy, like that accidental, sometimes fluctuating glory that we humans give Him; and all this inherited from St. Ignatius. What a blessing to be his daughters!

Thousands of considerations were made in those months, contemplating that beloved emblem. Soon she and her sisters began to perceive that the rays, in addition to being reflections of the glory of God, were pointy protrusions that easily snagged fabric and caused other problems. For that reason, she returned to the silversmith. She said, "Look, Mr. Capdevila, we are excited about the medal, but we have this little problem ... would it be possible to fill in the gaps, making a solid circle on the back?" "Of course, *Madre*. Great idea," he said. "And in the center of the circle, could we put the likeness of St. Ignatius?" asked Madre Félix. "Sure. That will not be a problem," he replied. "We can copy his profile from these medals, what do you think?" Madre Félix answered, "Magnificent, he has a beautiful expression, looking toward Heaven, with the Constitutions tight to his chest."

"And in the circle that goes around him?" Mr. Capdevila asked, "What would you like us to put?" He obligingly proposed to personalize each medal with the name of the religious sister and the date of her profession. Madre Félix smiled. "I think it's a very good idea. But you know what? We will put the name of each and every one of our sisters, because all of us, the current ones and those to come, have the same name: 'For the greater glory of God.'"

Time for Laying the Foundation

While all this was happening in Barcelona and Madrid, in Lleida several well-known couples from the Aige family, along with some former students of the Academia Nueva who remembered with admiration "Miss María Félix," were exploring whether it would be possible to open a school of the Company of the Savior in their city. Madre Félix prayed, asked for insight, consulted with the first members of the Company, got advice about the educational needs of the city, etc. She was persuaded to create a foundation there. She asked permission and recommendations from the bishop of Barcelona, on whom the congregation depended, and took the request to the bishop of Lleida, Bishop Aurelio del Pino. She wrote the petitions with eager anticipation mixed with a certain amount of suspense because she remembered so well how before the tabernacle of the Academia Nueva, in Lleida, "some women were consecrated through a vow to serve the Lord our God for the first time in 1934 on the day

First chapel in Madrid, 1945.

of the Assumption of the Blessed Virgin. This consecration was a beginning point for the current Company of the Savior."[34] Would they now be officially received by the diocese that saw them born?

The bishop must have considered these sisters, who wanted to "offer themselves to God in the sacrifice of Catholic teaching,"[35] to be a gift sent straight from Heaven. Not only did he accept them in Lleida but he entrusted them with much more. Since they had so many college graduates, he asked them to run the Church's Teacher Training College, which he was about to establish. This warm reception in Lleida was a great consolation for Madre Félix because at that same time she was experiencing difficulties in the other houses.

In Barcelona, the direction of the Escuelas del Sagrado Corazón was complicated. Although the relationship with Fr. Sola, a Jesuit, and his successor, Fr. Savall, had been magnificent, the third chaplain of the institution did not quite get along with the director or the other religious sisters in charge. He preferred to deal directly with the teachers from Catholic Action and was bothered by what he considered to be interference from the *madres*. Even with Madre Félix's intervention, the relationship was not smoothed over. She, with her lively spirit and quickness to react where she felt there was an injustice or a lack of truth, ended up making things even more tense, much to her regret. In the end, in August 1948, the Jesuit superior, Fr. Romañá, arrived at their residence very troubled to tell Madre Félix that the Jesuits had decided to end this collaboration in the area of ministry and to leave the Escuelas del Sagrado Corazón to other religious sisters. He was obviously embarrassed. He knew Madre Félix well because he had collaborated with her in the Lauria Academy. After having lived through those times of martyrdom together, needing to give this news was not easy. In addition, he was an astrophysicist, not a diplomat. Madre Félix, as usual, put herself in his place and tried to make things easier. It took a few days to let Madre Aige know. She took advantage of the reply she owed Madre Aige for wishing her a happy birthday and wrote:

[34] Petition to the Bishop of Lleida, December 8, 1947 (AGCS F 504.01.A,002).

[35] Petition to the Bishop of Lleida, December 3, 1947 (AGCS F 504.01.A,001).

> Fr. Romañá has come to tell us to leave the schools. The visit was very cordial. I think he suffered because his role was not very pleasant, but thanks be to God I was very calm and kind. I thank you very much for wishing me a happy old age [she was turning forty-one]. It also comforts me to see that time passes so quickly. What does not comfort me so much is to see the eternal sinner I am.[36]

And it was true that she felt like an eternal sinner, so much so that she deeply desired to leave the office of superior general so as not to be a cause of scandal for her sisters. She felt like a bad apple among them, with her volcanic temper, with her mood swings that made her appear abrupt and dominating when she had to exert her authority. If the bishops who dealt with the Company of the Savior heard her confession, they would surely depose her immediately. She felt that would be a gain for the Company, for sure. However, Fr. Mazón had already told her years ago not to repeat such nonsense. She had already gone to confession once with Bishop Díaz de Gómara, spilling out all her faults. With a simple "Anything else?" and a blessing, the holy bishop had wiped away her debt. The priest, when she told him about the matter, advised her to stop making such a spectacle of herself and to carry the cross that God had given her, which for her was the best one there was. She had to resign herself and continue in her service.

At the same time, from Madrid Madre Aige communicated her concern for the way things were going at the residence. The sisters who ran it were devoted and good, but they did not quite connect with the young women. Many university students had left, and the discomfort of those who remained was growing. The religious sisters, who noticed it, were depressed to see the external result of their efforts. Madre Félix wrote to her first companion, trying to comfort her with these heartfelt words:

> What you say in your letter does not surprise me. I already knew it. The lack of personnel is currently the greatest thorn in my side and has been for many years. Yet I believe they are fit for other things,

[36] Letter to M. Carmen Aige, August 26, 1948 (AGCS E 20,083).

and I believe very sincerely that they will give much glory to God and will greatly help the Company in other ministries. For now, we have to have patience and much charity. They suffer more than we do because in addition to everything we see and experience, they also suffer the humiliation of their inability to carry out what they have been entrusted with and the sting of responsibility. I tell you this because I have experienced it and I still experience it in myself. There is no heavier cross than to hold a position for which one has no aptitude.

Remember that they did not ask for this position, which they perform out of obedience. If they could follow their own will or if they had been consulted, they would do something else. Nevertheless, they most willingly strive to do their part as best as they can. May you be for them the Good Samaritan who softens the inmost wounds of the inferiority complex created in the face of their own involuntary inability. Be a patient mother in teaching them once and a thousand times the same thing without great success. Just as a mother, be enthralled with a correct answer, and consider it a favor from God for His daughters and boast about it. Take mistakes as very natural things. Be the mother of your subjects. God has given you the heart and intelligence to know how to be a mother. For every feeling of tenderness, benevolence, and compassion that you promote, the Lord will make you feel in the depths of your soul the treasures of the love and mercy that He holds in His Most Sacred Heart. You will feel not only paid for your efforts but also indebted to Him, so you will make new efforts in return.

With these conquests of ours and with this journey toward the imitation of Christ, we will move the Lord to increase the number of us who are of His Company and to give us what He needs for His work. Then those who now offer the Lord the most complete self-sacrifice might be assigned to other occupations of greater visible return. Because now is the time for laying the foundation. It upholds but is not seen[37]

[37] Letter to M. Carmen Aige, May 16, 1947 (AGCS E 20,041).

Because of all this, because she knew they were laying the foundation, she looked at Lleida with affection and with a lot of hope. She could not believe how easily the arrangements happened. Although she had to do a lot of juggling to pull off providing teachers to the new school without drastically stripping away the other houses, in September the Mater Salvatoris School opened its doors. In January the Escuela de Magisterio de la Iglesia began as well, in a new building in Ricardo Viñes Square. If the idea of a new school excited her, the work of training educators in the Escuela de Magisterio exceeded all her expectations and filled her with holy awe. She was impressed that the Church would entrust to the Company of the Savior, which was not even a canonically approved religious institute, the intellectual formation and pedagogical training of the faculty of other religious institutions. Of course, it could be explained by the lack of the Church's means, but she deeply sensed the Lord's Providence and His overwhelming trust.

"What About the Glory of God?"

The foundation of the house in Lleida and, above all, the beginnings of the school were exciting endeavors, but not always easy. Madre Félix was well aware that they were setting the course of the future schools of the Company of the Savior. This would be the first, but not the last, of the Mater Salvatoris Schools. There, in Lleida, but also in Barcelona and Madrid, there were many people waiting to see how everything would work out. Some Jesuits and very fond parents said that it was going as well as any school of the Sacred Heart, but they could not let themselves be impressed by flattery. Hopefully it was true. Were they all really working for God's greatest glory? Was the holiness of the students the educational goal they unanimously pursued? Was there an assiduous and generous effort on the part of the teachers to tie together academic quality and striving for virtue? Did the love of Christ truly reign in the classrooms and among the religious sisters? If she was honest, not always, and not in everyone — not even in herself. The latter hurt her deeply.

It seemed to her that, at times, there was a lack of religious spirit in the house. There was initiative, but it was not always open to obedience. Some made generous efforts giving themselves to the apostolate to the point of exhaustion, but sometimes these were short sprints and they got tired along the way. She saw that students were scandalized when they were scolded harshly, more out of self-love than for their good; or when, on the contrary, the sisters were too lax so as not to displease the students. The task of educating, passionately beautiful, was as difficult to teach as it was necessary to learn.

Mater Salvatoris pupils sewing at School (Lérida, 1948).

Madre Félix suffered, but she was not too scared. When things were difficult for her; when projects did not move forward; when she did not succeed in figuring out how to communicate her vision — which was set so high — to a group of women of goodwill, but who knew little of being true religious sisters and educators; when it seemed that everyone, including herself, was advancing so slowly on the path of holiness — what then would she do?

> Try to understand what would be the most perfect way, which would give the most glory to God. Nevertheless, I also understand that I cannot ask for great sacrifices from my sisters if I cannot give them the grace necessary to make them. Therefore, I cannot impose what seems best to me, and I also cannot fail to pursue the greater good. I resolve this by praying hard that I may contribute to increasing the capacity of my sisters to receive more grace and that the

> Lord may desire to increase in all of us the grace to know and fulfill His most holy will.[38]

Madre Félix also used external means. She studied pedagogical methods, consulted the most knowledgeable people, practiced what she was proposing in order to show that it was possible, preached by example, and waited patiently for the time to come. In the meantime, with Christian realism, she took on the humbleness it entailed to have to encourage others when she herself was sometimes discouraged and to receive — especially from those closest to her, those who knew her from the beginning — more than one reproach for striving to put the ideal into practice.

Receive humiliations as the mud that cures the blindness of the soul. Welcome them. Let yourself be cleansed by them as by bleach in a washing machine. For a long time, these thoughts had often assaulted her during prayer, especially during the previous two years. On the feast day of St. Claude La Colombière in 1946, while preparing herself spiritually for her personal consecration to the Sacred Heart of Jesus, which she was going to make on Holy Thursday, she received a very important grace that guided her in this direction. As she entered into prayer, she saw Jesus with the eyes of her soul, with that particular clarity with which she was allowed to see Him at times. He had in His hands, among several pearls of different sizes, three very large ones that He showed her one by one — to her great joy —, while helping her understand that verse of the Gospel that says: "All things have been handed over to me by my Father" (Matt. 11:27). Madre Félix, without words, understood that each one of those large pearls corresponded to one of the three things she had been asking from Him for a long time: much suffering, much humiliation, and to completely fulfill His precious will. Nevertheless, she asked Him about each one: "What is this pearl?" And she understood that it was the Company of the Savior. With the most vivid insight, she perceived that the Company would be an opportunity for her to suffer, to humble herself, and to fulfill the divine will. She did not know what it was going to be like, but if she was faithful to God, it would come true![39]

[38] Personal Journal, March 10, 1942 (AGCS M 202.05,001).

[39] Personal Journal, February 15, 1946 (AGCS M 202.12,001).

She remembered that grace, which she had understood as a promise from the Lord, often, especially when the little daily disagreements hurt her deeply. She was aware that she did not have to endure great humiliations, but her sharp sensitivity would come together with her immense desire for everyone's holiness and make her perceive any lack of charity between sisters as a terrible thing. Even more so, any lack of charity toward the superior — not so much because it was her but because of what she represented. She thought, "that which erases the seal of Christ's disciples, which scratches the very heart of God, is not something small."[40]

This contrast between the glory she wanted to give to God and the concrete fulfillment of her life and that of the Company of the Savior was habitually a kind of inner martyrdom. That . . . and being in charge. Even if her sisters did not see her this way, she still felt she was a bad superior: rough, commanding, extremely unfriendly, and naturally inclined to vanity and control. How was she to represent Jesus Christ, meek and humble, who became the servant of all? Several times, with a few months between each letter, she wrote again to Fr. Mazón, telling him of her desire to renounce her position because of her bad example and because she feared being an obstacle to God's plans for the Company. The Jesuit's response to her most serious attempt, in 1949, came quickly. He said if there had to be a resignation, the first would be his — irrevocably — as her spiritual director. If she wanted to do much penance to atone to God for her faults and to obtain graces for her community, she had a perfect means with which to do so. She knew it well. It was as simple and as complex and difficult as writing down the story of God's mercies toward her. They had already spoken about it before, and it was time to undertake the work.

Madre Félix trembled just thinking about it. The best way to prevent something from being known is not to tell it, much less to write it down. To expose her intimate life, to reveal to someone besides Fr. Mazón her infidelity to so many graces and, above all, those same graces received from the Lord, repulsed her greatly. Why did the Lord push her insistently to write them down?

[40] Letter to the Community of Mota del Marqués, December 24, 1956 (AGCS E 31,019).

"What about the glory of God?" Gently, not abruptly, but firmly, the assurance that God wanted it was seeping into her soul. Didn't she want to glorify Him? Didn't she want to show the whole world His mercy and her wretchedness? It would be enough to write down the path they had traveled together, the one that had led to the foundation of the Company of the Savior, the one that had led her to want nothing but to glorify Him. She committed herself to record all of the wonders God had accomplished, and she felt peace and strength. It was not about her but about Him and His glory.

María Félix in the year of her perpetual vows (Barcelona, 1952).

She had consulted Fr. Mazón, and the Jesuit clearly saw that it was a motion from Heaven that she had to obey. What kind of gift was it to God, if she gave Him whatever she wanted and not what He Himself had taken the trouble to ask her for? Thus began a series of notebooks, addressed to the priest, in which she poured out her grateful memories of the Lord's mercies.

Frustrated Foundations

Be grateful to God. Anything short of boundless gratitude seemed petty to her. Therefore, when Fr. Mazón told her that Central America was lacking missionaries and that the Catholic men and women religious there were fighting against superstition and cult, the first thing she thought of was a foundation. She communicated this to her councilors and tested the attitudes of the sisters by bringing the topic up in a conversation at one of the community's recreation periods. What fervor! They all wanted to be one of the expeditionary sisters sent out on the mission. Before the week was out, she sent a letter to the superior of San José College in San Salvador to see if he thought it would be possible to establish a house of the Company of the Savior in Latin America. Afterwards, she wrote to Fr. Mazón to tell him about the step she had taken, asking him not to be too angry. She hoped that it would make that fine priest take her holy desires seriously. Fr. Mazón was extremely surprised. This woman never stopped surprising him with her outbursts of generosity. He called her on the phone and tried to dissuade her by all means. How was she going to create a new foundation in South America, when they still did not have enough religious sisters trained in Spain? Faced with this argument, which she could not refute, Madre Félix reluctantly agreed, although she still felt quite upset. Her appetite had been whetted, and she was determined to have a foundation on the other side of the ocean as soon as the Lord paved the way.

This was not the only foundation that remained a beautiful dream. Madre Aige's health — she suffered from a pernicious anemia that a couple of times had made her fear for her life — made Madre Félix think about opening a nursing home. Madre Aige, a homebody like no other, loved the idea of a house in the countryside for an occasional retreat and to care for the sick. Of course, Madre Félix could not conceive of a house of the Company of the Savior that did not also have a direct apostolate. That is why she thought of founding the proposed nursing home in the Pyrenees Mountains, allowing her to work in a rural school for the daughters of miners and employees of the Ribagorzana hydroelectric plant. However, when it came to making her dreams a reality, she again encountered the usual difficulty: too few professed sisters and too few university students. They were not ready for another foundation at the moment.

She had to give the same response to the archbishop of La Serena, in Chile, when he asked for religious sisters for his diocese — although in this case there was the added problem that he was asking for them to direct a shrine and a rectory, two apostolates that were far from the educational apostolate toward which the Company of the Savior was oriented.

Each of these attempts at foundation, which forced her to wait for God to open the doors, widened her heart, making her more obedient to God's plans. At the end of her life, she would harvest the ripe fruit of this waiting. During the Spiritual Exercises of 1992, in the light of contemplating Christ's hidden life, she would write: "He was God and Master and Redeemer and was hidden for thirty years! And here I am wanting to evangelize immediately, dictated by my own desires? All in God's time."

"I Am a Religious Sister!"

December 1951 was God's time for canonical approval of the Company of the Savior. That same month, Madre Félix had been talking with a person who could support them in Rome. However, Providence had moved forward and, before her benefactor traveled to the Eternal City, the secretary of the Congregation for Religious, Father Arcadio Larraona, C.M.F., had signed the *nihil obstat* of their Constitutions. This precedence of the Lord regarding things of His Company gave Madre Félix such consolation!

The bishop did not take long to communicate. On January 9, 1952, the personal secretary of Bishop Modrego called the house in Barcelona asking for the superior general. Madre Félix was in Madrid, and Madre Linés called her to tell her the news. This was written by Madre Félix herself, in a private essay entitled *Memories of Great Days*:

> "Phone call, *Madre*!"
> "Who is it?"
> "Barcelona on the phone!"
> "What's going on, Madre Linés?"
> "The bishop wants to see you."
> "What is the matter?"
> "I don't know how to tell you. It is a very big and very good thing."
> "Well say it quickly."
> "I'm afraid the shock might be too much for you."
> "Is it news from Rome?"
> "Yes, Mother!"
> "Did the approval come?"
> "That is what Mgr. Muñoz insinuated."
> "My God! What great news!"
>
> And I got a lump in my throat from the emotion, and I could not make a single sound. Madre Aige picked up the phone and continued the conversation. Like a wounded deer, I took refuge at the foot of the tabernacle, falling apart in sobs from the deepest part of my being. Depart from me, Lord, for I am a sinful soul. Depart from me! I could not say anything else; I had no other feelings. What a shock, Lord! How can this be when I am such a sinner? Depart from me, Lord, so much light, so much happiness. Is Your mercy so great that, forgetting my wretchedness, You let me see the fulfillment of Your promises? Joy, confusion, surprise, admiration, gratitude, fear. An inexplicable complexity, an expression of the unspeakable. A feeling that annihilates and gives monumental life that was not even dreamed of. On the outside trembling like a wounded deer and sobs of mixed feelings. How poor is human nature that it can barely withstand a flutter from Heaven![41]

She quickly notified the other houses and Fr. Mazón, and the joy spread at such speed that even the girls of the school in Lleida applauded, not knowing why, when they saw the great joy that had captivated the *madres*.

[41] Personal Journal, December 21, 1951–January 9, 1952 (AGCS M 202.20,001).

Although Madre Félix had been sick in bed in Madrid, she quickly took a train to Barcelona with Madre Aige. There they officially received the news of the approval. The Sacred Congregation for Religious and Secular Institutes had left intact many of the clearly Ignatian points, but there were two key elements that were left out for the moment: The fourth vow of obedience to the Holy Father and the name of the Institute, which they had translated as "Society of the Savior" when translating the text from Latin: *Societas Salvatoris.* The latter was easy to remedy, the former would be a little harder.

The bishop, seeing them, congratulated them wholeheartedly and told them that he wanted to erect the congregation as soon as possible and that he himself would receive the vows of the superior general. No sooner said than done. On January 31, 1952, the "Religious Congregation of Diocesan Right of Sisters of the Savior" was canonically erected, and on February 2nd, the first seventeen nuns made their canonical vows: Madre Félix, as superior general, made them at the hands of Bishop Modrego; afterwards, she herself received the profession of her sisters. Her face, on that day of glory, said it all. Swept up by God, she could not believe that she was finally and forever a religious sister.

María Félix receiving the canonical vows of one her sisters (Barcelona, 1952).

Sisters who took their vows, on the staircase of the Archbishopric (Barcelona, 1952).

For the vow ceremony, the families of the religious sisters, the university students from the Mater Salvatoris College, and a representation of the students from Lleida gathered in the chapel of the episcopal palace. The next day, after the whirlwind, Madre Félix wrote to her spiritual director, who had offered to God the important sacrifice of not being able to attend the Mass of profession:

> Do you not see the hand of the Lord our God in everything? Do you not see how everything of ours is fully and completely His? Do you not feel how the supreme goodness and wisdom of God our Creator and Lord deigned to begin this tiny Company of the Savior? Do you not trust fully in Him, the only one who will preserve it and govern it and carry it forward in His holy service?
>
> The Lord has given me such an intimate, strong, and effective persuasion that nothing overshadows my joy, not even that I was elected to the office of superior general. If, in spite of me, the Lord has brought the Company to the point where it is now, to the point where I myself am — I who am so unworthy —, through my

> religious profession, what can I fear? Only one thing do I fear now: to not be faithful to the Lord our God in what He wants of me, that is, in my total and absolute surrender to His action and to His precious will. May He never leave me. May He make me what He wants. The governance of the Company does not worry me. It belongs to the Lord and the Blessed Virgin. I only need to abandon myself in His hands and remain united with Him as a docile instrument.
>
> I do not think my innermost feelings have surfaced yet. I hold them within me in a constant, sweet, and irrepressible outpouring toward the Lord our God. In reality, I live split into two beings: a physical and rational being, and another, intimately spiritual, being. Sometimes all my strength is absorbed from the inside, dazzled and strengthened with infinite desires for holiness, to love, to suffer, and to work. As for the entire Company, it lives full of joy, fervor, and gratitude to the Lord our God, to the holy Church, and to the bishop. The Company receives from the Lord our God an abundance of all kinds of benefits. It feels like the property of the Church, and lies not only in the arms but in the very Heart of the Savior.[42]

In the face of God's action, only three notes, like the echo of a chord, resonated in her soul: ardent love, immense gratitude, and unlimited trust.

[42] Letter to Fr. Mazón, February 3, 1952 (AGCS M 301.52,002).

Chapter 8

Growth of the Company of the Savior 1952–1961

"The Love of Christ Impels Us"

The joy of her religious profession was not as hidden as Madre Félix supposed. She carried it within her as a constant, gentle, and irrepressible outpouring toward the Lord our God. She transmitted it in all her gestures, her words, in her apostolic projects, and above all in the way she encouraged her sisters to be truly holy.

She had always held the profession of religious vows of poverty, chastity, and obedience in very high esteem, but now it had become "her cause." She needed to transmit it to others. To the sisters in Madrid, who congratulated her on her profession and expressed their desire to make their profession very soon, Madre Félix wrote:

> [Here are] just a few words to show you how much joy all of your enthusiastic letters give me. I thank the Lord so much for the graces that He pours out upon all of you. I pray that you will know how to be faithful to them until death and beyond death. Because for us death is not an end, it is a link between shadow and light, between what we desire and what we have, between fluctuating weakness and permanent holiness.[43]

[43] Letter to the Community of Madrid, February 11, 1952 (AGCS E 21,032).

In light of her religious consecration, everything had taken on a new color. She knew she was mysteriously chosen by God to be a witness and to give testimony of the holiness of the Church, and this, together with the trust that the Lord had placed in her, overwhelmed her. He entrusted her with the salvation and the holiness of other people! More than ever, she considered the apostolates — especially education, which sometimes left even the strongest religious sisters exhausted — as being entrusted to them by God, which led her to write:

> Thank the Lord with all your souls for entrusting you with fashioning souls, in a way, as mothers of souls. Model and nourish them according to the Divine Heart. One strong blow of the engraver's chisel can spoil the best work of any good artist. In the same way, a lack of balance in the educator can blur the image she intends to engrave in the soul of her student.[44]

That is why she encouraged those in Lleida to take care of their health:

> With our mind and heart set on the Lord our God — for whose love and glory we have set our hands to the plow — we are convinced that the better we plow His fields, the greater our spiritual and physical balance will be.[45]

Was she telling them to take care of themselves or wear themselves out? Whichever helped the most for each sister and for the souls entrusted to them to be united with God. She wanted all her sisters to be strong, serene, dedicated, full of that joy that is freshness, vitality, and friendliness on the outside; and on the inside to have a clean soul, to forget themselves, to feel God's presence, and to love souls. That is why, when considering her vows, she thought:

> Everyone in the Company of the Savior should take a private vow of the virtue of joy and make a public and solemn profession thereof

[44] Letter to M. Victorina Jené, April 13, 1952 (AGCS E 27,093).
[45] Ibid.

> and should care for this vow with the same love and care that they take care of the other vows.[46]

Those who live continuously in an intimate relationship with God have joy and a sense of humor; they can look at life from the loving perspective of God the Father. That is why Madre Félix could write letters like this one to Madre Aige. She wrote this after an exhausting overnight train trip from Madrid to Barcelona:

> As I told you, my trip was very good. I prayed, read, had dinner, I did my daily prayers, I prayed again, and then I fell asleep perfectly upright and poised. My fellow travelers stretched first one leg and then the other; they leaned to one side or the other, painfully eager to find a position as close as possible to being horizontal without ever reaching it because of the discomfort of the location. It wasn't until six o'clock in the morning, when light flooded the train car, that I woke up. My fellow travelers had been watching me, and with a tone mixed with envy and admiration, they scolded me and greeted me at the same time with: "You took quite the nap! And perfectly upright without moving!" "Well, that is the secret," I answered. "Sleep sitting up so you are in a normal position. That way your body rests evenly and can last a long time. However, if you lie in an abnormal position, the distorted parts of your body soon start to hurt and you have to look for another position." "You are an expert!" said one of my fellow travelers. I smiled and started to pray. "Oh, Lord, what a feeble honor! An expert at sleeping! I think I am actually just being trained in the art of sleeping on a train and, although my specialty is not very successful, I thank You Lord my God. Because I owe You my expertise and training in this and in everything, if there is in fact something else that I am good at."[47]

[46] Personal Journal, 1952 (AGCS, M 202.21,001).

[47] Letter to M. Carmen Aige, 1952 (AGCS E 21,049).

Happy to belong to God and to live for Him, she laughed at herself and thanked God for the nice little moments of life. Complaints were not part of her vocabulary. During the vacation for Holy Week, she gave the superior of Lleida an infinite number of tips to take care of the sisters who were in poor health — dispensations to get up later, more pleasant and gentle work, concrete patterns regarding meals, — but then she reminded her:

> Once there was a perfume maker who responded to those who thought he smelled strange: "What do you want me to smell of when I am around perfume all day?" We should answer the world, the devil, and the flesh, when they find the cross and sacrifices repugnant: "What else would my life be full of, if I am freely and willingly co-crucified with Christ?" Complaining about the cross, protesting sacrifices, facing work or pain with long faces is inappropriate for us. It would be as absurd as taking the northbound train in Madrid and wanting to end up in the cities of the south. And, as we observe and reflect, we see all the people of the world are subject to the law of pain and contradiction. In reality, there is only one difference between them: some hate that universal law and others love it. Nonetheless, all are bound by it: the first group raging against it and the second sanctifying themselves and sanctifying others. We have been called to be of that number, of the few. May we be consistent. The greater the cross, the greater the joy. Above all, may we have joy on our faces, in our words, and joy also in our hearts and in our spirits. God is our Father, and He will not permit a burden heavier than we can carry.[48]

This is how she herself tried to live, making both the small and large setbacks of life into a stepping stone or a springboard to raise her heart to God.

Her characteristic fortitude met its match with the foundation of the novitiate house in Mota del Marqués, a small town in the province of Valladolid, in northwest Spain. If St. Teresa of Ávila was called in her time a "restless, wandering nun," Madre Félix must have felt like a railway sister during that time

[48] Letter to M. Victorina Jené, March 30, 1952 (AGCS E 27,089).

immediately following the approval of the Company of the Savior. This foundation in Mota del Marqués meant that she would travel there by train a couple of times a month for about two years. She was living temporarily in Madrid, where the student novitiate had been since 1951. The routes from Barcelona to Madrid, Lleida to Madrid, and Madrid to Valladolid became very familiar to her. The reason for this foundation was that Fr. Mazón was going to acquire for the Society of Jesus the former Jesuit novitiate, which at that time was owned by the Spanish government. It was in the small town of Villagarcía de Campos in the province of Valladolid, and Madre Félix dreamed of moving the novitiate of the Company of the Savior to some nearby town. She wanted the novices, in addition to being attended by the Jesuit priests of the house, to know firsthand the stories of Fr. Bernardo de Hoyos, Fr. Baltasar Álvarez, and other worthy saints and Jesuits, as well as to get excited about the Ignatian spirit that emanated from this prestigious novitiate. The former mansion of Mrs. Magdalena de Ulloa in Mota del Marqués, half destroyed but its structure still intact, seemed suitable for her plan. Fr. Mazón suggested it to Madre Félix, who soon arrived at the town with Madre Aige, to see for herself the possibilities for a foundation and an apostolate.

Novitiate in Mota del Marqués (Valladolid, 1954).

The building had seen better days, of course. The large courtyard, which could be enclosed, had a balustrade that was half-broken. The roof tiles were ruined in some places and required intensive care. In one of the upper rooms, the floor had fallen, leaving a huge gaping hole between one floor and the next. The main rooms on the ground floor had been converted into a root cellar and had a terrible stench of rotten potatoes. Nevertheless, Madre Félix fell in love with it. She could already imagine it. The dimensions of the mansion were perfect for a novitiate, the apostolate of a school, meetings of the apostolates, and study circles with the people of the village. She was concerned about the cost. She considered it seriously. The Jesuits helped a little by lowering the price and, although it was expensive, it was still simpler than building a novitiate from scratch. In addition, they could start a farm, and with the permission of the bishop, they could open a vocational school. The income from both would contribute to the expenses of the remodeling necessary.

When she was finally able to move the novices, in 1954, they called the building the "Mice Mansion." However, Madre Félix's joy made the cold water and the lack of heaters bearable, and the work of the impromptu masons, painters, and farmers became a reason for joy, singing, and laughter. In the time she spent personally supervising the organization of the house, a few months at a time, Madre Félix took the opportunity to inflame the hearts of the aspirants. Her presence and conversation were enough to alleviate the difficulties and encourage them to work for the Kingdom of God while they made shoes, gleaned the fields, painted the pig pens, or bathed the single pig they had. In the evenings, during recreation, she would ingrain in them missionary ideals that would soon take shape. For Madre Félix, these were months of authentic happiness. She felt in her element with all these young women determined to belong to God, organizing manual labor that reminded her of the life of Jesus in Nazareth. Years later, she mentioned it with affection in the context of a conversation with Madre Gazo. She was a superior and novice mistress who had asked Madre Félix about her participation in the simplest tasks of the community:

> We would always mop whenever it was needed and wash out the pig pens and do other humble tasks. Madre Martínez could not do as

> much because of her poor health, but I did these tasks whenever I thought I should. I told her that I did not earn anything with them, because I enjoyed it. I would like the superiors to carry out humble tasks with simplicity, with naturalness, in good time, just as mothers of families do in their homes; not as a humiliation, nor as an act of special virtue, nor as an ostentation. None of that. In the Company of the Savior, the nobility, distinction, and honor of the office or position depends on the degree of love for God and love for neighbor that each woman puts into her own work. If we value things with the spirit of the world, we do not have the spirit of Christ. If we still consider domestic chores as lowly and humiliating, we are perfectly anachronistic and ridiculous people that are unaware that the social structures of the twentieth century are no longer the same as four centuries ago.[49]

They were all aware of Madre Félix's influence in generating joy and peace. She was the first to strive for them. Her joy was at the same time a gift from God and from her own hard work. The great sensitivity with which she perceived everything, together with an extremely delicate conscience, made her experience significant displeasure and forced her to look to Heaven when human relationships, even the most holy ones, made her feel contempt or herself misunderstood. In her writings from this time is found a precious paragraph about joy. She wrote:

> How poor is human nature: even the creatures we love bother us, even the creatures who love us make us suffer! God is never bothered by us. God never fears us. He is infinite love, who calls for and desires the love of all His creatures. He alone is unchanging, without being restricted by vain fears. He alone attracts us without repulsions of any kind. Happy is the human condition, ours and that of the creatures that surround us, since our hearts are restless and that moves us to seek rest in God — the real, true, and only center where we can enjoy resting in time and in eternity! Let us not

[49] Letter to M. Pilar Gazo, January 28, 1961 (AGCS E 37,029).

> expect creatures to fill our hearts. Let us not ask creatures to satisfy our hearts. Poor creatures! They are finite, small, and insignificant. Even if they wanted to, even if they worked hard, they could not fill the immense capacity that God has given our hearts to fit Him in our love. Only He is great enough to completely fill us. Let us not ask creatures for what they cannot give us. Let us be grateful for the smallness they offer us, and let us not hope for anything more.[50]

This is how she overcame her worst moods and, looking at others with tenderness and gratitude, radiated friendliness and cheerfulness.

Years later, after much practice, she was able write to another religious sister who was having some trouble:

> I would like you to abide by the following plan: When you wake up, say: "I am content, I am happy because I am a daughter of God and He loves me," and then repeat a lot: "I am content, I am happy," even ruminating on it. At meal times: breakfast, lunch, snack, and dinner, repeat more times: "I am content, I have a reason to be, I am happy; everything that I eat is good for my body and my soul. I eat it with pleasure and joy because it helps me to be healthy, and so I will work for God and for souls. This food is given to me by my Heavenly Father because He loves me and wants me to be strong, lively, and joyful." When you walk or rest or go to recreation in community, repeat: "I am happy, God loves me; God has done beautiful and good things for me. My sisters and my congregation love me, and I love them; and the supreme motive is the love of God, who loves us all and unites us all. This is always true, as it is true that the sun always shines, although clouds and storms prevent us from seeing its light and feeling its heat." When you pray, repeat again, strongly: "I am happy, I am content because You wait for me at every moment to hear me say that I love You, that I am Yours forever, even if I seem lethargic, cold, and gray." Repeat many times: "I am happy, I am content to be a beloved and favored daughter of

50 Personal Journal, 1952 (AGCS M 202.21,001).

> God and of the Blessed Virgin." Try it out. If after one month of this treatment you do not find relief, do not lose hope. Start another month and write to me.[51]

Tough Times for the Company

Madre Félix belonged to God and was happy. Nevertheless, God, whom she knew and felt was such a Father to her, did not spare her trials. He did not spare His Son either. Between 1955 and 1957, some difficult things happened within the Company of the Savior that made Madre Félix go through a bitter ordeal.

The first thing was an ordeal with the bishop of Lleida that could have been avoided. Madre Félix, who was attentive to the guidelines of the Magisterium and sensitive by nature to social problems, had decided to end a custom that was typical of schools at the beginning of the century but seemed archaic and unnatural to her in their school in Lleida. Since its foundation, the school had had two classes of students: paid students (some residents and others day students) in the main school and a free school for girls from disadvantaged families in an old and more precarious location. Madre Félix ordered the free school to be closed. Although she took some precautions for the good of the students, she was resolute. She said that all the girls who were intellectually prepared and able to keep up would be enrolled in the school with the paid students, providing them with a scholarship to pay for their studies. The reaction came quickly. Some families that did not like the decision complained to the bishop, and he demanded an immediate explanation from the superior of the community. Madre Jené, very embarrassed, wrote to Madre Félix. Her response was basically, "It's okay, don't worry about it":

> Let people say what they want, and don't try to justify yourself. We have merged into one school and this, besides being practical, is more Christian than that hateful separation into two locations so close to each other. I am increasingly happy that we have done so. You can tell

[51] Letter to a Religious Sister, June 28, 1978 (AGCS E 43,172).

> them that I ordered it and therefore I am the one that can give an answer to whoever needs one. Don't worry about the rest.[52]

Bishop Aurelio's warnings continued for a few months. The prelate even asked other bishops for reports on the performance of the Company of the Savior in their dioceses. The ever obedient and respectful response of the *madres* and the favorable information from his brothers in the episcopate won his approval in the end. Meanwhile, as always, Madre Félix sought to shoulder the responsibility and guarantee the peace of her immediate collaborators. The worries she carried on her shoulders were already quite numerous.

On the one hand, the weight of the financial situation always accompanied her. The novitiate, with its small farm in the making and the meager contributions of the candidates, was nothing to write home about. The house in Madrid was opening a school, a new Mater Salvatoris, but it only had one grade at this point. In the school in Lleida, they were asking for support to make renovations and to have better materials. The same thing was the case in Barcelona, where it seemed necessary to offer the university students some unique programs of study or other attractions that would make the college stand out among others.

Another subject that weighed heavily on her heart was the family situation of Madre Carmen Aige's sister, María Josefa Aige, whose husband had left her and their eight young children. Although this distressed Madre Félix, at least she could do something about that one. With great affection she offered María Josefa to welcome three of her young girls in the boarding school of Lleida or that of Mota del Marqués, depending on the season, in order to make caring for the others easier and to provide these girls with the means and the education they needed.

What worried her the most, because she did not manage to improve the situation, was the internal tension she perceived in some of the communities and the widespread distress that caused the departure of several religious sisters. The trouble had begun when two young professed sisters left the community. They were both capable and had shown promise. At

[52] Letter to M. Victorina Jené, 1956 (AGCS E 28,094).

first they were enthusiastic, but they had become disillusioned, perhaps by some unconscious expectations with which they had entered religious life. Shortly after finishing their studies, they left with great disgust and began a strong campaign of criticism against the Company of the Savior. They involved their relatives and a Jesuit who was close to them. They wrote to those who remained inside, obscuring their judgment about their own vocation. It was undoubtedly a spiteful outburst that was getting out of control. The pandemonium that arose almost put an end to the religious life of some other young women in formation. Madre Félix prayed, remained silent when she saw it useless to give explanations, and wrote to the promoters of the problem with great charity. She urged them to give up this attitude, which was as detrimental to them as it was to the Company, and to seek with sincerity the will of God from now on. For her part, they could count on her forgiveness, prayers, and help in anything they needed. However, the hardest thing was yet to come.

January 1957 was a month of poignant contrasts. On the one hand, Madre Félix received the happiest news that the Holy See had granted the Company of the Savior a special grace: they still could not take the fourth vow of the Jesuits, but if they wished, they could make a promise of special obedience to the Holy Father along with their perpetual profession. Madre Félix could not contain her joy. It was a caress from God after so many trials. Having regained her lively tone, she assured Fr. Mazón:

> Surely no one and nothing ties the hands of the Lord our God, and where I see them most free is in the Company because it is very much His and He does and undoes whatever He wants in it. Nothing gives me greater peace than this thought.[53]

She needed that certainty. That same month, she was told about the departure of one of her general councilors from the institute. She was very dear to Madre Félix and had been with them since the founding of the Company. It was completely unexpected. Madre Félix knew that she had been upset recently. Some

[53] Letter to Fr. Mazón, January 13, 1957 (AGCS M 301.57,001).

projects had not moved forward in the school in Madrid, which she directed. There were tensions in the community of which she was superior. However, Madre Félix could not have imagined that the standoffishness she had noted in recent months was hiding so much frustration and distrust as to take it to that extreme. She tried to talk, to clarify things. It was all useless. The decision had been made. With immense pain, Madre Félix let her go, convinced that a true vocation was lost.

These problems depressed Madre Félix. More than once during those days, her pain, sadness, and bad mood were evident. She herself — and only she — came to wonder if she was unbalanced. Her restless heart caused her to question her own capabilities so many times! She needed to ask Fr. Mazón, whom she could approach as a father, in confidence. Surely, he would tell her if she was the source of these problems, or if she was lacking the capacity to handle them if that were the case. In this way, she might finally have a serious reason to resign her office and would live under obedience; moreover, she would have an arena in which to toil for the rest of her life in developing interior ascetism. With these sentiments, she wrote to him on February 5, 1957, with moving simplicity. In her letter, she assumed that she suffered from an imbalance but continued:

> Well, the Lord has given me this "wrinkle" to force me to surrender to following Him, to His will, as well as to be able to follow the will of a creature — ultimately a fragile reed that would break if I sought to support myself on it. He wants me to give myself body and soul to the fulfillment of His most holy will, which is the will of the Heavenly Father. He wants the fulfillment of this mission to be my mission and the mission of the Company of the Savior. Because of the great Mystery of Christ, my "wrinkle" — which, if left to my own devices, would throw me into disgusting egomania and the horrors of despair — can be an instrument of redemption because it is a particle of His Passion that freely runs through me, a mystical member of His Body. I offer the passion of not being freed from the imperfection of my "wrinkle" and the most painful passion of not being able to free

> myself in spite of my efforts. I offer it for this world that I carry so deeply in my heart: for the young university students, for the many of them that are also threatened and are victims of this great psychological disorder of the current mentality. One more thing, and with this I will conclude. I feel a joyful balance, a luminous peace, and a deep joy because I feel God's action in me. It is not a "sublimation" of psychologists that frees me from my "wrinkle," which since it is on such a human plane, is of a much lower level and totally different from God's action. It is the grace of God that is given to me and invades me. It is the love of Christ that unites me to Himself as a member of His Body. It is something that is not in me but rather is above me, that possesses me. With our poor human strength, we can only ask for grace and cooperate with it — and even this we cannot do without a previous grace. We could never produce divine grace, nor can any "sublimation" ever change its action.[54]

Fr. Mazón, vice-provincial of Venezuela at the time, surely leaned back in his chair, in the city of Maracaibo in northwestern Venezuela, and smiled once again at Madre Félix's notions. He did not believe that it was a psychological disorder. What he did fully agree with was that this heart and its strong waves were made with the purpose of obeying God and cooperating generously in the redemption of mankind.

That is why he was infinitely happy when Madre Félix, a few months later, on the eve of the Sacred Heart, wrote to him in a very different tone. At last, she had finished reviewing the text of the Constitutions to send a copy to Rome that had been adapted to the indications that the Sacred Congregation for Religious had given when approving the Company of the Savior. In this letter from June 27th, Madre Félix's true spiritual image could be seen. Neither the "wrinkle" of her psychology nor the strokes of genius defined her. She was also not fully defined by her maternal tenderness or her acts of heroic generosity. If anything gave unity to this woman's life, it was the gift of God's love, which she had the courage to recognize and act on. She wrote:

[54] Personal Journal, August 27 1951–February 20, 1957 (AGCS M 202.18,001).

On the last day of May, late in the evening, I finished writing the amendments to the Constitutions. Since the finished Constitutions were the gift I wished to offer to the Blessed Virgin, I took them just as they were, still in rough draft, and went down to the chapel. There, by the tabernacle, in that hour of solitude and total silence, I placed the Gospels on my head and heart and kissed them fervently, declaring before my Lord and my God that all we wanted in the Company was the spirit of Jesus Christ, His love, imitation, and glorification. I did the same with the Missal because we want to be daughters of the Church and because our life must be Mass: Eucharist and sacrifice. In the same way, I repeated it with the Constitutions of St. Ignatius, and I begged our father very much that he would present our Constitutions, from his younger daughters, to the Blessed Virgin and to the three Persons of the Most Holy Trinity. In the end, I took that handful of pages and in spirit put them in his hands, and I entrusted to him their path and the approval of everything that was according to God's will and the annulment of that which was not.

It is true that I only desire one thing with all my soul: the glorification of God. This is the great desire that the Lord has placed in my heart, this is His great gift, the great grace He has granted me. This great desire, which is sometimes fire and is always light, is the one that lifts me up when I fall, the one that sustains me in danger, the spring that puts me back on my feet, the impetuous force that fills my soul with infinite desires for souls and holiness. It is what makes me feel in a unique and ineffable way that longing for God alone, which although sometimes it is martyrdom, is the only thing that gives meaning and fullness to my life.

When I started writing, it was not my intention to tell you these feelings; but it does not matter, it has been an outpouring of the kind that my soul only knows how to have with Your Reverence because God wants it and because Your Reverence lives according to His heart. Tomorrow is the feast of this Most Sacred Heart, and I would very much like to love Him and to remedy what displeases Him. We creatures are such small things to love God and to remedy

> what displeases God.... Nevertheless, He asks for it, and I would like Him to use me however He wants.[55]

That was really important. In a few months, the Company of the Savior was going to make a geographical and qualitative leap that required complete openness to God's will.

"Strong Desire for Missions"

The pope had spoken. There was no doubt anymore. That is why they had made a special promise to adhere to his Magisterium and indications. The dream of making a foundation in South America had to be possible now since the Holy Father wanted it. Pius XII was very clear. He had written to the bishops of Latin America about his desire for men and women religious to collaborate in the pastoral action of these particular churches, his concern for the abundance of harvest for so few priests, and his interest in the fruitful collaboration with religious and lay catechists to give birth to a new impetus for the Church in the Americas. Couldn't the Company of the Savior do its part? Moreover, as if that were not enough, now Fr. Mazón was vice-provincial in those lands.

The priest liked the idea, but under one condition: that they send people who had already been formed. They needed to start off on a good foot, and also life in Venezuela was very expensive compared to Spain. There was no way their houses of origin could cover the expense of their studies. If they agreed, Madre Félix and Madre Aige could travel there to do research. They could put feelers out with the bishops and with the landowners and landlords. They would see what could be done. A good school or a resident college would be a sure fit in the city of Maracaibo or the capital city, Caracas.

Said and done. The superior general and her vicar traveled for the first time across the ocean on August 22, 1957, on the feast of the Immaculate Heart.[56] They traveled by plane in first class because when they entered, they were the last ones and there were no more seats left in coach. It no doubt reminded them of that trip to the city of Palma on the island of Mallorca, almost

[55] Letter to Fr. Mazón, June 27, 1957 (AGCS M 301.57,008).

[56] This date is the Feast of the Queenship of Mary in the new calendar.

twenty years ago, looking for companions to found the institute. Now they were religious sisters, but they continued dreaming of giving themselves more to God. They imagined the missionary Company of the Savior in the jungle areas in the interior of Venezuela.

They did not suspect what awaited them in Caracas. They were surprised from the moment they landed in the country until the end. The first surprise was Fr. Mazón. He was waiting for them at the airport so that he could throw some *bolivars* (Venezuelan currency) over the fence for them to use to pass through customs. He had prepared accommodations for them in a residence of religious sisters and urged them to write down some commitments in their expeditionary agenda. The first was a meeting of Catholic educators in which they could verify the prestige of the Jesuits in the city. Madre Félix was very amused to see how several dozen religious were watching Fr. Mazón's gestures out of the corner of their eyes to applaud or reject the proposals according to what he did. With such an advocate, they would be very secure. Then he introduced them to several Jesuits of the vice-province who could collaborate with them depending on where they settled. Finally, on September 6th, he accompanied them to see the archbishop of Caracas, Archbishop Rafael Arias Blanco, warning them that they should not have many illusions. The prelate, who usually did not allow foundations in the capital, intended to make an exception for them. He wanted them to start a school. The best in town.

Somewhat self-conscious because of the archbishop's expectations, Madre Félix and Madre Aige paid their respects to him and expressed their wishes for the Company of the Savior to found a school in Venezuela. Archbishop Rafael was extremely friendly and expressed his concern about the need for Catholic schools in Caracas, particularly in Las Mercedes, a residential area of high socioeconomic status. They answered that they were there for whatever the Church needed. Of course. What about the jungle? What about the poor neighborhoods and slums that they had seen on the way from the Maiquetía Airport? Madre Félix felt that, in that highly developed city, she needed "to work with the poor, just as we need air for our lungs." The archbishop replied that they should not forget about the poor. Surely later they could do something to help them. For now, they should study English and open a practically bilingual school; that endeavor would do a lot for Jesus Christ and His Church.

In a couple of weeks, the school year would begin, but Madre Félix was not discouraged. They would start that year even if it was a little late. In November, Madre Ribera and Madre Sagüillo arrived by plane, and a few days later, the other three assigned to the foundation arrived by boat. Upon their arrival, they found the *madres* settled in the Garbiñe house. It was a small five-room house on Madrid Avenue, with a beautiful sign out front announcing: "Mater Salvatoris Children's School." Just like that. As if it had been open forever. The school began with seventeen students, primary school girls and preschool boys and girls. Almost all of them were children of acquaintances of Fr. Mazón and attended for free because Madre Félix was the one who received those coming to register their children.

This is what Madre Sagüillo, one of the first religious sisters in Caracas, remembers:

> Madre Félix was the one who received them, and the rest of the community was in the kitchen-dining room listening to the conversation,

First Missionaries sent to Venezuela (Madrid, 1957).

> excited to find out if they would stay. Madre Félix, with her characteristic friendliness, spoke about everything until the mother would ask about the price. Immediately Madre Félix would say: "Look, since she is one of the first to register, your daughter will be our guest of honor." Those of us who listened as Madre Félix convinced the woman to accept the offer were surprised, and Madre Aige with her practical sense later said to Mother: "But how are we going to live if the students do not pay?" Madre Félix answered like a witty little girl: "You will see how many students will come. . . ." They laughed and stopped worrying. Madre Aige gave in and trusted that Madre Félix was prophetic, which she was. We finished that first year with twenty-five students, and we had to look for a new house, something bigger. It was the Laura house on Las Mercedes Avenue. We ended up with more than a hundred students. The number kept increasing until we went to the Gladys house, which was the pioneer of new houses: Sacromonte, Toluca, Bellita, Lola, and Trinidad. They formed a small colony, with the yard of the Gladys house in the center.[57]

After only two months in Caracas there was a flood. The Guaire River overflowed, and the sisters had to evacuate their house in the middle of the night and spend the night in the house of some neighbors who invited them to take refuge on the top floor of their house. How could Madre Félix leave these poor daughters of hers? In light of the situation, she knew she could not return to Spain so soon. Aware that this foundation was such an adventure, she decided to turn Caracas into her provisional headquarters for at least a couple of years. From there she would go back and forth to Spain, but it was important to help the Company create a strong foothold in Venezuela.

Her presence among the junior sisters — the sisters in temporary vows who were being sent from Spain — was a great incentive for everyone. It was no wonder. Madre Félix as usual was empathetic, cheerful, open, highly spiritual, demanding — yes — but understanding, maternal without ambiguous tenderness, and if possible, even more of an apostle than in the days of the founding of Mota del Marqués. She knew how to enkindle in them

[57] Testimony of M. Concepción Sagüillo, August 10, 2001 (AGCS M 503.01,018).

the desire for the most heroic holiness, making them see that it was not so necessary to multitask and do more things, but rather to cultivate their union with God. To a young woman who had just made her profession, Madre Félix gave this advice:

Mother Félix during a First Communion (Carcas, 1958).

> Spend a lot of time with Him, intimately in the depths of your heart, constantly talk with Him. This is the spiritual life, and the love of Jesus Christ that is cultivated in it transforms our life imperceptibly, almost without realizing it. For this love we sacrifice the cultivation and gratification of our worldly "grace and finesse" and instead receive the grace and finesse of the saints, like St. Teresa of Jesus, St. Francis de Sales, St. Pius X, and so many others received them. That love of Jesus Christ makes us sacrifice the eagerness and curiosity of external things and gives us the knowledge of the intimacy of the human soul together with the knowledge of God. It is by that sacrifice that such gifts reach us so we can bear fruit in souls.[58]

The way she became absorbed in prayer, the fervor with which she spoke about the girls and their families, and her heated exhortations to work tirelessly and without hesitation for souls, all gave them a glimpse into what Madre Félix was experiencing. Their intuition was correct. In her personal notes during this time, she wrote:

> In Caracas my soul came to life again. If I am not a holy religious sister, what am I? What am I here for? Nothing on earth moves me in this way: it is only the voice of Christ in the depths of my soul. The Company awaits my direction while I play around and Christ cries out in my heart. He cries out because He has shed His blood for souls and I do not catch it to apply it to them. He cries out in my heart for the souls that walk around blindly and have no one to guide them, for those that are lost and there is no one to look for them.

No. Madre Félix did not play around. However, she wanted to be a thousand times more serious, more consistent, more devoted to the service of God. This was what she asked of those who were preparing to come to Venezuela:

[58] Letter to M. María de la Cruz Vaquero, March 14, 1958 (AGCS E 43, 124).

> Look, if we are not saints, we are nothing. Saints of flesh and bone, not as those painted images on the cheap holy cards with beatific smiles but as those that are full of energy, those who get up if they fall down and, because of that fall, tie themselves more tightly to the Cross; and if they fall down again, they get up and love with a new love that is more intense, more total, and of greater dedication to the Lord our God. Saints who measure time with eternity and the earth with infinity; for whom the time of work and struggles, of sufferings and humiliations is a short second on the clock of the merit and of the love for God and souls; for whom the surface of the entire earth is so small, that it is not even enough for them to lean their hearts on; so small that when it comes to offering it to God, it seems to them like the head of a small pin, and they wish they had millions of worlds to offer to Him because one is so small. This is what the Company needs: saints of this caliber, courageous and fervent, of an open and strong spirit, striving for the greater glory of God and for the salvation of souls. That is how the Lord wants you; that is how all of you must be.[59]

She wanted to be one of those, and she begged God for it with all her soul. That is why she was not intimidated in January when the fall of the dictatorship of Marcos Pérez Jiménez was accompanied by a clamor of bombs, arson attacks, and other kinds of turmoil. To Madre Isabel Martínez, the novice mistress, and to the novices who were being formed in Mota del Marqués, Madre Félix wrote simply:

> For now, it does not seem that they want to throw us out of here, and if they do not throw us out, we should not leave. We have come here for souls and for the Church, and as long as one or the other needs us, we should not think about leaving. It would be a desertion.[60]

She would never consider desertion. However, she had no choice but to return to Spain herself, at least during the summer, to prepare for the second General

59 Letter to the Community of Lérida, August 28, 1957 (AGCS E 32,004).

60 Letter to M. Isabel Martínez, March 13, 1958 (AGCS E 31,054).

Chapter of the Company of the Savior, six years after that first one on February 2, 1952. Would she finally cease to be superior general? Could she be assigned to Venezuela — perhaps to the school they had been asked to lead in the residential area of Tamare — as just another member of the community? She confided in Fr. Mazón that she would be very happy if she were to be assigned to those lands for the rest of her life. She had upright and pure intentions.

There was a lot of work to prepare for the General Chapter. So much so that she even had to attend to some matters during the Spiritual Exercises immediately before it was held. However, she did not lose sight of the needs of all the houses. She also followed the health of her spiritual father closely.

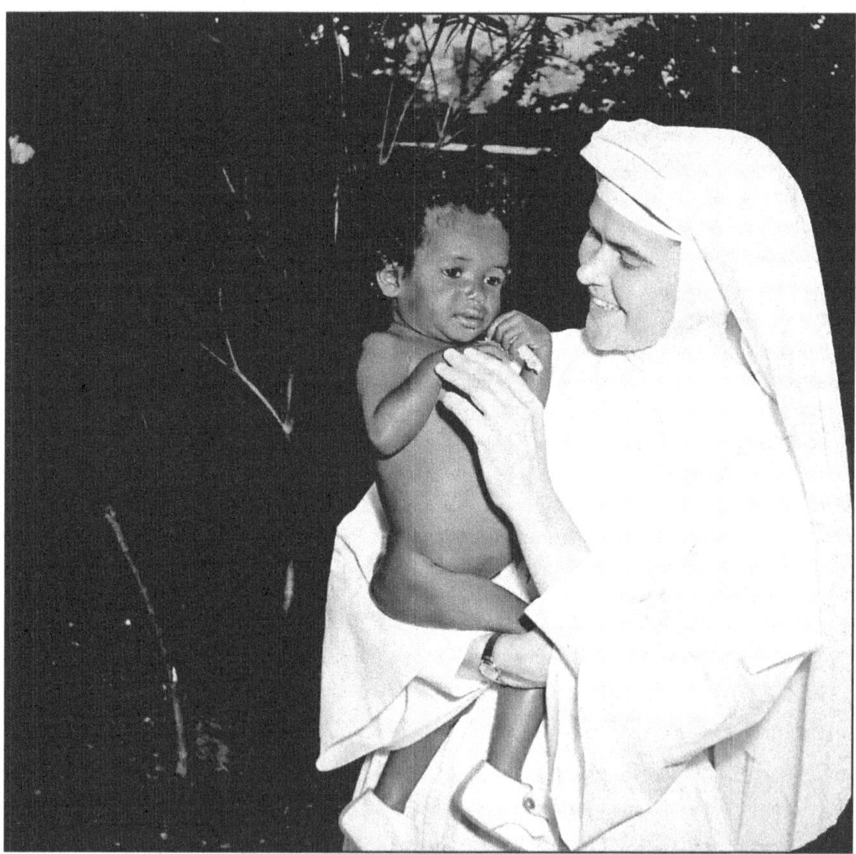

Sister's apostolate among the poor (Carcas, 1959).

When she had left Venezuela, he had an infection, and she could not rest until she did something for him. When she arrived in Spain, she consulted doctors, bought medicine, and quickly sent it to Caracas. The priest's answer did not take long:

> The spots are gone. That is all it was. Now stop worrying and thinking nonsense. It was all my fault. Ask the Lord to make me more consistent in taking my injections. Don't send any more medicine. I thank you with all my heart for it because I know you meant well, but know that I will not take them. Do not waste any more money.[61]

Madre Félix paid no attention to his harshness, nor did she give up. In the middle of the Chapter, on the eve of her dreaded reelection, she replied to Fr. Mazón saying for God's sake not to give up and to be consistent in taking the medication, just as the doctor told him. Then she went on to tell him about her fears of reelection, the trust she had in Divine Providence, and her desire to do God's will and to go to Venezuela for the rest of her life. However, the Lord had other plans for her, and she was not going to return to Caracas until September of that year, and only for a visit — as superior general.

As planned, before the end of the Chapter, the sisters' assignments were discussed. Madre Félix wanted to send six to Tamare, four to Caracas, and three to Maracaibo to found another school there. However, when he was consulted, Fr. Mazón again encouraged her to pull back. She should not make any more foundations until they had more college graduates and sisters with doctorates and who knew more English. Only the one in Tamare would prosper for the moment. Tamare was a new residential area created by the Creole Petroleum Corporation for its managers and workers. It was on the edge of Lake Maracaibo near the city of Ojeda, about four hundred miles west of Caracas. They wanted a good religious school for boys and girls. They entrusted that area to the Jesuits and through Fr. Mazón, they offered for the Company of the Savior to take on teaching the girls. The agreement was made. On November 16, 1958, the first five religious sisters arrived. On the

[61] Letter to Fr. Mazón, July 22, 1958 (AGCS M 302.58,004).

18th, Madre Félix and Madre Aige arrived for the start of classes. The latter was going to stay for a long time in Venezuela as superior of Caracas and delegate of the superior general for the houses of the Americas. As for Madre Félix, she would be freer to travel often to visit the houses. It was another example of her detachment. She knew how to sacrifice her most holy affections whenever the good of all her daughters required it.

"The Authentic Social Revolution" (1959–1961)

The world was changing. The Company was too, at least in its number of members and works. The sisters could feel it, of course, and wondered what God wanted from them in an increasingly global and increasingly divided world. It was the time of the Cold War and the Vietnam War. The *madres* fantasized about going to Russia to preach about Jesus Christ. What about in the meantime? Meanwhile, the poverty and inequalities they saw with their own eyes astonished them. The sisters in Caracas had begun to attend to a residence for young students with few resources, and on Sundays they gave catechesis in the slums around the Catia neighborhood. In Tamare, the sisters dedicated the weekend to giving catechesis and general instruction in the indigenous villages, though they wanted to do more! They were disheartened to see skyscrapers and miserable shanties just a few yards apart from each other, and to walk through poor neighborhoods on Sundays and then on Monday find out about some lavish trips the girls in their school took. It was the same way in Spain. There were tensions in Barcelona and the area around Lleida. It was the same in Madrid, around the university. Madre Linés, from Barcelona, and some of the other first companions, from different assignments, confidently asked Madre Félix if she thought the initial character of the Company of the Savior — of being open to any mission — was fading. They had so many paid schools, there was so much emphasis on pedagogy and English, so much planning for the exchange program for the girls to stay in Ireland and France, so much eagerness to open a high school in Madrid and for the cultivation of university women in Barcelona. Should they not also be trained for the social apostolate if they wanted to respond to the need of the times?

Madre Félix understood. She herself had insisted that the first thing was to be Ignatian and the mission would come from there, which the Lord would

Community of Tamare, 1958.

show them! Even so, she saw the hand of God in the way in which events had been happening. If she was being sincere, He had always led them in one way or another to evangelize through schools and other educational centers. Moreover, their activity was to form educated women who could serve the cause of God and transform society, and was there any better way to pursue it? Therefore, in view of the facts, she replied:

> It comforts me greatly to be able to answer you with joyful contemplation about the master lines that the Lord has engraved in the Company and considering only the greatest service of the Church. Without a doubt, by serving it in the field of teaching, the Company contributes in the most effective and most Christian way to making men and women into brothers and sisters of the same class: HUMANITY. We give them awareness of the high dignity that can come through their divine filiation.

And, in this same letter, she confirmed these principles with experience:

> In our school in Madrid, girls who are aristocratic live with others who are not. In Caracas, daughters of millionaires live with others

> who cannot pay the monthly fee. In the school in Lleida, middle-class girls are with others of humble class. This life together in our houses is achieved without problems and without complications because of the way our sisters run the schools. Besides that, in Tamare, we fight hard against roughness that borders on savagery. In Mota we fight against another kind of roughness that affects only external forms. Most of the time that roughness conceals an exquisite sensibility and a high spiritual level. In our congregation and in many others, it is the case that the lowest sister has been chosen by them to preside over all. Let us be aware of the social work of our Church. The authentic social revolution—which makes all men and women brothers and sisters, with all its consequences, and children of God, with all its rights—is the seal of Christ, the Founder of the Church, and the seal that He has imprinted on all those who are His. The Church has been doing social work since her foundation, although not through demagogy. The Company, assimilated by the Church its Mother, has been doing social work since its foundation, although not through demagogy. This is something as innate in us as breathing air.[62]

And that is the social work that she gave herself to, body and soul. She had always had a preference for the poor, perhaps because, without being poor herself, she had seen her father earn a living by the sweat of his brow. She took care of the distressed parents who could not afford their children's school or medicine, of migrants who arrived with only what was on their backs to a country that did not want them, of the abandoned children who swarmed the streets, and of those who saw their elders suffer without being able to do anything to help them. That is why during these years that she was staying in Caracas she was the protagonist in very beautiful scenes that the junior sisters who lived with her would remember all their lives. In December, shortly before Christmas, she learned that the sisters had met a ten-year-old boy named Omar while they were teaching catechesis in the Antimano neighborhood. He had been abandoned by his mother. He had been sold to a criminal but, when the

[62] Letter to M. Inés Linés, January 30, 1959 (AGCS E 30,171).

criminal was arrested, Omar was left alone on the street. His mother did not want to take him back. He spent his nights on a front porch and bathed with water collected in discarded sardine cans. The mothers who were catechists insisted that she and her sisters help this child. Madre Félix was moved by the situation of the child and by the love of the catechists. She agreed to the unthinkable. Yes. They could bring him home until they found a place he could live. Thus, the orphan Omar lived among the sisters for a few days, until Christmas Eve. On the 24th, well dressed, "covered in talcum powder like a fish for frying" and dressed in new clothes, they took him to the Salesians, who had admitted him to their institution. Omar, saying goodbye to them, confided to the sisters that he doubted whether he would be a priest when he grew up. Maybe he would be the sisters' chauffeur and so help them to keep doing good by giving catechesis in his neighborhood.

Other situations were less dramatic but equally significant. For example, Madre Félix tried to help several families from Cuba by giving scholarships to the girls or by hiring their parents in the school. She gave a young French woman a place to live and a job at the school to get her out of danger because she was beginning to have a morally compromised situation with the father of the children she was caring for. She offered the bus manager of the school in Caracas free writing and spelling classes to ensure access to studies. She helped other employees send money to their families. She provided financial aid to the parents of several religious sisters. She provided one of the sister's brothers with the contacts and means to emigrate to Venezuela. At Christmas, she invited the school workers who came from other countries to celebrate with the community the birth of the Lord after Midnight Mass, eating some sweets and singing Christmas carols, to ease their nostalgia of the celebrations in their homelands. Her social sensitivity was not some abstract idea. It was a concern for people that was equally displayed in both big and little things.

She did these things while also pleading with the Lord to show her His will for the Company of the Savior. Madre Félix was not an oracle. She was a woman of God though, and she tried to follow His will with the light that He was giving her:

> I have been entangled in a sea of pros and cons without seeing anything clearly. With much anguish and darkness, when they told me white, I said white, and when they told me black, I said black. When they told me nothing, either I cried in the shadows or I tried not to do anything. However, last night, since I could not sleep, I began to read our Constitutions. When I read the special purpose of our congregation it seemed to me that the sun rose. I slept with a hope of figuring things out. I resolved to assist at many Masses in order to be enlightened by the Lord, to pray many prayers, and to be very good. This morning everything was very different. Everything seems easy; everything is illuminated. In Barcelona we will continue with the college, and in Madrid we will also continue with the high school. What we have to do is work well in our field with well-defined goals and with a well-chosen method. What I have to do is to move less and to pray more because Our Lord wants me to rely more on my knees than on my head. I have been given such a desire for prayer, to remain recollected, and not to lose the presence of God that I wish I could stop time and always be like this. I have so much joy and happiness that I would like to devote my entire being to all those who suffer and to all those who struggle.[63]

The Foundation in the U.S.

Shortly after writing, "I would like to devote my entire being to all those who suffer and to all those who struggle," she was going to devote her attention to a servant of God struggling to expand people's devotion to Mary.

In March 1961, when she arrived at the Caracas airport to pick up Madre Aige, who was coming from Spain, Madre Félix met an American priest who was waiting in vain for someone to come pick him up. She struck up a conversation with him. He was a religious priest, from the Congregation of the Holy Cross, and his name was Patrick Peyton. He had come to prepare a campaign for the recitation of the Rosary by families. The motto of these massive gatherings, which he had already held in other countries, was: "The family that prays together, stays together." He had been in communication with some

[63] Letter to Fr. Mazón, April 2, 1959 (AGCS M 301.59,002).

people by letter who were interested in bringing this initiative to Venezuela. However, there must have been a mistake because his host had not appeared at Maiquetía Airport. Madre Félix, in her typical way, offered him lodging, saying that he could stay at the school as long as was needed. When the crusade took place in July, she offered to help him with whatever else was needed. There were some consecrated missionary sisters who accompanied him. Well, they were welcome too. They could stay in the house that the school had just acquired and set up their central office in the community building. If the Company of the Savior could help the projects of the Blessed Virgin in any way, he should consider them already paid-in-full.

Madre Félix was happy. She could not believe the opportunity God was giving her. For a couple of years now, seeing the political instability in Venezuela and the number of girls who moved with their families to the United States, she had been thinking about opening a home in North America. She had told Madre Aige that hundreds of times. She had contacted the bishop of Miami just in case. She had inquired about the political situation and educational possibilities in Florida, New York, and even in Canada. Then, here she found herself, through an act of Christian charity — giving shelter to a poor priest abandoned at the airport — with the best of advisers regarding a future foundation right in her home. The priest turned out to be a saint, in love with the Virgin, very simple and affectionate. In reality he was not American as he seemed, but Irish. He was shy by nature, despite having become a media phenomenon just like Bishop Fulton Sheen and rubbing shoulders with the big Hollywood stars. With the sisters, however, he felt right at home, and it brought out his most human side. His return to the United States was lamented by the whole community. Since Fr. Mazón was back in Spain and they only knew about him through letters, they had been greatly helped by the preaching and example of this saintly religious priest, a squire of the Virgin. Nevertheless, Fr. Peyton left with an idea in his head: to help these sisters of the Company who had devoted themselves to him and his mission. He spoke with his provincial superior, based in Bridgeport, and with the bishop of that same diocese that bordered New York. From there, he proposed that Madre Félix make a visit in May to become acquainted with the United States.

We can see how much she desired this foundation in a letter that she sent in March to her spiritual director. In it, she told him about the providential way she met Fr. Peyton and said:

> I ask for prayers for this intention of America, even more than for the house on Ganduxer Street. It is absolutely necessary that we go there. I have not wished for anything more in the world except for the approval of the Company. I desire it intensely, and I believe that this desire is from God.[64]

In May, Madre Félix traveled to the United States, accompanied by Madre Carmen Aige and Madre María Luisa Baró, to inspect everything. She could not have been more pleased with what she saw. Connecticut is beautiful in the spring. The Jesuit University of Fairfield, the landscaped spaces, the discipline of the schools they saw ... everything excited her. In addition, the bishop of Bridgeport, Bishop Lawrence Shehan, received them wonderfully. He sent Fr. Victor Torres to pick up the sisters at the airport. He was a priest of Puerto Rican origin who showed them around the diocese. The bishop's idea was for them to learn English for a year and then they would consider. He was very interested in their proposal to open a school, but without English it was impossible to think of such a thing. Meanwhile, they could stay with the Sisters of Mercy at St. Joseph's College in Hartford. During the week they could study with them and at the university. On weekends, meanwhile, they could collaborate with Fr. Torres's apostolate with the Hispanic faithful. That is the agreement they made with him. By the following September, the first American sisters of the Company of the Savior would be sent there.

"An Apostle of the Council"

In the same letter in which she informed Fr. Mazón about the planned foundation in Connecticut, Madre Félix wrote a precious paragraph about the greatest dream of her life: to see Christ reflected in the Company of the Savior. She explained:

[64] Letter to Fr. Mazón, March 31, 1961 (AGCS M 301.61,04).

> Sometimes I think that the Company is still somewhat unformed, like a little child in its early childhood, and that now it is going to begin to acquire its adult physical features. With Ignatian traits, it must show strong signs of the features of Christ, the Founder and Head of the Church, Savior of all mankind, infused with the greater glory of the Heavenly Father. It must also have features softened by those of the Blessed Virgin, which do not clash with Christ's because she is His Mother. I feel the desire to contemplate this appearance embodied in the Company, which corresponds to its spirit, to its inheritance. What a joy it will be when I see Christ in it! I already see Him in its soul, but I want to see Him also in its physical body.

For this reason, and because of her interest in everything related to the Church — "the work of Jesus Christ, the work of my loves" — Madre Félix felt that the convocation of the Second Vatican Council was a providential opportunity. Pope John XXIII had announced it in January 1959, but on Christmas 1961, he promulgated the Apostolic Constitution *Humanae salutis,* with which he called for its celebration. Its aim was to infuse the veins of a troubled humanity with "the life-giving and perennial energies of the Gospel."[65] To make Christ, who is in the Church, visible in the Church, recognizable in her structures, and above all in each of her members. Madre Félix was enthusiastic about this initiative of the Holy Father and encouraged everyone in the Company to support it:

> We would not be daughters of the Church if the movement coming from the Vicar of Christ did not have an intense impact on each of our souls and the whole Company.[66]

That *feeling with the Church* was something she had learned from St. Ignatius and his beloved Society of Jesus. Hence Madre Félix wrote to the superior in Barcelona, asking her to ask Fr. Mazón what the Jesuits were going to do: were they going to pray something special for the fruits of the Council? She was very excited because she had great hopes for this ecclesial event:

[65] John XXIII, Apostolic Constitution *Humanae salutis* (December 25, 1961), no. 3.

[66] Circular Letter, December 30, 1961 (AGCS R 403.01,017).

> Just as a spiritual retreat and a review or examen do much good for the soul, so the Lord our God asks the Church from time to time to do [or reflect on] a review, an examen, a doctrine, some directives. That is what the councils are. The Church comes out of them more like the heart of God, more enriched with truth, charity, and supernatural life.[67]

For this reason, she congratulated a religious sister who was going to take her vows in March 1962. Madre Félix invited her to consider how God had blessed her, allowing her to make her profession in a year of such importance to the Church:

> You will take your vows on the feast of St. Joseph, Patron of the Universal Church, in the year of the Council. This will be a solemn assembly of the Church with transcendental consequences. Everything seems to indicate that the Lord wants you to pay special attention to your quality as A DAUGHTER OF THE CHURCH. You are already a daughter of the Church by your baptism, and more so after you take your vows because you will be a religious sister. However, you will be a daughter of the Church in an even more special way because you will make a special consecration as a professed sister in the Company of the Savior, which is particularly consecrated to the service of the Church. I would like all the sisters of the Company to love the Church very much and to love the pope very much. To love the Church and the pope is to love Jesus Christ, her divine Founder, Head, and High Priest, whom the pope represents. To love the Church is also to love our brothers and sisters, the living Church, and to love God's will — as the laws and dispositions of the Church are God's will.[68]

In almost all her letters during these years, she ended with similar words of farewell: "Do not forget the Council," "Keep praying and sacrificing for the

[67] Ibid.

[68] Letter to M. Concepción García, February 10, 1962 (AGCS E 37,002).

Church and the Council," "Pray for the Church, for the Council, and for the pope," and so on.

On the other hand, her apostolic vocation did not allow her to restrict her enthusiasm to the small group of the Company of the Savior. She wanted the university students in Barcelona and the students of the other schools to be aware of the historical moment in which they were living. To Madre Jené, when recommending that she spare no expense for the formation of schoolgirls, Madre Félix said:

> There is no need to suppress formative events because we must not lose sight of the particular purpose of the school. It would also be advisable to organize a workshop on the social doctrine of the Church, presented by a specialist, and another on the Ecumenical Council. Those are topics that a Catholic university student these days must know about.[69]

She also encouraged the sisters of Tamare to do the same thing for the students of that school:

> During this year, pray in a special way for the fruits of the Second Vatican Council. Each of us must consider ourselves apostles of the Council. We have to pray a lot for this assembly, and we should have our girls pray. We also need to explain to them what councils are and what the pope wants from this council.[70]

Only a month later, she insisted in a second letter and asked what concrete initiatives they had put into place to learn about and help others know about the Council.

Even when writing to her mother and her brother Pepe for their birthdays, she made them see the importance of the Council for the good of the Church:

[69] Letter to M. Victorina Jené, August 28, 1961 (AGCS E 29,093).

[70] Letter to the Community of Tamare, February 15, 1962 (AGCS E 39,182).

> Take good care of yourself, *mamá*. Do not go out in the cold. Do not work too much on crocheting or embroidery or other tasks. Take it easy. Pray a little, like someone who speaks to God our Father who is in Heaven, and pray for your children, for your granddaughters, for the whole world, and also pray for the Council that will be held in Rome. In this council, the pope wants all Christians to convince ourselves that we must be more Christian. He also wants us to realize that all human beings are our brothers and sisters and that we should serve one other on an international scale. All of us should pray to God for this to happen, and we must strive to make it a reality.[71]

In time, God was going to fulfill those desires of giving the Church an apostle of the Council. What Madre Félix did not suspect is that she would be this apostle, experiencing firsthand the conciliar doctrine.

[71] Letter to Florentina Torres Fumás and José Félix Torres, March 8, 1962 (AGCS, Madrid, M 604.01.A,027).

Chapter 9

"Suffering and Doing His Precious Will" 1962–1970

Remediating Needs

Madre Félix was very motherly. She was also very much a daughter. The two things became apparent in the first half of the 1960s.

Shortly after arriving in Bridgeport, she had to turn her eyes to Spain and take charge of the circumstances that her mother Florentina was going through. *Abuelita Flor,* as she was called in the family, had a complicated situation. Until now she had lived in Albelda with her son Pepe, who had been separated from Carmina, his wife, for many years. However, Pepe had fallen in love and was going to move to Andalusia in southern Spain. He and his new family were more than willing to have her come with them. But Abuelita Flor felt out of place there, so far away, where she had no roots. Neither could she live permanently with Ángel, who lived in an apartment with his wife and children. She would prefer to live alone in the village, but everyone considered it to be a bit dangerous for someone her age. Madre Félix tried to encourage her to leave with Pepe, but she could not force things. She considered a residence for the elderly. It broke her soul, but she asked around in many residences run by religious sisters to see if they could welcome her mother. She was not successful. She who had helped so many families of the sisters of the Company now presented herself to the General Council with her limitation. She could not decide what to do in her own case. She asked them to decide what to do about Abuelita Flor's petition: could she stay in one of the houses of the Company for a few months at a time? She would pay a woman to live there with her and attend to her. Madre Félix asked that the vote be secret and that they act with complete freedom as they would in the case of any other sister. They did so with pleasure. At last, they could give something back to their mother who had gone out of her way for each and every one of them. Starting in 1962, Abuelita Flor moved around, living for a few months at a time in the houses in Barcelona, Mota del Marqués, and Madrid.

Madre Félix with her mother and nieces and Madre Aige (Barcelona, 1955).

But Madre Félix, who was an endearing daughter, was above all a mother. She knew that her heart and her eyes had to be focused on the sisters of the Company and on the people that God had entrusted to them. That is why, during those years, she did not remain by her mother's side. Rather, she wrote to her frequently, keeping her mother up to date on all her adventures. In her letters we see Madre Félix traveling through Spain and America and guiding the different communities in person and through letters. For example, the sisters in Bridgeport needed her to hold them by the hand. They had been in the United States for only a year when the Cuban

Missile Crisis shocked the world. One time, when they were sick, they received a surprising letter from Madre Félix. She wrote them a complete care program, down to the number of eggs and amount of sugar they should eat, and ended with:

> Do not neglect your diet because if you are weak, you will not be able to do much and you will easily fall victim to any infection. If we do go to war, we will have to suffer hardships and the lack of necessary things. If that trial comes and you already have weak health and no reserves, you will not be able to bear it very easily. You will not be able to do anything to help others.[72]

The objective was clear.

Madre Félix had to do the same with the director of the sisters in temporary vows who was overwhelmed because she was also the superior and director of the school in Madrid. It was similar with the sisters in Caracas. They were exhausted by the school work, the programming, and the validation exams that were added to the development of the classes. Some of them were showing signs of nervous exhaustion. Madre Félix went about prescribing care, proposing transfers and job changes, and remedying needs. It was what she herself learned in her prayer when she contemplated the way Jesus treated the apostles. This is what she told the superior of Tamare:

> He, who wanted to clothe Himself with our bodily weakness and limited energy, understood His disciples well, and He understands us well who follow Him with filial love. That's why He prepared a breakfast of bread and tasty fish roasted over a fire on the seashore. He, who not only gave bread but also fish to that crowd that followed Him and asked nothing for Himself. He, who was entirely love and mercy, poured Himself out—and is still pouring Himself out. Just as a mother pours herself out for the wellbeing of her children. Try to guess everyone's tastes and provide them with these little comforts without them noticing, without their having to ask

[72] Letter to the Community of Bridgeport, October 28, 1962 (AGCS E 37,038).

> for them. That way they don't feel so weighed down by their nature and will walk more lightly and courageously on the path of the supernatural.[73]

This is how Madre Félix acted, the way she saw Jesus act.

But her maternal providence began to encounter a completely new difficulty during these years: the generational change. They were no longer as young as when they first began, although at fifty-five years old, Madre Félix was no old woman and neither were her first companions. They were in the prime of their strength and full of valuable experiences. Perhaps that is why they were so concerned when the young twenty-five or thirty-year-old women began to take the reins of some of their projects. Would they be up to it? Would they know how to maintain the way they did things in the institute and its schools? Could they be entrusted with missions of responsibility? To one sister who doubted it, and gave her reasons, Madre Félix answered full of affection and magnanimity:

> I would like for you, who are older, more "solid," and more educated, to take the first step in opening a wide path of understanding, charity, softness, patience, and meekness between all of you. You and I are realizing that young women are coming of age and taking their place in life. This novelty may shock us at the moment, but we have to accept it as a fact of life. It happens to parents with their children, to grandmothers with their grandchildren, to mothers-in-law with their daughters-in-law or their sons-in-law. The same thing happens in religious families. We must understand young people just as our parents understood us, with big hearts, very happy to see the growth of those who come to relieve us. This attitude will provoke in them a filial feeling of affection, interest, respect, almost pampering. When we rejoice in the breaking of their rosy dawn, they will respond by rejoicing in our golden twilight. That is the circle of life. The same sun that illuminates the dawn of maturity also illuminates its drawing to a close. This sun in religious life is

73 Letter to M. Margarita Ribas, June 22, 1962 (AGCS E 41,032).

> none other than CHARITY, THE GOD OF LOVE. So, resist those annoyed moods and be magnanimous with the young women. Until now we have shown them how to live with the fullness of our strength and our faculties. Now, we have to teach them how to live during the downhill slope of our life. This is the most beautiful teaching, the most worthy, the sweetest, and most effective. To exercise it takes a great dose of holiness, a great sweetness, and a great intelligence. But the grace of God will be sufficient.[74]

"To Be *Partners* of Christ"

Between 1962 and 1964, the growth of the schools in Madrid and Lleida, which was a great joy, was also an important concern. Where could they put so many students? And with what money? They needed a large place for school activities for the good of the students. Madre Félix wanted to provide it. Just as a mother sacrificing herself for her children, she sought what was best for the students, even if it meant making sacrifices. She wanted everyone in the Company to love the students more and more throughout their lives. She considered these girls their offspring, more numerous than the stars, which the Lord promises to those who are consecrated virgins out of love for the Kingdom of Heaven. She wanted the best for girls and their education but not for herself. When she founded the house in Venezuela, she had gone to look for materials in Belgium and sought out native English teachers in the United Kingdom. Now, in the same way, she wanted suitable locations for schools, with large yards and corridors full of light. And, as a good daughter of St. Ignatius, she loved more through works than words. So, she began to look for land suitable for the construction of two great schools, inspired by those she had visited in the United States.

She had to work very hard to finalize the budget and obtain the necessary loans. She was extremely generous but not naïve. She had a great capacity for foresight and was perfectly aware of the magnitude of the project. Be that as it may, she had experienced how God blessed their poverty and trust during the

74 Letter to M. Concepci6n Junyent, July 21, 1963 (AGCS E 38,038).

early days of the Company. Antonio Cámara was the architect who was in charge of the construction of their schools in Madrid and later those in Mota del Marqués. Many years later, he recalled how surprised he was by Madre Félix's intuition, her decisiveness, and her organization when it came to focusing on construction of that caliber. He was impressed by her attention to the current laws and her very clear vision of financial matters. She was so realistic that one of the people who dealt with her for the purchase of the land in the Aravaca neighborhood in Madrid commented with admiration: "I like this nun who is not content with a simple 'may God repay you.'"

That year, 1964, the job fronts started overlapping. In addition to the work that was involved with transferring the schools of Madrid and Lleida, they were considering building a new and modern building to expand the older school that had gotten too small on Ganduxer Street in Barcelona. She wanted to save the first house of the Company, but by attaching new construction that would frame the historic building in a harmonious, elegant, and functional ensemble. She also wanted to do it without going over budget. As if that were not enough, in April she visited the houses of America and immersed herself in the preparation for the Third General Chapter. There was much to prepare, among other things, her desire for someone to succeed her as superior general.

In the Spiritual Exercises before the Chapter, in July, she felt a great desire to live a hidden life, retired and obedient. It seemed so easy to be a saint in the shadows! But this, like the desires and promises of humiliation that she frequently recalled, was simply another example of God stockpiling provisions in her for later on. For now, she was put forward again as superior general; she was still in governance.

Madre Félix accepted it and got down to work. In Caracas they also had to buy land and build an extension onto the school as soon as possible. In Lleida the land had already been acquired and the construction had to begin so they could take advantage of the aid offered by the Ministry of Education. They needed to obtain the permission of the archdiocese of Barcelona to request the loans. She also wanted to discuss with the bishop of Bridgeport the opening of a second home in his diocese. And this is not to mention the hundreds of personal letters and business that accumulated every day on her desk. Undaunted by the work, she wrote:

> Will there be a plot of land? Will there be a new building for the school? Of course, there will be everything. Have complete assurance. It is God's thing and God never fails. The thing is that sometimes the Lord our God and our true Father asks us for some personal contributions in order to raise us to the category of being His partners in His business of saving souls. This contribution is made either as holiness in cash or through the Cross — the Cross is holiness in promissory notes. Nevertheless, do not be afraid because it is very nice to be PARTNERS of Christ, to be other Christs, daughters of the HEAVENLY FATHER, coheirs of the Kingdom with HIM, collaborators with HIM.[75]

Now the Lord was going to ask her for her contribution "in promissory notes," in redemptive acceptance of the Cross. On March 12, 1965, Madre Félix — who was in Madrid — had a bad night. She did not want to wake her sisters, but at dawn, when she let them know something was wrong, she was already swollen and agitated. She was unable to articulate a single intelligible word, and half her body was paralyzed.

To the immense shock of Madre Aige and the others, she tried to smile reassuringly, but it was clear that they needed a doctor. They called him, he saw her, and the next day he had her transferred to the hospital. There she was diagnosed with a cerebral embolism that had led to mild hemiplegia — from which she soon recovered — and aphasia.

Since she could not speak, they began to doubt her mental state. She suffered immensely because she understood everything. She could see the reservations of the doctors; she understood perfectly what they showed her in the newspapers to verify that she was in her right mind; she perceived the enormous concern on the faces of her sisters but was unable to communicate a single thing. What an achievement it was when she was able to ask for

[75] Letter to the Community of Caracas, January 15, 1965 (AGCS E 43, 098).

glycerin for her hands by writing its chemical formula on a piece of paper! Impressed, the doctor recognized that Madre Félix was fully aware of herself and the situation, and he was encouraged to try therapy.

In collaboration with the neurologist and the speech therapist, two sisters took turns during her time at the clinic to help her learn to speak again. She had to create a new language center in her brain. That was almost impossible, of course, but the doctors did not know how much tenacity she had. The most painful anguish came when she finally — after making much progress — managed to get her "little daughters" to let her record what she was saying to see how her babbling sounded. Hearing herself, without uttering a complaint, she began to cry. However, after that good cry, she did not give up. She asked for more hours of rehabilitation, as many as were necessary. She even tried special education methods in case that would help her.

After a month, she was able to write to Fr. Mazón with the help of another sister. As was typical, her main motivation for writing was to ask about him and her beloved Society of Jesus, which was celebrating its thirty-first General Congregation and the election of the new superior general at that time. On May 18th, she wrote again:

> We continue to pray to the Lord for Your Reverence and the General Congregation. We are eager for news, and we read the Spanish press to see what is published about the Jesuits. I'm better thanks to our Lord. On Saturday I went to confession with the help of some paper, and I missed Your Reverence. On Sunday, the second part of the Hail Mary came out of me with a normal and fast voice. Then I sometimes said the Our Father and the Hail Mary very well.[76]

The trial was difficult, of course. Madre Félix really suffered and had to overcome it so she would not abandon herself to sadness. She confessed to Fr. Mazón that she repeated to herself a thousand times, "God wants it," and then:

[76] Letter to Fr. Mazón, May 18, 1965 (AGCS M 301.65,02).

> There are times when the black and gray clouds give way, and I see a blue and cheerful sky. In the blue sky I see the will of God that conforms me to Christ, and I feel the joy of a supernatural birth, of grace, and redemption. If my blue sky is covered, my soul freezes, and I feel how romantic dreams and illusions fall away. I only ask God, my Father, for the gift of FAITH on the days of light and on the days of darkness.

How many times in these months she must have repeated the very brief prayer that Fr. Mazón had written down for her before he went to Rome: "Peace in the FATHER, joy in the FATHER, trust in the FATHER, in JESUS and in MARY, my Mother!"

From this incident, in addition to immense gratitude toward her doctors, she was left with a certain difficulty in expressing herself, which made some think she was a foreigner. For her it was a mortification that sometimes she could not find the right word, but for others it was the opportunity to see her as an example of patience and humility. The future Jesuit cardinal, Fr. Urbano Navarrete, who visited her shortly after her aphasia occurred, recalled more than forty years later:

> We talked for quite a long time in the hall. Madre Félix spoke with notable difficulty. The words did not always obey what she wanted to say. I was impressed by the extraordinary serenity reflected on her face and the way she expressed herself, without dwelling particularly on what had happened. When a word did not come to her, without getting the least bit impatient, with great self-control, she even cracked a serene smile, a reflection of the deep peace of her soul and an expression that the cross — a very heavy cross with serious consequences for her apostolate — had been fully accepted. Many years have passed since this visit, and I remember it as if it were yesterday. Such was the impression made on me by the peace, self-control, Christian strength, and total acceptance of God's will, which reflected all of Madre Félix's attitude in the face of the harsh trial she was going through.[77]

[77] Letter from Fr. Urbano Navarrete, S.J., December 13, 2006 (AGCS M 503.02,029).

The difficulty was evident, and Madre Félix saw her hour had come. She could not continue as superior general. She told the Council so but left the timing of her resignation in their hands. On several occasions throughout that year and the following year, she brought together the members of the Council for that purpose. She even wrote to the archbishop of Barcelona, through Fr. Mazón. However, since no response from the chancellery has been preserved, it seems that the priest did not deliver the letter. For their part, the consultors, after delaying the matter as long as they could, unanimously opposed her resignation. The Extraordinary Chapter for the adaptation of the Constitutions to the renewal requested by the Second Vatican Council was about to occur. Now more than ever they needed Madre Félix's presence and her guidance as their foundress.

Meanwhile, as she was diminishing, the Company of the Savior continued to grow. In Venezuela, the archbishop of Maracaibo had strongly requested that the Company take charge of the college that the Ursulines left in his diocese. At last, a second Mater Salvatoris school would open in Venezuela! Madre Félix had dreamed about it from the beginning! However, the lack of personnel was, as always, a burden. In order to accept this request, a great sacrifice had to be made. They had to close the house in Tamare. The State was going to appropriate their school there, so they would move this community to Maracaibo.

As for the school in Madrid, the new center in the Aravaca neighborhood was half-built. The construction had been delayed, and Madre Félix decided to find a solution. She ordered that the classes of the new school year would begin in "El Rosalar," a house surrounded by rose bushes next to the new school grounds, which was intended to be the residence of the sisters. In the 1965–1966 academic year, the community was divided between the house on Límite Street and El Rosalar. They would open the provisional location with the sisters together with the preschool and primary school students. Combining school activities and community life in the same house had its complications. It led to some amusing scenes in the early days. There were classrooms that turned into bedrooms at night, outdoor painting lessons due to lack of adequate spaces, etc. However, everything was done for the good of the students, who were still waiting in the house on Límite Street because the main purpose was to speed up the progress of the construction. Indeed, in one year the new building was finished, and all the students were able to move to their wonderful new school.

Madre Félix with Sister Ramos visiting construction works (Madrid, 1966).

Madre María Félix at a school celebration (Madrid, 1968).

Thus, Madre Félix was a partner in the works of her Lord. With work or with resignation and hiding, what difference did it make? She was a partner of Christ. Now, through pain, just as at so many other times that were full of joy, she could pray: "May the Lord be glorified in me or in whom He will; but may He be glorified."

The Beginning of the Pain

"Without a cross there is no glory, / nor with a cross, eternal weeping, / holiness and cross are one, / there is no cross without a saint, / nor a saint without a cross." Felix Lope de Vega, the author of that poem, had a turbulent life, but he also had the luminous faith of the Spanish Golden Age. He knew well that all saints have a turning point in the story of their lives. Everyone meets the cross. The cross in its pure state, without palliatives, apparently absurd. A cross that, uniting them to Christ, brings them with Christ into the depths of God.

In the late 1960s, Madre Félix also had her turning point. The cause came from the two great loves that God had placed in her soul: the Church and the Company of the Savior. The Lord had warned her. In 1946, when she was preparing herself spiritually to consecrate herself to the Heart of Jesus, when she dreamed of great humiliation and much suffering with Him for the salvation of souls, He told her about valuable pearls, jewels of His own treasure that He was willing to share with her if she wanted. She had understood it then. She would endure much suffering and much humiliation in order to completely fulfill His precious will, in exchange for the Company of the Savior. She had understood it well and had recalled it many times. Now the hour had come. But "the hour" does not usually arrive with ecstatic or apocalyptic tones. At least, it did not for Madre Félix.

It all began with a word of light uttered by the Council: the Church called for renewal. This renewal, fruit of a greater knowledge of the ecclesial vocation itself, had to reach everyone, including men and women religious. Their consecrated life needed to make Jesus Christ more visible in the face of the Church. The Decree *Perfectae caritatis* of the Second Vatican Council gave them guidance. It asked the orders and congregations to revise their rules of life, seeking at the same time an ongoing return to the sources of all Christian life and to the original inspiration of the institutes. It also asked them to make accommodations for the current conditions. Times had changed. The institutes, especially those that had been founded centuries ago, had also changed. Perhaps some customs and procedures had crept in over the years that were not rooted in the Gospel. It was time to examine and refresh their fervor.

This invitation fell as a lighted match on a pile of tinder. The expectation for the changes was intense inside as well as outside the Church — political personalities, the media, members of the ecclesiastical hierarchy, religious, lay people, believers, and nonbelievers. Everyone began to voice their opinions on the direction that the *aggiornamento* (updating) should take. There were so many personal expectations involved! Madre Félix, open and enterprising by nature, this time preferred to wait. She observed how some institutes with a long history were moving ahead to change their structures of governance, their apostolic works, their familiar accents, and sometimes, unintentionally, their spirit, and she was concerned. The Holy See had given them three years to convene the Special Chapter to handle the revision and adaptation. Well, the Company of the Savior would make the most of that entire time. It was better to lag behind and see the result of the changes so they could learn from the experience of others.

She asked the sisters of the Company for patience and work. They also had a desire for renewal, especially some of the original sisters who felt decrepit in body and feared they were also decrepit in spirit. The lack of vocations seriously worried them, and they wondered if it was due to having antiquated structures and remaining on the sidelines of social issues. On the sidelines? They were not on the sidelines. In Maracaibo they had just opened a technical school, and in Mota del Marqués, a residential school for girls from the villages was going to be opened. Within the Company, steps were being taken to improve the academic instruction of the sisters from humbler origins that had hardly studied before they entered. No, they were not on the margins of a changing world. However, there was the question of leaving behind the schools and taking a substantial turn. "In times of desolation, never make a change" is the maxim given by St. Ignatius in the *Spiritual Exercises* for the one who finds himself in tribulation. Madre Félix, forged in this school of thought, put on the brakes. At least for now, they would continue as before. The Special Chapter was going to be postponed and held in two stages between 1968 and 1969. In the meantime, everyone could and should become familiar with the Council documents, respond to opinion questionnaires, participate in series of conferences organized by other institutions, hold assemblies of superiors and those in charge of the apostolates, consult experts in religious life and canon law, and, above all, pray and observe.

Madre Félix was concerned about the winds of independence and secularism that were afflicting all religious life, including the Company of the Savior. However, she did not attribute them to the Second Vatican Council or to the ill will of the people. She was concerned, of course, by the factions and mistrust that were beginning to be perceived in some communities, but she trusted in God, in the discreet and effective intervention of the superiors, and in the desires for holiness of each of her sisters. To the superior in Bridgeport, she wrote:

> I am optimistic about the future of religious life. The Council was and continues to be given to the Church by God's Providence. The Council has stirred up the deep waters of our ecclesial society in order to purify the environment and separate the debris that has been deposited in the Church by the actions of man over the course of the centuries. When our society is stirred up, our waters appear to be murky, choppy, and threatening. Let us not be afraid. After this cleansing, the waters will be crystal clear, still, and the beauty of God and the beauty of the Church, our Mother, will be reflected in them. Let us purify ourselves, let us be mirrors of God, may the Lord imprint Himself in our soul and in our life, and may we await the end of this trial.[78]

At last, the Chapter arrived. In 1968, on the eve of its celebration, Fr. Mazón and many other wise and prudent religious men visited their school in Madrid, such

[78] Letter to M. Pilar Basallo, C.S., November 8, 1966 (AGCS E 35,046).

as the Servant of God Fr. José Antonio de Aldama, S.J., and other distinguished Jesuits, such as Fr. Cándido Pozo, Fr. Jesús M. Granero, and Fr. Eduardo Fernández Regatillo, and the Claretians Fr. Pedro Franquesa, Fr. Gerardo Escudero, and Fr. Timoteo Urquiri. Madre Félix had asked for them to give lectures on different aspects of religious life for the participants in the Chapter and for the whole House of Formation. To some Chapter participants it seemed excessive. What role did the novices have in such a serious matter? Madre Félix did not insist. She would have liked everyone to benefit from these talks, but when things were not essential, she preferred not to impose her opinion or authority.

The Chapter took place in two stages: the first from August to October of 1968 and the second in the summer of the following year. Everything had to be reviewed—the identity of the institute, the admission and formation of the members, the specific apostolic activity, the structures of government, etc. — and put into a rule of life. It was obvious that they were not going to finish in only a couple of months. Between one session and the next, Madre Félix worked unceasingly. She moved the generalate to Madrid, which was a better connected and more central city than Barcelona. She had recently installed the novitiate there. She supported the efforts of Madre Jené, the superior of Maracaibo, who asked to be relieved from her position given the difficulties of the school. Madre Félix decided how to collaborate with the charitable school that the students' parents in Caracas wanted to entrust to the Company, and continued attending to the day-to-day needs of the congregation.

Finally, at the end of 1969, the Special Chapter was able to bring its work to a conclusion and issue their new Constitutions and Directory. It had been a strenuous task to review the completed questionnaires that had been sent to all the religious sisters, to attend to dozens of personal and community proposals, to integrate the documents of the recent Magisterium into the previous text, which was so richly christocentric and Ignatian. Although the draft could be improved — as the prologue itself said — they could still be satisfied enough. Practically all the final votes had been unanimous, and this was a triumph of harmony and a personal success — one cannot deny it — of Madre Félix's motherly diplomacy.

As the Council had recommended, these texts were to be adopted *ad experimentum* (that is, for a trial period), with plans to ratify them at a later date.

And here came the problem.

The Response

From the very moment the Chapter ended, some of the sisters expressed a certain displeasure with the new Constitutions. It seemed to them that they had anchored the congregation to a preconciliar model, which was slow to change, as harsh and lifeless as a granite monolith. Their objections focused mainly on four aspects: the Company's apostolate, their lifestyle, the devotion to the pope, and obedience.

With regard to the apostolate itself, it was more of the usual: the desire to be more effective and attractive for young women by implementing new initiatives, of a social nature, appropriate for the times. That would mean reducing personnel in the schools, but even if they wanted to, they knew they couldn't do everything. They saw it as necessary in order to give witness to the poverty so vividly desired by the Church and by the Company itself. As for the lifestyle, they felt stifled by the notoriously traditional common life. Ringing the bell to attend community events felt misplaced in an institution of free women who already knew the schedule by heart. Insisting on using habits made the sisters equal, indoctrinated them, and prevented the free expression of each sister's own personality. Moreover, that was one of their distinctive characteristics ever since the origins of the Company—they were able to dress in habit or not. There were also a few more things that needed to be reviewed. The promise of obedience to the pope, for example, did not seem so necessary since the pope was never going to explicitly call on a minuscule institute such as the Company for a specific mission. Such a vow sounded grandiose and ridiculous in a microscopic congregation. As for obedience, that was something so characteristic of St. Ignatius! Of course they wanted it, but they indicated that it had to be limited. It would be better for the supreme bodies of governance to take into account that the foundation had been carried out by a group, not one person. Therefore, the Company should be governed with more dialogue, conferring about the different opinions until reaching an agreement, so as not to infantilize people by deciding things about their lives for them from above, in such a vertical way.

Madre Félix attended to these grievances one by one. She answered the letters with equal motherly love, both from those who defended these viewpoints and those who reported them, frightened by the disturbed atmosphere that they perceived. But every new letter was like a nail in her heart. In the manner in which these objections were being proposed, she saw an underlying problem of faith. Without faith, everything in religious life falls apart.

To try other apostolates when God was exponentially increasing the number of students in their schools seemed to her to be a rejection of His blessing. Why be partial to the soul of one person or another, when God has so clearly entrusted these ones to them? Of course, they had to bear witness to poverty. This also worried her. However, nothing deprived them of being truly poor inside, in community life, while providing schools and students with an environment and means suitable for their academic and professional preparation. She wrote to the sisters in Maracaibo about it:

> Do not see triumphalism in the new building; rather see only an instrument of work, a talent, as in the parable, that the Lord is going to ask us to multiply. Consider it also a sackcloth for the Community and for the Company because, while building facilities is a joy in part, paying for the buildings is a difficulty that we take on due to the responsibility of paying the debts we have incurred. They tell me that the building is simple, functional, austere, and dignified. Blessed be God for such a good success! Continue in this same line of austerity and dignity. The education of our girls must be directed toward, among other goals, the love and practice of austerity as a means of achieving Christian justice, lived out through charity. They need our example of kind, humble, and gentle austerity. We must hide how hard it is for us and demonstrate our understanding for those who shun all sacrifices. If we are authentically austere, but humble and balanced, placing our hearts in God, we will be educators according to the heart of Christ, meek and humble.[79]

[79] Letter to the Community of Maracaibo, April 20, 1970 (AGCS E 29,196).

As for the lifestyle, she did not see a reason to abandon practices that had borne such good fruit in religious life. Calling the sisters to community acts with a bell served a practical purpose — she knew well how caught up she got working that she had even forgotten to eat. However, it was also a way to exercise detachment to "our" things in order to attend to God's call. As far as the habit was concerned, they were right. This was a change from the original plans of the Company, which many had experienced. Madre Félix herself had valued very positively the ability to dress with or without a habit based on the judgment of the superiors about which best suited the apostolate. However, if they wanted to be consistent with the "signs of the times," now it was best to heed the invitations of the Holy Father and the bishops, who encouraged religious to use habits to show their consecration.

As for the promise of obedience to the Holy Father ... that one did make her tremble. Love for the Vicar of Christ was an essential characteristic of the Society of Jesus and the Company of the Savior. Had they not been favored by the Lord by being able to seal it with a special promise? Why were they going to despise that promise now, while waiting for the day to ratify it with their actions? No one deprived them of knowing and defending the Magisterium of the pope, who was being attacked so much at that time. Nothing prevented them from praying for his intentions, supporting them from afar. Why not put their energy into living their promise well instead of no longer making it?

The problem of authority and obedience continued to pulse in the background. Madre Félix was not surprised. The events of civil unrest in May of 1968[80] had not only been a problem for the students in Paris but the tip of a colliding iceberg that shook the foundations of Western society. However, she did not want to belittle the request. Neither had the Chapter done so. Rather it had sought to expand the powers of the consultors — the advisors to the local superior — making the structures more flexible. This required more virtue from everyone, including the superiors, who had to know and appreciate the

[80] The student and worker protests in May 1968 in Paris (occupation of universities, strikes, riots, barricades, etc.), were the symbol of a broad movement of protest against the Western lifestyle, characterized by capitalism and traditional civil, cultural, and religious institutions.

opinion of those who helped them in governance. However, in the end, what could not change was the supernatural motive of obedience: the ecclesial mediation of the will of God. For this reason, she did not want the superiors to decline their authority, nor did she want them and the rest of the sisters to stop obeying. This was what she indicated to Madre Batlle when she had recently been appointed as superior of the house of Mota del Marqués. Madre Félix advised her:

> Be humble; learn to rule by asking your superiors, and practice consultation in a spirit of collaboration and of seeking God's will.

She also reminded Madre Batlle that:

> All positions of governance in the Company are of service, work, and responsibility, and never of honor. However, it is necessary to distinguish between authority and honor, which are very different in themselves, even though in the world they are confused. Honor is not necessary; but authority is a quality without which one cannot rule in any society, especially in a religious one, which is anchored in the obedience of Christ, who became obedient unto death, even death on the Cross.[81]

She asked the same thing from the superior of Maracaibo, who had recently acted somewhat distantly toward Madre Félix:

> Set an example of true, loyal, and cordial union with your superiors even if they are garbage in every way and far inferior to everyone in human and divine gifts. The virtue of obedience and supernatural communion have a foundation: Christ, who was obedient and united to His Heavenly Father. Their foundation is not in people, however holy they may be. The person constituted in authority to represent God in His salvific plans is like the signs in the mystery of

81 Letter to M. María Batlle, March 12, 1970 (AGCS E 35,149).

> the sacraments. Understanding it is a gift of faith; practicing it is CHARITY that leads to everlasting life.

She knew well what she was advising them and why. The foundations of the Company of the Savior were also being shaken. One of the Company's first religious sisters, perhaps not completely aware of the damage it implied, was encouraging a campaign against the Constitutions and the general government. The influence she had over the others, and the way her demands were in sync with the general environment of opposition of the times, made a major impact. The problem grew to the extent that the visitor of religious sisters in Madrid took action on the matter: She and two others had to be invited to leave the congregation or be formally expelled. This decision, which Madre Félix would have preferred to avoid by all means, deeply harmed the spirits of various communities. Letters were even sent to the archdiocesan curia of Madrid questioning whether Madre Félix, after the aphasia, was a sound mental state.. At last, the Lord gave her those three precious pearls He had promised long ago: "much suffering and much humiliation in order to completely fulfill His precious will."

Madre Félix felt exhausted. Where was that serene fraternity, the crystalline joy of the beginnings of the Company? And as if that were not enough, in the face of the palpable tension, the visitor of religious sisters advised that they should not hold the Ordinary Chapter, which was to be held in 1970 to elect a superior general, until the situation had calmed down. Madre Félix should continue to govern for at least one more year. During this unforeseen extension, she increased her charity with everyone and tried to redirect the women who were restless in order to save their vocations. Madre Félix herself felt quite useless, but she asked them:

> Be aware, have peace, and put all your trust in the Lord our God and in the intercession of the Blessed Virgin Mary, who is the perpetual and true Mother Superior General of the Company. Her poor representative has done it quite badly, but Mary, full of grace, covers the smallness of her daughter, and the Treasure of Holiness of her Divine Son, our Savior, will redeem my faults and my imperfections without diminishing from the Company that she governs. The

> Company belongs to God. Be certain of its hidden strength, of the virtue of so many of our sisters. Cheer up your hearts! With God we can do anything, even be holy. That is a difficult thing, but with true love, it is easy and beautiful.[82]

It was not a hollow exhortation or a flaunt of false humility; it was almost a personal confession of her most intimate convictions. She explained it to Fr. Mazón in these terms:

> God my Father helps me a lot with everything. I have dreamed all my life that God wanted me to walk a path marked with the spirit of the greater glory of God, of service to the Church, of help to souls. I have also dreamed that my path would be marked with the pieces of my alabaster jar, full of my passionate, deep, and overwhelming love poured out at the feet of Christ, in love for Him. Now, at the end of my life, it seems that the Lord lifts the veil of my true path of holiness: a string of unwanted offenses that I have committed. Before, I sought God in the summits; now I find Him in the valleys. He set His eyes on St. Ignatius, on Mary Magdalene; now, on Dismas, a true criminal but crucified with Christ and forgiven by Him. My ticket to my future life is not the strategy of St. Ignatius, nor the aromas of Mary Magdalene; it is the misdeeds of Dismas. But there is one point in common: LOVE. I am happy and I have peace.

In the postscript of the letter, she clarified:

> I have received very uplifting letters from you-know-who and in very good spirits. I tell you so that you do not suffer because if I tell you only what people are unhappy about from the Special Chapter you will have an incomplete vision. The Company is fine and has wonderful daughters. The one that hinders things is me and little by little I will disappear. Amen.[83]

[82] Circular Letter from June 21, 1970 (AGCS R 403.01,014).

[83] Letter to Fr. Mazón, April 11, 1970 (AGCS M 301.70,06).

Chapter 10

"The One You Love Is Ill"

1971–1975

Vicar General

At the beginning of 1971, the rejection of the Constitutions persisted, but the Ordinary General Chapter had to be held sooner or later. Given the situation, the outcome of the election of superior general was particularly delicate. Madre Félix, who really wanted to disappear, feared she would be elected again but was just as concerned or more about a change in direction of the whole congregation. Her fears soon dissipated. In August the Chapter was held, and Madre Carmen Aige was elected. As for Madre Félix, she remained as vicar general. Although this could not yet be suspected, exactly the same thing would happen in 1977 and 1983. In addition, just a month later, Madre Aige appointed Madre Félix as superior of the General House and director of the sisters with temporary vows. It was clear that the Company was still in need of its foundress and was well aware of it.

But this eloquent choice, which manifested the support of the participants in the Chapter, did not fail to represent a change for Madre Félix. For the first time in her life, at the age of sixty-four, she began a novitiate: learning to obey. She had been superior general for almost twenty years, not counting the years before the foundation, in which she was already at the helm of the group of Ignatian women. With humility, she wrote to the visitor of religious sisters in Barcelona:

> It is the first time that I am a subordinate in religious life. I am still a novice in this state, but I hope in Jesus and Mary for the inner grace of tasting that mystery of Christ who "was obedient to them," as it says in the Gospel of Luke.[84]

Of course, it was sometimes strange and even difficult, but for several decades she had asked God to live under obedience, and how she thanked God for this situation today! To the sisters who sent her birthday wishes shortly after the Chapter, she replied with satisfaction:

> From time to time, I encounter a spiritual treat in my conscience, when a conversation like this happens:
>
> "Do this."
>
> "What ...!?" Then I consider, "Who is the one giving me orders?"
>
> "It is Christ who commands me!" I respond with great joy.
>
> Yes, it is Christ without confusion, without complications, when I hear the voice of the superior. I do not doubt what God wants. Before, in order to know God's will, I had to take stock of so many things, and now it is so easy to know! I am like a novice sucking on candy.[85]

Madre Félix understood the obedience she had preached and defended so much. It could cost her, of course. She was counting on it ahead of time. However, what she wanted before as well as now was to detach herself from her own will in order to know God's will. She said the same thing in her letter to another house:

> I have changed positions of service in the Company, but I have not changed the Lord whom I serve, nor the parcel of land to which He assigned me, nor sisters, nor anything that is my life. Nor has my

[84] Letter to Bishop D. Gabriel Solá, Visitor of Religious Sisters, September 17, 1971 (AGCS E 47,109).

[85] Letter to Five Religious Sisters, September 16, 1971 (AGCS E 40,147).

> affection changed for all of you and for all the works of our congregation.[86]

No one would have guessed that among the recipients of these loving letters were some of the sisters from whom she was receiving the greatest opposition.

As for her new position, Madre Félix was very clear about her role. She knew that God was counting on her to help Madre Aige in governance, making easier any task that Madre Aige found less agreeable. That is why Madre Félix sought to prepare the sisters' hearts to gently accept Madre Aige's decisions. Madre Félix would be the one to give the most bitter news or the most difficult assignments. She also tried to advise, guide, and offer the superior general the unparalleled support of her knowledge about people and affairs, but always without forcing anything on her. In fact, when she felt that she had overreached through her natural assertiveness, she simply asked Madre Aige: "Forgive what seems to be 'little advice.' I just want to help you and help the Company, but you should act on the ground however you see fit."[87]

A Shock Wave in Caracas

At the end of 1972, by Madre Aige's orders, Madre Félix returned to Caracas. She went as a representative of the superior general to buy a house that the school had been renting. However, she knew she would probably have to deal with other, more serious matters. Madre Félix herself had foreseen the possibility that "the problems that existed in our homes in Spain after the Special Chapter might also be found in Venezuela, in one shade or another."

When she arrived, the nature of the problems became clear. The day after she landed, on December 11th, the regular assembly of parents and representatives of the students met. Mr. Alfonzo, as president, explained to the sisters the opinion of several families that were concerned about the doctrine that one of the teachers taught in religion class. They knew that this professor, a Jesuit priest, was very dear to the Company and the brother of one of the sisters, but they were not willing for him to educate their

[86] Letter to a Religious Sister, September 16, 1971 (AGCS E 32,141).

[87] Letter to M. Carmen Aige, June 28, 1974 (AGCS E 23,098).

daughters in a way they considered to be truly harmful to them. He was a young, eloquent, and very attractive priest to the young women, who were dazzled by his very enthusiastic words. Nonetheless, the parents had found out that in matters of sexual morality, he proposed his own way of reading the Dutch Catechism, which was ambiguous in matters relating to contraception. His ideas regarding sexuality and family life were more than progressive. He also had no qualms about instilling in the girls his political positions, which were communistic. To that end, he brought in speakers — priests and young activists — of whom the parents did not approve. In addition, he urged the students to be the pioneers of social change, rebelling against their parents and their environment if necessary. Faced with this situation, they were willing to take their daughters out of the school if things did not change. Of the sisters, on the other hand, they had no complaints, except for their passivity in relation to this matter.

Madre Félix thanked them from the bottom of her heart for their sincerity and promised to learn more about the situation and gather them again when a solution was found. It wasn't going to be that easy. Both the Jesuit priest and the sisters of that community were wary of Madre Félix, as if they had been warned about her and perceived her as a threat.

Something similar happened with the community chaplain. One of the first days Madre Félix was there, he proposed changing the Our Father in the Liturgy for a text by Louis Evely. He consequently had a major clash with Madre Félix, and after that he changed the content of his homilies and ceased to depart from the rubrics in the celebration. Madre Félix noticed that there was a groundswell happening, but she did not know where the heart of the matter was. Several times she tried in vain to visit the building of the high school where the Jesuit priest taught his classes. She was afraid of upsetting the sisters by going against their wishes since they insisted on dissuading her. At last, she went during the Week of Prayer for Christian Unity, and she was amazed at what she saw:

> There was a mural made by our students that said it was to celebrate the Octave of Christian Unity. It looked like a powder keg of

> communist dynamite for its words, depictions, and drawings without any reference to the unity of Christians, neither to Christ, nor to God, nor to anything related to the Church.[88]

Later she told Madre Aige:

> For this reason and for other things that happened when we talked about the norms of the Holy See on the Mass, there is a certain tension between us, but they respect me, and I am careful and gentle with all of them.

And at the end of her letter, she recommended to Madre Aige:

> Do not suffer, but pray and make others pray. If we can get through this crisis, the authority of the Company will win, and there must be authority, even if it is exercised with meekness, with humility, with understanding, with charity, seeing God in everything, and seeking God in everything.[89]

A few days later, in the face of new disagreements in the house — since several of the sisters in the community had spiritual direction with this priest — and new petitions from the parents, Madre Félix chose to visit the superior of the Jesuits and the bishop. They recommended that the professor be dismissed. That is what she did. Trying to be polite with the priest, she preferred to go herself to the Catholic University to ask him to turn in his resignation, rather than go through his provincial superior, Fr. Jesús Francés, who had offered to handle it. The conversation was tense but fruitful. The difficult part came later. Half of the community saw the dismissal of the professor as an injustice. Then the other issues that had been worsening the relationships between the older and younger women for months reemerged. The young women felt that the general government of the Company of the Savior did not listen to them; that the superiors only cared about

[88] Letter to M. Aige, January 26, 1973 (AGCS E 23,086).

[89] Ibid.

the results of their work in the schools and were neglecting their formation; that things were not the same as before, and so on. Now the dismissal of this professor meant leaving them without the support of a priest who understood them well. This frustration reached the older students of the school, who on February 13th showed up at the door of the sisters' residence with banners, chants, and graffiti of "*¡Félix, fuera!*," demanding for Madre Félix to leave and for their professor to return.

And how did the community react to this event? It remained divided, so much so that the bishop decided to appoint an external visitor, the Jesuit priest Fr. Leocadio Jiménez, a confrere and close friend of the professor who had been dismissed. Conversations, meetings, and Masses of reconciliation followed. In the end, the bishop himself recommended that the best thing was to break up the community, transferring several sisters to other communities, and that Madre Félix leave Caracas for a while to ease the tension. She obeyed. It was somewhat humiliating because it was tantamount to deeming her a "part of the problem," but she gladly abided by it. That same day she traveled to Maracaibo, not out of spite or in order to flee but rather to show her firm will to obey the Church and to do everything for her part to solve the crisis. She traveled even though she was sick. For the first time in her life, she had asthma. Nonetheless, she also had a love for her sisters and the Company that was even greater than before. From there, in Maracaibo, she learned that Madre Pilar Basallo, who had been appointed as interim superior of Caracas, had received a warning from the nuncio. It said that if the unrest spread to other houses, they ran the risk of the Holy See dissolving the congregation.

This did hurt her. But she knew how to turn to the heavens. She was ready to give everything to the Lord once again and was so grateful to Him! She wrote to Fr. Mazón about it:

> Thanks be to God I have not lost my peace and I have great confidence in Him and in the Blessed Virgin. They watch over the little Company and its daughters. Still, if the time came for our congregation to disappear by God's will, I think I would calm down immediately with His help. In any case, my whole life must

> be a continuous act of thanksgiving for the many graces that He has dispensed to us, especially for this tiny Company. If the great grace of being RELIGIOUS SISTERS is and has been possible, and if every day we feel greater desires for the greater glory of God, for following Christ in love, for love and service to the Church as a Mystical Body and as a divine institution, and for devotion to her visible Head, His Holiness the pope, we owe it to God our Father and Lord. We have not lost anything, even if the congregation disappears. On the contrary, we have gained much if He is happy with us.[90]

It was the same attitude that she had admired many times in St. Ignatius. During the time of Pope Paul IV, who was unfavorable to the Society of Jesus, St. Ignatius had said:

> I thought about what could make me feel melancholy, and I found nothing. Only if the pope disbanded the Society altogether. Even with this, I think that if I gathered myself in prayer for a quarter of an hour, I would be as joyful or more than before.[91]

Some notes from Madre Félix's prayer during these months help us to see her inner experience of the events. Truly worried about figuring out what God wanted for her daughters, on February 6th she wrote:

> I do not want to be the one who acts but rather may it be You, Lord. Let's make a deal: I'll be watching You, loving You, seeking Your will, conforming myself to You, forgetting about me, seeking only You; and You take care of the Company, or annihilate it, whichever is better for Your greater glory. I want only this: Your greater glory, the greater glory of God our Father.[92]

90 Letter to Fr. Mazón, April 9, 1973 (AGCS M 301.73,01).

91 *Monumenta historica Societatis Iesu: Fontes narrativi de S. Ignatio de Loyola* (Rome, 1943–65), 1:638. Translator's version.

92 Personal Journal, 1973–1974 (AGCS, M 202.31,001).

And the next day, meditating on the Gospel passage of the resurrection of Lazarus:

> Is there a crisis in the Church, in the world? Is there a crisis of obedience, that is, order, co-responsibility, etc.? "Master, the one you love is ill!" [John 11:3]. I believe in You, in Your love, in Your power: save the Church, the world, the Company of the Savior![93]

The same thing on February 8th, contemplating the healing of the daughter of the Canaanite woman (see Matt. 15:21–28):

> I have asked for faith and great trust in the power and love of Christ to heal the Church, our Company, and the house in Caracas. Christ can. The Canaanite woman humbled herself, trusted, and nothing else; she was not even present at the time of her daughter's healing. The Canaanite woman only humbled herself, loved, trusted; there was no external, direct action for that healing. I simply ask, love, and trust.[94]

Madre Félix knew that the salvation of the institute had to come from God. The only thing that was up to her was to try to be faithful to Him and sincerely seek His will. She left the success or failure of her actions in His hands. This union with God was visible on the outside and impressed those who knew or sensed how much Madre Félix was suffering. One of them was Fr. Francisco Arruza, S.J., vice-rector of the Andrés Bello Catholic University and community brother of the professor who resigned. This religious man knew well his religious brother, who taught classes in the university as he did, and also had interactions with the sisters of the Company. Because of his familiarity with them and with the diocesan bishop, Bishop José Alí Lebrún, he was an exceptional witness to all the events. Madre Félix's way of proceeding impacted him. He had never seen anything like that. That is why, when he returned to Spain almost twenty years later, he did something surprising. He visited the new superior general,

[93] Ibid.

[94] Ibid.

Madre Amelia Lora-Tamayo, and Madre Félix, with whom he had a very pleasant conversation, full of good memories. Upon leaving, once Madre Félix had taken her leave, he gave the superior general a signed testimony about Madre Félix's heroic virtues observed by him in the 1972–1973 school year. He knew that sooner or later that testimony would do some good, and perhaps he would not be in a position to provide it at that time. This is what he wrote:

> Before the Lord our God and swearing that I speak the truth, I want to leave my testimony for whenever the sisters of the Company of the Savior believe it is convenient to make use of it. It is about the virtue, which to me has seemed heroic, shown by their foundress, the Reverend Mother María Félix Torres, during the events that occurred in the community of the Mater Salvatoris School in Caracas during the 1972–1973 academic year, during her intervention in the conflict between some priest professors of that school, sister teachers of the same school, and parents and representatives of the students.
>
> The Reverend Mother Félix had to make resolutions to dismiss these priests and to give a new assignment to certain religious sisters to avoid greater harm. As a result, there were accusations, insults, and contempt, due to the disease she suffered, on the part of those affected.
>
> The reactions against her were manifested in opposition to what she determined based on the incompetence they attributed to her given her condition of cerebral embolism with aphasia (which she had already overcome by then). Therefore, in contempt of her intervention and as a final resort, they insulted her speech impediment (since they could not attribute any defect to her thought).
>
> The undersigned attests to all this and was consulted by her regarding the conflict and its solution. In this process, I want to testify about three virtues that reverend mother showed on that occasion:
>
> 1. Her strength of spirit to carry out the mission entrusted by the reverend mother general, letting go of everything that could be said about herself. She only sought the good of the

congregation in general and of the school in particular. She sought everything with prayer, meditation, reflection, and dialogue.

2. She demonstrated to the highest degree a great, if not heroic, charity toward everyone. I never heard a single word against the priests or the sisters whom she had to separate from the school. She always talked to the undersigned of this statement without accusing such people of anything dishonorable. She always excused them from any guilt and considered that the whole conflict was due to misunderstandings, to the circumstances, and so forth, even if some definitive measures had to be taken to resolve it. For the undersigned, her charity for everyone in the conflict was extreme and delicate. That charity resulted in the third point.

3. The heroic humility she showed because she received so many insults. For example, she accepted the disdain she had to endure because of her illness with a smile. I still remember how, smiling and without attacking anyone, she told me that she believed they were right to consider her incapable and that perhaps she was not the best fit to solve the problem, but she would comply with what obedience had commanded her.

Not even at that moment was there a complaint against those who despised or insulted her. She smiled, and it seemed that before God she rejoiced at this humiliation. There was not a single word, gesture, or attitude that indicated that she wanted to impose herself because she was the foundress of the congregation. It would seem that she considered herself the least of the congregation but the person who had been ordered to resolve the conflict that arose.

For the undersigned, her strength of spirit was extraordinary. Her charity was delicate and evangelical; but in humility she was heroic because throughout the whole conflict, in which I had to intervene and of which I had to inform His Eminence Cardinal Tarancón, I did not see in her a single gesture of impatience, of displeasure, of protest at the way the Reverend Mother Félix was treated. For me it was a clear example of a degree of heroic humility that came from what St. Ignatius of Loyola calls the third degree of humility.

I give this testimony before God, in Caracas, on the 7th day of October of 1992.

Francisco Arruza, S.J.[95]

The Unrest in Madrid

In his testimony, Fr. Arruza acknowledged that he had to report the facts to Cardinal Tarancón, the archbishop of Madrid. That is what happened. Upon returning to Spain, Madre Félix found a more cordial welcome but not a more promising outlook. Complaints about her and about the general government of the community had been sent to the chancellery of Madrid, on which the entire Company of the Savior now depended canonically. The reason was the same as always. They were accused of centralism, of being closed off to change, of excessive recognition of Madre Félix as foundress, and lately, of having tested the vocation of two Venezuelan junior sisters, the only ones in that country who had entered the congregation by that time. The situation was that Madre Félix, as their director, and Madre Aige, as superior general, had decided that their vocations should be confirmed before making their perpetual vows by spending a season at their families' homes. It was permitted by canon law and was recommended by prudence. This last decision, at a time when vocations were lacking, had upset some of the sisters in Spain, who felt overwhelmed with the work and the outlook of the schools. They questioned whether Madre Félix was capable, after the aphasia, to actively collaborate in the general government and to decide things about the people in the juniorate. This is how things were put forward, through letters, to the archbishop of Madrid.

June of 1973 was particularly hard for Madre Félix. On the 1st, Abuelita Flor died unexpectedly. It happened in little more than three hours. She had

[95] Francisco Arruza, S.J., Testimony About the Heroic Virtue of M. María Félix, C.S., on the Occasion of the Events That Took Place in the Community of the Mater Salvatoris School in Caracas, 1972–1973 School Year, October 7, 1992 (AGCS R 902.04,001).

spent years with different ailments, but nothing made them foresee an imminent death. She woke up a little dazed, but she didn't look seriously ill. At noon, she unexpectedly entered a coma, and three hours later she died, leaving Madre Félix deeply shaken. Her mother was buried the next day. To that pain was added her concern for Madre Aige. She had a suspicious lump and was informed on the 4th that it seemed to be breast cancer. It was not the best day for such a diagnosis. They had been summoned by Fr. José María Martín Patino, S.J., the vice vicar general of the archdiocese of Madrid. That same afternoon, Madre Aige and Madre Félix were to account for the charges brought against the general government.

This summons was followed by the visitor of the religious sisters surveying the sisters and houses involved, and several visits to the chancellery. Cardinal Vicente Enrique Tarancón himself took an interest in the matter, questioning the reason for Madre Félix's repeated reelection to the general government. He assured Madre Félix that he would do whatever it took to receive an adequate explanation. He even said that, if the mother was sick and could not come to see him, he would go visit her to receive the pertinent explanations.

Once again, Madre Félix sought to put God above all and to live through these circumstances as she had done before: in silence, in truth, with humility, and with sincere charity toward everyone. While awaiting the dispositions of the ecclesiastical authority, she wrote to one of the sisters: "Count on my understanding, on my love, and on my trust. My heart and arms are wide open to embrace you and all the sisters who confront and enrich me."[96]

She felt pressured from above and below, but the initial coldness of the cardinal was not going to temper her love for him and for everything of the Church. Quite the opposite: It increased her desire to show her adherence to her diocesan shepherd, to the ecclesiastical hierarchy that had been so challenged during those times, and above all, to the Holy Father. If this was the suffering experienced in the dioceses, how much suffering must the pope endure when he sees the situation of the Church

[96] Letter to a Religious Sister, September 19, 1973 (AGCS E 42,092).

in the whole world! In July, Madre Félix wrote to Fr. Mazón that she would like to proceed with the pontifical approval of the Company of the Savior. She inquired whether the priest remembered that they had spoken about it — half fantasizing and half seriously — back in the sixties. In November she wrote again, full of joy, that she had discussed the papal approval with Cardinal Tarancón and that he had accepted her intentions and was visibly satisfied. By then, the cardinal was beginning to get to know Madre María Félix.

In spite of everything, by the summer of 1974 the tensions within the Company had not quite subsided. The visitor of religious sisters, Fr. Hermenegildo López, encouraged them to celebrate a "Day of Renewal and Reconciliation," with moments of common prayer and multiple exhortations, gatherings, and assemblies. They discussed in his presence the topics of the disputes in recent years, and gradually the flood waters receded. Madre Félix listened a lot, attended to everyone, worked to restore trust with her sisters, and even proposed some of those who still felt offended by her for positions of responsibility. She took advantage of every occasion to show them that she still trusted them, that she was not scandalized by people's faults, that she understood perfectly her own and others' fragility. In November of that year, without taking any credit, she wrote to Fr. Mazón: "Little by little we can see shining forth the joy of peace and religious life in common in good spirits. This is largely due to your prayers; may the Lord repay you for everything."[97]

The priest was not able to go see them. If only he could have been closer in recent years! But he had grown very old and, with the meekness and acceptance that the saints have, he had gradually withdrawn from the scene. He only replied to her letters — and if he was delayed, he would accuse himself of being lazy — and received some visits at his retreat house in Villagarcía de Campos (the small village near Mota del Marqués in Valladolid, Spain). Madre Félix could not have imagined that in a little more than a year and a half she would also lose this priest who was so dear to her and to the congregation.

[97] Letter to Fr. Mazón, November 28, 1974 (AGCS M 301.74,03).

On June 1, 1976, just three years after the death of Abuelita Flor, Fr. Mazón died. Madre Félix was in Caracas. God, who had plans to give her another fervent Jesuit as spiritual director in His good time, once again stripped away all her human support.

What did Madre Félix have left after this time of such great pain? A more lucid knowledge of her own weakness and a heart widened by the effort of charity. Not bitterness. If anything, shame for not having done better. She did not talk about the subject even with her closest collaborators, then or in the following years. As she had done at other times, she wanted to:

> [Cover] those tortures with a wide, thick, white, and happy veil. Anyone who wants to look at this question from that time will undoubtedly find this veil. I do not want it to be a sad veil because what it hides is not sad in the supernatural order, since those sufferings are little splinters of my cross and the Cross is a treasure.[98]

What she did speak of was simply what she had learned through all this suffering: the way to be united with God, the pearls of His treasure that Jesus Christ shares with those He truly loves. Emma Reyna, a young Venezuelan psychologist who asked to join the Company of the Savior in 1976, recalled this from her conversation with Madre Félix:

> Among the things she shared with me, she told me that there are white pearls that are precious and the most common color but that there were other pearls, which were more rare, that were black. These, due to their scarcity, are not so common, but they are of great value, much more than the white ones. The days in religious life are like that: there were going to be white pearls and black pearls. She perceived that I did not grasp the matter very well and said to me: "I will give you another comparison. Oil in Venezuela is black gold. Its color and other characteristics are not attractive, but we cannot be misled by our impression or repugnance."

[98] Autobiographical Writings, Notebook C (AGCS M 201,003).

> That is how she emphasized once again the meaning of the dark or difficult moments. At that moment those did not seem to be very inspiring words for someone who was asking to enter religious life. However, I am deeply grateful for the sincerity and clarity of her words, her honesty, and above all for her teaching me to value, and offer up as valuable in God's eyes, those things that in human terms can be more difficult. I always remember the graphic image of black pearls and oil, and I can't help but smile and accept it.[99]

Forty years later, the woman who wrote these lines would die as a sister in the Company of the Savior after a long and painful illness. In her dying moments, she asked them to read to her the following writing from Madre Félix:

> Impelled by Jesus, I dare to offer what is left of my life and my death, together with the agony and death of my most precious Lord, to save souls, so that sanctifying grace may be poured out abundantly on the world, so that the Heavenly Father may be greatly glorified.[100]

[99] Testimony of M. Emma Reyna, November 19, 2006 (AGCS M 503.01,055).
[100] Spiritual Exercises, November 3–10, 1950 (AGCS M 202.16,001).

Part Three

"Hidden with Christ in God"

Chapter 11
Trying to Hide
1975–1989

One Step Behind

Since the election of Madre Aige as superior general, Madre Félix went out of her way to help her in every way she could. She was so grateful for the burden Madre Aige had taken on! That is why she tried to help and disappear at the same time. We see that in a particularly eloquent way during 1974 and 1975.

In those difficult years, the Company of the Savior was offered two foundations in Latin America: one in San Juan, Puerto Rico, and another in Cerro Chato, Uruguay. Each had its own beauty. The one in Cerro Chato — requested by the bishop of the diocese of Melo through the vicar for religious sisters of Madrid — was a lively mission for the most disadvantaged. They would be managing a parish school — or two, if they accepted another — whose students were at real risk of being excluded. Cerro Chato had doubled its population in the last decade and had many children who were not in school and with family situations that necessitated the provision of a boarding school. It would be a hard mission due to the lack of material resources, but gratifying because of its importance to the lives of these children. If the sisters took on this task for a few years until the institution took shape, it would be an invaluable service. As for San Juan, the archbishop, by his own initiative, had asked them for a school. He offered them the possibility of teaching or taking part in the management of the former Sacred Heart School, which ranged from primary education to university degrees. Madre Félix would have loved to have gone to these new missions being offered to the Company of the Savior and especially the university apostolate she had always dreamed of! But it was no longer her time, but that of her successors. That is why, although she was full of enthusiasm, she remained at all times a step behind Madre Aige.

Madre Félix shared the work of studying the proposals, weighing the human and material means required to take them on, and following up on the correspondence about matters related to the houses. However, she always preferred that Madre Aige make the exploratory trips, while she remained in Madrid in her position as vicar — so much so that she never ended up traveling to Cerro Chato, since it was a temporary mission and only lasted four years. She would not visit San Juan for the time being either, but she followed what happened with the foundation from a distance. In her conversations with the archbishop of San Juan, Madre Aige realized that the school was beyond their capacity since he was asking for religious sisters with degrees in philosophy and other natural and human sciences. At the moment they could only set foot on the island by opening a kindergarten as the beginning of a school that would grow at the pace of its students. Madre Félix, from Madrid, wrote to her first companion with some sorrow:

> What a shame we can't attend to the college. You know that it has always been my desire to work with university girls with a certain autonomy. Everything will move forward, even if I do not see it in this world; but from Heaven I will see many university centers under the apostolic influence of our sisters.[101]

That was not going to prevent Madre Félix from being excited about the school and all the adventures that could come with the foundation. Finally, in the early 1980s, she would see it with her own eyes. But she did not visit of her own accord. It was because Madre Aige insisted that she do so; she wanted to provide the houses in the Americas with a canonical visit presided over by their foundress.

[101] Letter to M. Carmen Aige, January 23, 1975 (AGCS E 23,102).

Foundress. Here is another field from which she wanted to disappear. She knew that she had only been God's sometimes very imperfect instrument, which He had used to start a project much greater than she. She had always sought to consider the foundation as something of Bishop Modrego, the bishop of Barcelona who granted the approval, or of Fr. Mazón, or of the group of the first women ... anyone but herself. Since she had to take on her role as the foundress to avoid the institute changing course in the years after the Council, this moral authority was a much greater weight on her. That is why she insisted on becoming just another sister, one among many. She fended off any devotion to herself that could tarnish the glory of God and was especially vehement about doing so after the accusations she had suffered. She said that if she had done anything it was to convey a message, but that the important thing is the message, not the messenger; the letter, not the one who delivered it. She explained to the sisters that she was just the phone, an old and ugly and even noisy one, through which God had spoken to His Company. No one would think of being fascinated by the phone. Anyone who came up with the idea of being fascinated by her or contemplating her too much ran the risk of upsetting Madre Félix, who had not yet completely lost her strong temperament.

The documents that were sent to Rome to process the pontifical approval of the Company of the Savior are proof of the seriousness of her intention to go unnoticed. Obviously, to take such a step, they had to send information in writing about the institute, its works, its members, and also its origin. Well, the name María Félix appears only once, as one of "those who made a vow of consecration to God on August 15, 1934." And what about the first feeling of the Ignatian vocation of the Company, that grace that Miss María Félix received back in the 1930s on St. Ignatius's feast day? It is hinted at in this way: "The first motions and feelings of the religious and apostolic vocation, typical of the Company of the Savior, were felt in Lleida, Spain, in 1931."[102]

Nothing more. Just that vague phrase to say that "someone" felt "something" in "a place." These roundabout expressions easily reveal the friendly

[102] Application Paperwork for the Pontifical Approval of the Company of the Savior, May 16, 1985 (AGCS F 140.02.A,016).

struggle of Madre Félix and Madre Aige in writing about the origin of their common vocation.

But it is easy to be humble on paper, in documents that will be buried on the shelves of an archive. Madre Félix was not satisfied with that. In her day-to-day interactions with her community sisters, she also sought to diminish her influence as much as possible. She wanted the spirit, the fragrance of the perfume to remain, but for the alabaster jar to be broken. If she had to stand out, she preferred it to be in closeness and simplicity of heart. Three of the first sisters of the Company — three who had made her suffer so much — now, after the storm, congratulated her on the twenty-fifth anniversary of the Company of the Savior. Madre Félix replied to them:

> The Lord our God inspired it in all of us, and He carries it out through the merits of Christ and through the intercession of the Blessed Virgin. With you I renewed my canonical vows, which we first made together on that blessed day, and I confirm my feelings toward you just as on that day, extending them to our other early companions. With Christ, one heart and one spirit.[103]

Basically, with these attitudes she only sought to be consistent with her old and solemn conviction: "There was nothing extraordinary in me, nothing supernatural, I was a sinner."[104]

Joy in Weakness

Sinful and weak. That was how she felt in practice, especially now that her health was beginning to fail. Ever since the problems in Caracas, she suffered asthma, as her father had. Little by little, other aches and pains were added. In 1977, she had to have surgery to remove a benign tumor in her left leg. The tumor disappeared, but over time a large lipoma began to form on her thigh that, apart from being her regular penance, would take her to the operating room several times in the following decade. When her brother Ángel called her in August, she told

103 Letter to Three Religious Sisters, February 7, 1977 (AGCS E 29,222).
104 Autobiographical Writings, Notebook C (AGCS M 201,003).

him humorously: "The doctor came to see me. He says that I suffer from a disease for which there is no remedy; only resignation and holy patience." Ángel, very much alarmed, asked: "And what kind of disease is it?" She replied, "The disease of seven." "Seven? I do not understand. What do you mean, María?" he asked. His sister answered, "That at seventy years old, we must arm ourselves with patience. By the way, how are Maruja and the kids? How about you, are you still writing poems? You were always such a good writer . . . ."

This exercise of moving from personal suffering to looking at the material and spiritual needs of others, or to the apostolic possibilities of offering up that suffering, was one that she had been doing and recommending for many years. She knew that it came with fruits of joy and holiness. That is why she tried to live it out and gave it as advice to other sisters on their birthdays:

> We certainly cannot dance a *muñeira*, but we can applaud it with joy. We can mend and patch up our physical ailments. Believe me, if we do it right, we will look as new. "When you fast," — from youth, from health, from physical strength — "anoint your head and wash your face" [Matt. 6:17]. Jesus said it so that the world may be more beautiful and the angels may sing "glory to the Lord" and so that God our Lord, who sees everything, may be truly loved. The internal and external joy and rejoicing of a soul that fulfills the divine will with poise, her head held high, and a heart in love with Christ crucified, glorious in His Resurrection, is a treasure in the Church and in the Company.[105]

She generously shared this treasure of inner joy in the midst of her weaknesses with the novices, who had been entrusted to her since 1974. They were the hope of the Company and a great joy for Madre Félix, although at times she was disturbed to see that so few entered (only two between 1974 and 1979) and wondered if it was because of the sins of their director. In El Rosalar, the community residence in Madrid a few yards from their school, she gradually taught them the customs and especially the spirit of the Company of the Savior. She wanted them

[105] Letter to M. María Blanca Campo, March 28, 1980 (AGCS E 36,107).

to be loyal to God, in love with Jesus Christ, imbued with a family spirit marked by charity toward all, simplicity, obedience, joy — all for the sole purpose of giving much glory to the Lord. She listened to them with infinite interest, sometimes understanding hidden heart strings that they did not even know about themselves. She gave them confidence. She quickly put into words what they wanted to say but did not know how to express. She would ask for their opinion about some internal matter. Or she would risk getting in the car with a novice driver with the same joy with which she would have done it with the most experienced one. She devoted her attention, her prayer, and all her time, as was needed, to them. She was not overly sweet or overly emotional. She was sensitive, though. Sometimes the aspirants would be touched by how thoughtful she was, asking about their families and other questions that revealed her sincere interest in everything about their lives. Nonetheless, she corrected them, and she did it strongly, when she saw a lack of religious spirit that had to be corrected before it became a normal habit. Everyone knew that if Madre Félix started a conversation praising the qualities of the person she was talking to, that person had better prepare herself! She was paving the way for some kind of correction. What many of them did not know was that whenever someone left her office crying, Madre Félix did not come out immediately because she was crying herself.

She loved them very much and wanted them to be holy. That is why she was a little worried when she considered their formation. She was worried about being a bad example for the novitiate, especially now that she was getting older. As a result of her breathing difficulties from asthma, her neuralgia, and other aches and pains, she spent many days in bed. That is why she asked several times to be relieved of her position. However, even though she wanted to retire, neither Madre Aige nor the Council thought it was time. "God directs me, and I renounce my own resolutions. It is He who leads me, and my reasons are not God's reasons. I will stop being a director when He wants, not when I want it."[106]

Through her obedience, her loving self-denial in order to do God's will, He worked wonders. One day she wrote this about the meetings in which she would explain the rules and Constitutions to the sisters in formation:

[106] Personal Journal, March 1, 1981 (AGCS M 205.01.A,013).

> I have a profound feeling that the Lord speaks through me, Balaam's ass (see Num. 22:21–33). It is a mysterious, indescribable sensation that gives me peace, security, humility, joy, and confidence. An aphasic, empty, poor woman who is less than an ass. I say what I did not think; they are His words using my poor voice. His words that burn me with the fire of love. They impregnate me and are the seed of supernatural life. Lord, do You speak for me or for Your novices? I believe it will be for Your novices so that they may know You, love You, and follow You to the Cross.[107]

The novices had only one complaint about these meetings, which helped them so much: Madre Félix did not let them take notes about what she said. She assured them that everything was in this book or that one anyway and it was better to go straight to the sources than to write down her mess.

Fr. Mendizábal

In 1979, three years after the death of Fr. Mazón, Madre Félix would entrust her conscience to a new spiritual director: Fr. Luis María Mendizábal, S.J., the national director of the Apostolate of Prayer.

She had known him for a long time, almost ten years. Around 1970, in the midst of the internal crisis of the Company of the Savior, Madre Félix heard about a Jesuit who was very devout and faithful to St. Ignatius. He had been a professor of ascetical and mystical theology at the Gregorian University and had just been sent to Madrid. The people who recommended him said he was a magnificent spiritual guide and a man forged in the school of the Heart of Jesus. He could be a providential support for the religious sisters, especially in those moments of pain and confusion. She consulted Fr. Mazón about this priest, and he gladly corroborated the information. Therefore, in 1971, through the superior of the Jesuit house in Maldonado, Madre Félix and Madre Aige asked Fr. Luis Mendizábal to give a retreat for the house of Madrid. The sisters all ended up very happy. Then they asked him if he could lead a series of Spiritual Exercises at Christmas; again, a

[107] Personal Journal, 1982 (AGCS M 302.35,001).

week of Spiritual Exercises in 1978, some sporadic retreats, and so on. Finally, in 1979, the priest was able to dedicate a long stretch of the summer to preach the thirty-day Spiritual Exercises of St. Ignatius to the Company of the Savior.

Her spiritual writings give some idea about what Madre Félix enjoyed in these Spiritual Exercises and the fact that, starting that summer, Fr. Mendizábal would be her spiritual director until her death in 2001. From the beginning, they understood each other perfectly. The spiritual connection between them, the fruit of their intense union with Christ, was as remarkable as the esteem they had for each other. Shortly after meeting him, she would write about the priest: "I believe that he is a saint and that the Lord makes him available to me in order to serve the Lord and to follow Him." He, in turn, would write about Madre Félix years later:

> I always had the impression that I was before a person of superior rank, an extraordinary woman in her intellect, in her greatness of heart, in her vision about things, in her elevation of spirit, in her love for Jesus Christ and for St. Ignatius, in her boundless self-sacrifice, in her fidelity to a charism that brought her many puzzles and problems but to which she remained faithful all her life, through many sufferings and also many joys that the Lord granted her.[108]

The priest would also comment with admiration:

> Madre Félix manifested a serene, penetrating personality. She had a certain clarity in her person, proper to those who have found their favorite resting place in the Heart of the Lord. That resting in the Lord's Heart was shaping in her the same attitude of generous dedication to others, with even more sensitivity.[109]

[108] Luis M. Mendizábal, S.J., "Búsqueda intrépida de la voluntad de Dios," in *Recuerdos de mi vida* (Madrid 2009), 5. Translator's version.

[109] Ibid.

Although he very respectfully kept everything related to her conscience strictly confidential, he did affirm this, which certainly reveals to us the style of their conversations:

> She was such an exceptional woman; above all her human qualities, the image I keep in my memory is of a person devoted to God: a woman of God. What stood out was her simplicity of spirit, her kindness, and her intimacy with the Lord, which often made her burst into tears that slid down her face when she spoke of the love of God.[110]

These meetings of spiritual direction, in which their sights and interests were those of Jesus Christ, were always marked by their origin in the Spiritual Exercises of 1979. In those days of retreat, the themes that had accompanied her since her youth resounded in Madre Félix's soul with particular intensity: the glory of God, an intimate and unique relationship with each person of the Most Holy Trinity, the motherhood of the Virgin, the Church, the pope, the salvation of souls, and so on. She understood that what God, her Father, wanted was for her to immerse herself in trinitarian love as the true essence of her vocation and to extend this love to every person, thereby making it known.

Fr. Mendizábal knew how to place that entry into the love of the Most Holy Trinity very, very close to Jesus Christ. That is why Madre Félix, elated, wrote in those Spiritual Exercises: "The love of Christ is one of FRIENDSHIP. How sweet it is to be a friend of Christ! The love of Christ is transmitted to me, and if I let Him in and open my heart to Him, He overwhelms me and makes me happy, and in principle He transforms me, He converts me. I no longer live; it is Christ who lives in me. He loves me and I love Him." Madre Félix's desire for holiness had not diminished over the years but had increased, and at the same time she could write: "When will Christ be in me and I in Him? Peace and trust. In the arms of my Heavenly Father, I will arrive at the time God has planned."

[110] Ibid.

After these Spiritual Exercises and with the inspiration from Fr. Mendizábal's spiritual direction, the intensity of her spiritual life manifested itself even more than before. It was surprising to see her so enraptured in the chapel, very caught up in prayer, kneeling sometimes for more than an hour and immersed in God. Yet this transformation did not make her distant or self-absorbed. On the contrary, she was deepening her capacity to know the intimacy of mankind and to penetrate the hearts of those with whom she interacted. She herself wrote: "'Christ is the way to find the heart of man.' This thought from John Paul II in *Redemptor hominis* was a revelation. I must be an apostle, and Christ is the way to enter the human heart."

Mother Félix with Fr. Luis María Mendizabal, S.I., and Mother Amelia Lora-Tamayo (Madrid, 1997).

The simplicity of her external manners, in which the most extraordinary thing was to be taken for granted, was accentuated. Her tone, which was sometimes dominant, and her naturally intimidating personality had gradually been softened and gave way to the powerful meekness of the Heart of Jesus. Her conversations revealed something of the greatness of the inner life that she nurtured. Something was perceived in her that was special, difficult to define, and very discreet in appearance. Cardinal Eduardo Martínez Somalo, recalling his dealings with her during those years, wrote:

> From the time I encountered Madre María Félix, I had the impression of being before a religious sister who was guided by a profound spirit of faith, hope, and charity that crystallized in a coherence between what she believed, hoped, and loved. Her conversations reflected serenity, simplicity, and discretion. It was not difficult to sense in Madre María Félix her rich and solid interior life. It was also evident how and spiritual values and trust in the Lord prevailed in her and her judgment, allowing her to face any initiative or difficulty. She was moved and guided by the love of God and neighbor. The great ideal of her existence and the charism of the institute founded by her were precisely the greater glory of God and unconditional adherence and service to the Holy Father.[111]

Pontifical Approval

Madre Félix carried this service to the Holy Father deep within her. She had received it as a sacred inheritance from her father St. Ignatius.

She had always wanted to found a house in Rome in order to also be physically closer to the pope. Already in 1959, full of holy desires, she had wished to accept a house offered to them in the Eternal City. The work that was being proposed to them — attending to the service and administration of a center of studies for priests from Central and South America — was not very characteristic of the aim of the Company. For this reason, out of basic prudence, she consulted Fr. Mazón before embarking on the adventure:

[111] Card. Eduardo Martínez Somalo, In Memory of M. María Félix, Founder of the Company of the Savior, September 1, 2006 (AGCS M 503.02,028).

> You already know about my devotion because of what Rome means for us. I wrote to Madre Aige about this matter and told her to talk it over with Your Reverence. I am certain that no one else can advise us better.[112]

What did Fr. Mazón say? As he had at other times, he dissuaded her. He knew well how things went:

> You will have time to go to Rome.... What they are offering you is full of difficulties that come from every direction: personnel to serve, people that need to be served, nature of the occupations, responsibility, etc. No, definitely not. The best thing is to say that you do not have enough personnel.[113]

And so it was. At the end of that year, 1959, a Spanish religious priest who was very dear to the Company was made a cardinal: Father Arcadio M. Larraona, C.M.F. He had assured Madre Félix, during the time of the Company's foundation, that she could appeal to Rome to get permission to make the vow of obedience to the Holy Father, which had at first been suppressed in the diocesan approval of the Constitutions. By his encouragement, Madre Félix had set out to request the amendment, and thanks to this request, they had been able to make the "fourth vow" by way of a special promise of obedience to the pope in 1957. She considered Fr. Larraona to be the one responsible for her joy. Therefore, on the occasion of his installation, she traveled to Rome with Madre Aige and Madre Martínez to congratulate him and to talk to him about the pontifical approval. Fr. Mazón had predicted it when he wrote: "See whether you can be convinced to go to Rome. I have little hope, but sometimes God has His ways."

On that trip, the first she made to the city of the popes, Madre Félix was especially pleased to be able to visit the places where St. Ignatius lived, but she was also elated to see Pope John XXIII.

[112] Letter to Fr. Mazón, May 26, 1959 (AGCS M 301.59,013).
[113] Letter to Fr. Mazón, June 1, 1959 (AGCS M 302.59,013).

> In Rome I felt much consolation before the pope; I only wanted to see in him the Vicar of Jesus Christ, the visible Christ whom I profess to serve faithfully as the only commitment of my life; the visible Christ of our vow of obedience.[114]

Then she tested the waters with the cardinal, who was the secretary of the Sacred Congregation for Religious, to see if it would be possible to ask for the papal approval of the Company of the Savior. It was important for the Company. It would mean that its general government depended directly on the Holy See, which would allow things to go faster when it came to founding houses, taking on new apostolates, making internal decisions of the institute, and so forth. But, above all, it meant a closer relationship with the Holy Father, and for Madre Félix that was the most fundamental thing. It was almost an impossible mission because for this purpose, institutes were often required to have about two hundred professed members and houses in five dioceses. The Company at the time had houses in six dioceses, but only twenty-six sisters with perpetual vows. Cardinal Larraona, who had known and appreciated Madre Félix since the 1950s, smiled when he heard her request. She had already asked him years earlier for permission to appeal the vow of explicit obedience to the Holy Father, and now she came to him with this. He felt badly, but he had to say no. He would pray for them to grow in numbers so that the process for pontifical approval could be started.

And the years passed. More than a decade, in fact. Madre Félix did not try again until the 1970s. In 1974, with fifty-six professed members, it was still risky, but Cardinal Tarancón liked the idea, and the process began from Madrid. Madre Aige and the visitor of religious sisters asked for letters of recommendation from all the bishops of the dioceses in which the Company was working, prepared all the documentation, and such like. However, the number of sisters tilted the scale again.

"God has His ways." When the subject was already put on hold, a surprise happened that moved Madre Félix's tired and at the same time young heart. In April 1984, Monsignor Juan José Dorronsoro, department head of the

[114] Personal Journal, 1957–1959 (AGCS M 202.23,001).

Congregation for the Religious and Secular Institutes, suddenly appeared in El Rosalar in Madrid. He was the uncle of a student and was not a stranger, but they did not expect his visit. What was the reason for this? To ask a question. Taking advantage of the fact that he was in Madrid for Holy Week, he wanted to alert the superior general that the file containing their request for approval as a pontifical institute had been dusted off in Rome, and they wanted to know if they were still interested in asking for it? Of course, yes! Madre Aige rushed to tell Madre Félix, and she, who was sick and in bed, immediately got up to receive that unexpected gift from Heaven.

Since some modifications of the Constitutions were in progress in order to adapt them to the new Code of Canon Law, they agreed that they would wait for the final text of the Constitutions to complete the necessary documentation. Once the Constitutions had been approved, the request was processed, and on February 12, 1986, Cardinal Suquía — Cardinal Tarancón's successor in Madrid — finally called to communicate the joyful news: the Company was as closely linked to the Holy Father as it could be. Pope John Paul II had given the papal approval on January 30th. It was confirmed by the authority of the pope that the Company of the Savior was a gift from the Holy Spirit to the Church, that it could serve her effectively in the contemporary world, and that her Constitutions were a sure path of holiness. The decree of approval of the Pontifical Constitutions, which came later, would bear a date that was dear to Madre Félix: the Solemnity of the Most Holy Trinity. The text approved in Rome had a very important modification: the promise of special obedience to the Holy Father, without them having expressly requested it, now appeared as a vow. It was a gift of God's Providence.

Madre Félix could not contain her joy. She could not keep her joy and gratitude for the Lord to herself. When Madre Vaquero, the superior of the community in Mota del Marqués, passed through Madrid shortly after the news of the approval had come, the following happened:

> Madre Félix was in bed, and she picked up the commentary on the readings and said: "Look at the coincidence of the reading on the day we got our approval." With tenderness and with the spiritual

> joy with which she did all these things, she began to read the passage from 2 Samuel 7:18–19, 24–29. "King David went in and sat in the Lord's presence and said, 'Who am I, Lord God, and what is my house, that you should have brought me so far?' " At the end of that paragraph, she looked up and, between joyful and excited, turning and looking at me, continued: "And yet even this is too little in your sight, Lord God! For you have made a promise regarding your servant's house reaching into the future, and giving guidance to the people, Lord God!" She read the whole reading, and when she came to verse twenty-eight, with a strength that I cannot forget, she raised her voice, saying, "Since ... your words are truth and you have made this generous promise to your servant, do, then, bless the house of your servant, that it may be in your presence forever—since you, Lord God, have promised, and by your blessing the house of your servant shall be blessed forever." By the end we both had tears in our eyes, and she said: "Do you see the coincidence?" She repeated it to me several times, and I perceived the impression it had made on her and the delicate gratitude she had to God for this token of affection for the Company, her house.[115]

In December, taking advantage of a pilgrimage led by Cardinal Suquía, Madre Félix traveled to Rome with Madre Aige and Madre Amelia Lora-Tamayo to personally thank the Holy Father for the grace of pontifical approval. After the general audience, in a private room, they were able to greet him. Madre Aige's preparations were useless; as expected, her nerves made her speechless. Then Madre Félix came to her aid and, in a gush of veneration and affection for the pope, she eloquently expressed to him the gratitude of the whole Company. The cardinal, amused, could not believe his eyes. A few minutes earlier, Madre Félix had assured him that, with so much emotion, she would not be able to say anything.

She had already been following the Holy Father's every step with all her interest: his travels, his intentions, his Magisterium above all. After

[115] Testimony of M. María Cruz Vaquero, May 29, 1986 (AGCS M 503.01,014).

receiving pontifical status as a community, her esteem for everything that had to do with the pope grew even more. She read *L'Osservatore Romano* regularly and encouraged the other sisters to read it. She studied the pontifical documents in depth, took them to prayer, commissioned several copies for the community and sometimes even one for each sister; she collected the commemorative medals for each year of the pontificate, and enjoyed inventing new ways of placing them when they no longer fit in the display case; she asked for special prayers for the pope's most important trips; and she sent a generous donation to the Holy Father every year and dreamed again of founding a house in Rome so that devotion, obedience, and spiritual closeness could grow even more, reinforced by physical proximity.

Although she perceived herself as old and tired — she was almost eighty years old — nothing dampened her enthusiasm for serving the pope. In August she wrote:

> I am coming to the end of my days. Standing here, without merit, without fruit, poor, and useless. But You know that I love You, that I have loved You since You made Yourself known. Do not give me a denarius at the end of my mortal life. Give me Your love, and let me be with You for all eternity. I would like to bring many souls to You, I would like to serve my Church, I would like to obey Your Vicar, the Holy Father. I don't want anything, only what You want from me and from every soul.[116]

And in October of the following year, in view of the ecclesial events, she wrote:

> I have prayed for the Synod of Bishops. I have prayed for the Holy Father, my dear John Paul II, and Cardinal Suquía. Holy Mother Catholic Church, my Church! My Church is born of the divine Heart of Jesus Christ, my Lord and my All: she is born in Your Heart and remains in Your Heart; she springs from Your Heart and

[116] Personal Journal, August 26, 1985–January 10, 1998 (AGCS M 202.36,003).

> lives from You. My Holy Mother Church lives in You, she is Your Mystical Body. How much I love You and Your holy, beautiful spouse, my Church! Mother of the Church, Mater Salvatoris, place me and keep me in the living stream of the Church of Your Son, my Lord and my All.[117]

A New Stage

In 1987, Madre Aige's cancer returned. A malignant tumor that spread to her lungs began to seriously threaten her health. On March 13, 1988, as the disease was gaining ground and her strength was decreasing, Madre Aige presented to the Council her decision to resign from the post of superior general.

The consultors, seeing that there was barely a year and a half left before the next Chapter and that the vicar could take over her roles until then, considered it unnecessary to take this measure. However, Madre Félix, who had recently had a second operation on the lipoma in her leg, did not have the slightest intention of taking over. On the contrary, she pointed out her own inability and her intention to resign. Both had to be convinced that it was best for them to continue to serve the Company as they had until that point.

Madre Aige agreed, but Madre Félix was not convinced about her part. She asked the consultors to consider it again and postpone their response a little. At the next Council meeting, in April of the same year, they rejected her resignation again. Then Madre Félix, convinced that she was unable to carry out her duties but overcome by charity, "seeing the occupations of the other consultors and the difficulty of replacing them due to lack of personnel, and considering that there is only one year left until the next Ordinary Chapter," replied that she agreed to continue in the position of vicar, relying on the collaboration of the Council.

Her acceptance was providential because within a year — on January 26th — Madre Aige would pass away. During her long and painful illness, Madre Félix went out of her way to take care of her. She accompanied her to practically all her tests and hospitalizations and tried to alleviate the heat of summer by taking her to Mota del Marqués to rest. She made sure they had

[117] Ibid.

everything at home to deal with chemotherapy as best as possible, she increased her turns sitting by her sickbed, and so on. Her respect and gratitude for the superior general was joined by a profound spiritual friendship. She felt as if she was losing half of herself. She could never forget all they had enjoyed, suffered, and worked on together. Madre Aige had been her first companion and faithful collaborator in the founding and development of the Company of the Savior. By temperament and by Providence, her whole life had been lived somewhat in her shadow, and Madre Félix had made a serious effort these last few years to let her go ahead of her. Now she was really ahead of her. A few weeks before she died, lying in bed and seeing Madre Félix kneeling beside her, Madre Aige told her through gestures: "I ... first ... to Heaven." And she was right.

According to the Constitutions, as vicar general, Madre Félix was again at the head of the Company. It was up to her to announce and convoke the General Chapter. She wanted to convoke it as soon as possible, but even though she tried to set the dates in the middle of the school year, she did not manage to convene it any sooner, and had to set it for July 23rd.

School vacation finally arrived. One by one, vividly moved by the transcendence of the moment they were experiencing, the Chapter participants arrived in Madrid. Madre Félix received them all with immense affection and with fear and trembling because she sensed that they could choose her as superior general. That fear was justified. They did, in fact, choose her in the initial vote. But in her usual personal prayer time she had already talked to God about it. As soon as the first scrutiny was over, before the expectant eyes of her sisters, she said: "For reasons of age and health I cannot accept the position." Despite the insistence of the vicar for religious sisters, Fr. Luis José Alonso, who was presiding at the Chapter, Madre Félix maintained her stance about resigning and asked the Chapter to vote in favor of another sister. Madre Amelia Lora-Tamayo, who had been the general secretary until that point, was elected. Madre Félix accepted the result of the election with much devotion and joy. What an impression it made on everyone, especially for the young superior general, to see their foundress kneeling to kiss her hand!

However, to Madre Félix it seemed small compared to having avoided being appointed as superior general. She wanted to definitively close the door to her election for governance and proposed that the Chapter set age limits: age seventy to be superior general and age seventy-five for the consultors. She was eighty-two. Her proposal was not approved, and she had to accept her election as vicar general and the subsequent appointment of novice mistress as a service to God, the Church, and the Company. However, she only accepted to be a novice mistress and superior of the house of formation on the express condition that it be for a short time. In fact, within a few months, she reflected in her spiritual notes whether she was going to have to insist on resigning. But she must have remembered her dear Fr. Mazón and his saying, "Stop making such a spectacle of yourself," and she concluded: "I will not resign. I will express what I consider to be an impediment. Voluntary resignation is comfort and vanity. To accept being dismissed is the right and holy thing and is appropriate in religious life." Accept the dismissal. She was really expecting it. She would never have imagined that this "transitional appointment" was going to last almost a decade.

Chapter 12

Nunc Dimittis
1989–2001

"I Want to Love You and Nothing More"

In May of 1942, shortly after taking her vow of perfection, María Félix had written: "I want to love You and nothing more" Now she was getting closer and closer to living it. In recent years, her life could be summed up by St. Paul's exhortation in Colossians 3:1–3: "If then you were raised with Christ, seek what is above, where Christ is seated at the right hand of God. Think of what is above, not of what is on earth. For you have died, and your life is hidden with Christ in God." It was one of her favorite passages. It seemed to her to be a perfect synthesis of a life consecrated to God. She had mentioned it four times in the Constitutions: to seek together, in community, the greater glory of God, "hidden in Him with Christ, following the example of the Blessed Virgin"; to eagerly foster in all things that hidden life with Christ in God, which "both excites and energizes that love of one's neighbor that contributes to the salvation of the world and the building up of the Church"; to help aspirants to religious life, whatever their vocation, through the "testimony of a humble life hidden in Christ"; to form young religious women in something that is essential to the Ignatian vocation: "In seeking and encountering God in oneself and in all things and in learning to live the hidden life with Christ in God."[118] And, since she wanted to convey that, she had to experience it firsthand.

[118] Constitutions of the Company of the Savior (2000), nos. 33.2, 52, 81, 117.2 (AGCS F 204.02.A,006).

While with Madre Aige she had endeavored not to overshadow the superior general, Madre Félix's collaboration with Madre Lora-Tamayo was even more discreet and decisive. She had truly resigned, without taking away anything from her availability. The door to her office was always open to anyone from the most recent postulant to the superior general, for any matter whatsoever. In the meantime, she would help in whatever way they asked her, no less, no more. Her external occupations in these years were extremely simple. Of course, as vicar, she advised the superior general in the matters of the Company, and as a novice mistress, she continued to form the young women who joined the congregation. She also helped with the accounts, with the supervision of the reforms and works of the houses and schools, and so on. But, above all, she was the soul of the Company, as she had always been. She was and she knew it, even though she did not want to recognize it herself.

During recreation, the novices and junior sisters would trick her into telling them "things of the early days of the Company." They would not ask her specifically about her own vocation or her younger years, so that Madre Félix would not realize that they were asking about her. If she realized it, she would immediately cut the conversation short, and they were left without any stories. But they would not stop trying. That is why, on one occasion, Madre Lora entered Madre Félix's office and found her tearing up papers and notebooks. She asked, "Madre, what are you doing?" "All this has to disappear," came her reply. "They are God's mercies and my weaknesses." Madre Lora said, "Madre, how about if we keep it in a cabinet and forget all about it? But tearing it up isn't right." "Well, do as you wish," she answered her in tears. "You keep it." And there, on a shelf, was the autobiography, like a hidden treasure, for whenever its time came.

For her part, Madre Félix no longer wanted notoriety, nor to completely disappear. It didn't really matter anymore. As for public recognitions, the bare minimum. In 1995, the editor of the *Dizionario degli istituti di perfezione* (Rome, 1985) was planning a new edition of the work. He wrote to the superior general, sending her a brief biography of Madre María Félix to be updated. Madre Félix's displeasure was remarkable. After a while, she sent a response that she wrote herself: "You can't publish anything about this foundress because she is still alive and we don't like for her to be talked about." What a dilemma! How were they going to send that to a publisher? But, at the same time, how could they contradict Madre Félix? In the end they sent it so as not to make her any more uncomfortable. However, to the great consolation of her daughters, the editors did not take Madre Félix's response seriously and kept the entry "Félix Torres, María" in the new dictionary.

She didn't want to be given honors as a foundress in more restricted environments, either. The students of the school in Madrid, next door to El Rosalar, were unaware that this elderly religious sister who sometimes came to participate in Mass with the students had founded the Company. When they saw her arrive, some whispered among themselves and commented quietly: "Look! The holy madre! Here comes the holy madre!" But they did not know who she was or what her name was. Not even Dr. Luis Martínez Socías, the general practitioner who treated her for the last thirty years of her life, knew she was the foundress. He would find out in the end when he read her obituary in the newspaper.

Only in community, in those last years, would she admit it with simplicity. But she would speak about it in a way that the sisters would not look at her but at Jesus Christ. For this reason, she sought to strengthen their veneration for the Holy Father, for ecclesiastical superiors, and especially for the superior general of the Company. She prepared for and followed with real enthusiasm the visits Madre Lora made to the houses. She called them and wrote to the sisters who were going to receive her ahead of time and tried to ensure that everything — both the material aspects and the openness of their hearts — was ready upon Madre Lora's arrival. To the superior of Caracas, on December 21, 1992, she wrote:

> Before leaving your house to meet her at Maiquetía Airport, you should call me to make arrangements for Madre Lora-Tamayo's stay in Maracaibo. Receive Madre Lora-Tamayo's visit as the Lord. It is a gift of faith. She is a gift from our Lord.[119]

[119] Letter to M. Margarita Ferrán, December 21, 1992 (AGCS E 26,163).

What she wanted was to find God's will, in her life and in the lives of others. Therefore, although she dreamed that many young women would embrace the charism that God had entrusted to her, she was extremely careful to seek what God wanted for each one. A young woman who in 1996 talked with Madre Félix about her vocation, and who in the end would enter a Carmelite monastery, saw firsthand how Madre Félix's priority was the divine will. This is what she wrote when she recalled it:

> It was very important for me to discover the "will of God." It was not about where I was at ease or where I felt attracted but what God's will was for me. I had the impression that for certain people, even religious sisters or priests, this seemed to be a way of not wanting to commit. There, Madre Félix helped me a lot by telling me about her experience in the beginning, when everything seemed to indicate that she should enter the Handmaids, while she believed that God was asking her for something else; and all the difficulties she had to go through until that "will of God" was fulfilled. At the same time, I saw how she valued this as the fundamental issue in the consecrated life: to be what God wants you to be; that is what would give greater glory to God, which was her life's aim.[120]

Madre Félix wrote in her personal notes about another young woman with a vocation whom she talked to in those years:

> May my Lord's will be done. Every saint, all the saints, are the work of God and glorify my God and Lord. What does it matter where? What does matter is living in the love of my Lord. Help me Lord, help Teresita to live only in Your love in order to glorify You.[121]

Seeking and finding God's will was the only important thing. Hence the preferential care she gave to spiritual things. Until the end of her days, she valued and practiced the resources of Ignatian asceticism. Year after year, she carried

[120] Letter to a Discalced Carmelite, July 30, 2006 (AGCS M 503.02,024).

[121] Personal Journal, January 10, 1998 (AGCS M 202.36,003).

out with enthusiasm and seriousness the Spiritual Exercises of St. Ignatius, and in the monthly retreats and spiritual direction she reviewed the resolutions and determinations from those days of special grace. With loving fidelity, she kept notes in her personal notebooks about the virtues she was struggling with. She would keep track of observance of the schedule, which was a constant battle for her, as well as her efforts regarding how she treated the sisters, which she always wanted to improve; the attempts she had made to refine her humility and her care for prayer, the Rosary, the examination of conscience, and other daily spiritual practices. However, since she tended by nature to disorder, she would sometimes see that she did not have enough marks on her charts. With the recognition that she was limited, she would turn to the Lord and move on.

> Disorder in my work. When the Lord looks upon the work I have done, how and when, what will He think of the "gaps in my charts"? I think He will think that my concern is foolish. He wants me to accomplish my work with love and out of love and with all perfection humanly possible to me. The important thing is that I finish the work He entrusts to me at the time He wants.[122]

In her day-to-day life and in her travels, she was accompanied by fatigue, osteoporosis, and the lipoma in her leg. She never abandoned these instruments of penance because she desired to collaborate with Christ in the work of redemption.

To Whom Much Was Forgiven

This redemptive work in which Madre Félix knew she was immersed has for us a touchstone: the testimony of forgiveness. She knew herself to be a sinner and knew herself to be forgiven. That had been a constant in her life. With the particular light that people who are close to God have, she had felt her sins and imperfections deeply and had vividly experienced the Lord's mercy. "Bathed in the blood of Christ, God looks at me with mercy, with the love of the Father," she wrote in 1992. In the pontifical constitutions, she expressed

[122] Personal Journal, July 22, 1978–November 16, 1979 (AGCS, M 202.32,001).

the desire that all the religious sisters would approach the Sacrament of Penance seeking "contact with divine mercy and encouragement to love in knowing that they are forgiven because the one who has been forgiven the most loves the most, but "the one to whom little is forgiven, loves little" (see Luke 7:47)." She had experienced this ever since her first general confession, at the age of fourteen, and she kept her gratitude alive and burning for the mercy of her Lord.

This feeling of being a forgiven sinner, which made her feel a kinship with St. Mary Magdalene, St. Dismas, St. Augustine, and so many others, was a constant in her life that was reflected even in her way of joking around in the community. To cite but one example, one day, during dinner at El Rosalar, when she saw that Madre Lora was not eating dessert, Madre Félix with a mischievous smile got close to her ear and asked her: "Is it for my sins?" She would not have been surprised if it really was.

She lived immersed in the forgiving love of God; in a living love that made her write:

> I fall and I ask forgiveness from my Lord and my sisters, and I fall again. My agitation blurs the mirror of my soul and prevents me from contemplating my Lord. I pray for forgiveness; I look at Him and the mirror is clear and in it is reflected sweetly my loving Lord, who looks at me with love and forgiveness. This is repeated throughout the day. I fall and rise up again because of the mercy of my Lord and my All. Do these unwanted, unforeseen falls weave the armor of humility I need? There is something that does me good spiritually: my Lord loves me infinitely and wants me to be His, with nothing left of mine. What is mine is weakness, poverty, impotence. What is mine disappears, absorbed by the merciful love of my God and my All. Under this impression I am new, little, loved, completely of God, very happy. If my public failings are material for my humiliation, I should understand that it is good. Trust in the infinite goodness of my God. A deep feeling of my nothingness, with joy in seeing myself in this way. A very sweet experience that my Lord makes me His, very much His. My God!

> Is it possible that from my weakness You extract so much sweetness and good?[123]

That is why Madre Félix, who understood her own weakness so well, was unable to hold a grudge or a long-lasting anger that poisons the heart. On the contrary, her eagerness to transmit God's love fully reached those who made her suffer. She needed to overcome offenses in order to restore love to those who closed themselves off from her.

In 1993, when facing a lawsuit with a neighbor who had torn down the wall separating the property, she prayed to the Lord:

> My prayer yesterday and the day before was: "You are the Truth, show the truth of the matter!" Then yesterday and today I beg my Lord to convert my neighbor at the price of losing the case we are in. You are the Truth. Am I going to invoke the Truth in exchange for a right to material things? Is it not better that this expired right is lost and that my neighbor is saved, that he be Yours? Besides, it suits me to become "small," humble; You call me to love. For love of You I give myself to You, and I renounce forever everything that is not Your will. I pray to You for my neighbor, for his lawyer, for the court that has to judge the matter of the wall. How small is everything next to Your glory, next to the salvation of a soul![124]

And when she received the news of the judgment against the Company, she was very glad. With that the Lord had given her the sign that her request had been heard.

Her capacity for forgiveness was also manifested as acceptance. Throughout the 1990s, she corresponded with Carmina, her old childhood friend and her brother Pepe's wife, who had separated from him shortly after their marriage. That separation had caused a lot of pain to the whole family and, as in so many cases, had meant a long estrangement. But it could not be left in this way. In these last ten years of her life, Madre Félix resumed the relationship.

123 Personal Journal, June 22, 1996 (AGCS M 202.39,001).
124 Personal Journal, October 2, 1993 (AGCS M 202.38,001).

She wanted to comfort Carmina in her remorse and give her the best she had: her trust in God and in His mercy. This is how the last of her affectionate letters from those years ended:

> I would like to see you and comfort you and embrace you. It will help you to find peace if you meditate on the sacred Gospels and read about the life of Christ. Count on all my affection in Jesus and Mary.[125]

That is why the phone call she received in December 2000 was such a joy for Madre Félix's heart. Carmina, encouraged by the affection Madre Félix had put in all her letters, mustered the courage to call her shortly before Christmas.

> On December 15th, overcoming my usual fear, I found myself calling her on the phone. I had not given my name to the sister who had answered the call. I heard her say: "I am María, I am María." I said: "This is Carmina." She began to cry and so did I. Then I heard her say that she loved me, that she loved me, and I remember crying and answering thank you, thank you. She had the same tone of voice and laugh as always. I told her that and she laughed. I found it funny. We agreed that we would talk again after Epiphany because I needed to send her a photo from 1929 of her father, Ramón, and some other people. She had said: "Do not mail it right now because the mail is saturated at the moment; wait until Epiphany passes." The rest you already know: she died on the 12th, but she left me with that memory, that was the best thing I could have received.[126]

Yes, Madre Félix knew how to forgive; even the people with whom she or the Company had had problems years ago. The Jesuit professor of religion whom she had had to remove from the school in Caracas came several times to visit

[125] Letter to Carmen Quintana, September 13, 1999 (AGCS E 45,087).

[126] Letter from Carmen Quintana to M. Amelia Lora-Tamayo and M. Pilar Gazo, C.S., August of 2001 (AGCS M 503.03,007).

his sister in El Rosalar. She received him several times with true friendliness. None of the young sisters who milled about the house would have perceived even the slightest tension. Quite the opposite. They perceived that a priest very dear to the Company had arrived, the brother of one of the first sisters. The same was true of the visitor of religious sisters who had once mismanaged the problems in Madrid following the Council. For years she asked him to teach theology classes for the novices, aware that the job and financial help could be good for him. As for Cardinal Tarancón, who had treated her with such indifference during their first meetings, Madre Félix helped him generously in various diocesan initiatives, involving the families of their school in Madrid in the campaign to build churches. In her decisiveness to forgive and forget, she carefully avoided telling people about the problems that the Company had dealt with and that she had suffered as a superior, as a vicar, and as a sister. Even Fr. Mendizábal did not know what happened in those years until he heard from third parties, after Madre Félix's death.

As for the sisters from whom she had suffered the most, she always had a special affection for them that was again widely reciprocated. Madre Amelia Lora-Tamayo, when she found out about the most difficult moments of Madre Félix's life, also through third parties, commented in admiration:

> It impacted me tremendously when I learned that several of the sisters for whom she had the most affection and deference and who seemed to be her "favorites" were precisely from that group that made her suffer so much.[127]

She had managed to anoint the wounds and restore unity. A couple of months before she died, she wrote to one of these sisters a very humorous letter, in which she joked about both of their aches and pains:

> Let us thank God for you and for others of us who live on this earth, that we can live with Him, with joy or pain, but always with LOVE for Him, which is projected in fraternal love for the whole world, for

[127] Testimony of M. Amelia Lora-Tamayo, 2009 (AGCS M 503.01,083).

every created thing. We can be happy in the midst of our "ouch!" With "ouch!" and without "ouch!," I love you in Jesus and Mary,

María Félix, C.S.[128]

Teacher of Love

Some of the religious sisters who lived with Madre Félix during her last years say that they would not have thought to use the word humility when referring to her. One hears "humility" and thinks of a downcast gaze; a certain timidity; or even the radiance of someone who does not focus on himself. But in Madre Félix, humility took the form of a tremendous simplicity, straightforwardness, naturalness, and closeness of heart.

Madre Félix' birthday (Mota del Marqués, 1999).

It was common for people to say that they felt loved in a special way by Madre Félix: The way she received them with a smile, how she took the hands of the person who spoke to her, as if she wanted to put the whole person inside her heart, how she listened. Everything manifested an affection greater than herself. It was that love that made her write:

[128] Letter to M. Inés Linés, November 3, 2000 (AGCS E 30, 206).

How much You love me, my Lord! How much You have loved me! Let me be the conduit of Your love toward all souls. Your invisible conduit on earth. Only You, Love and Salvation. Everything in me, for Your greater glory.[129]

Gazing on the Holy Sacrament, during the Blessing of the Chapel in the Elementary pavilion (Madrid, 1994).

[129] Personal Journal, June 6, 1999 (AGCS M 202.40,001).

She knew herself to be very much loved by the Lord, and this vivid awareness sometimes made her burst into tears when she spoke of Him. That is why it was not uncommon for her to always convey a supernatural vision of events, a lens of faith. It was from her relationship with God that she came out as divinized, luminous, and at the same time delicate and extremely close. Put simply, the Lord gave her what she had prayed for so much:

> Oh Jesus, my Christ, flood me with Your light, clarify me, purify me, cleanse me, make me totally transparent so that, filled with You, the true light of truth and love, You may show Yourself radiantly through me to souls and the darkness of their spirit may be cast out; clarified and illuminated by You, may they may become Your messengers, messengers of Your light, and through them may You illuminate other souls until Your light floods the world. Amen.[130]

The source of this luminosity was the same as always: her moments in eucharistic adoration, which moved those who found her absorbed in God in the chapel of El Rosalar, her participation in Holy Mass, her habitual awareness of the presence of God. Fr. Rafael Hernando de Larramendi, Siervo de Jesús (Servant of Jesus), often celebrated Mass in the afternoon at El Rosalar and was impressed by Madre Félix's attitude at the Holy Mass:

> At Mass, she was at Mass. She used to have a serious countenance that sometimes reflected pain, as if she was experiencing Christ's surrender from within herself. I will never forget her serious, profound, and captivated expression.[131]

The same thing was noted by Begoña de Reyes, a professor and former student of the school in Madrid:

[130] Personal Journal, November 2, 1961 (AGCS M 202.24,001).

[131] Testimony of Fr. Rafael Hernando de Larramendi, S.J., January 7, 2004 (AGCS M 503.02,007).

> I remember it as if it were yesterday. I was at a meeting at El Rosalar, and we ended with Mass. Normally when you are at Mass, you are focused on what is happening, and I try to do so, obviously. But I do not know what happened that day, for some reason during the consecration I looked over at Madre Félix. I will never forget what I saw. She had an expression as if she were in another world. She was with God; she was with Jesus at Calvary. It was evident that she was experiencing what was happening on the altar. I did not know who she was so I asked a sister as I left. She told me: "That is Madre Félix." Since then, often when I am at Mass, I think of her, and she helps me to live the celebration seriously by trying to enter into the Mystery as she did.[132]

Did this perception respond to the reality of what Madre Félix experienced? Without a doubt. In her writings during her last years, she constantly alluded to the presence of the Lord in the Eucharist, her experience of the Holy Mass, her gratitude for being able to participate in it with the sacrifice of her own life:

> Everything is wonderful in my Lord and my All. Today I felt the sanctity of the mystery of the Holy Mass. This ever-new mystery of infinite love from my Triune God, visible in my Lord and my All.[133]

And yet the impression caused by her being immersed in the liturgy was accentuated by its contrast with her usual demeanor. Fr. Rafael explained his memories of Madre Félix during Mass:

> On other occasions she was very different. She went out of her way to be hospitable, to show interest in me and my loved ones and my apostolate. She was always laughing and jovial. She looked like a novice who seems to like everything.[134]

[132] Testimony of Begoña Reyes, June 3, 2021 (AGCS M 503.03,076).

[133] Personal Journal, January 15, 1996 (AGCS M 202.39,001).

[134] Testimony of Fr. Rafael Hernando de Larramendi, S.J., January 7, 2004 (AGCS M 503.02,007).

Yes, she liked everything and enjoyed everything. She especially enjoyed giving. She needed to devote herself to hundreds of acts of service and generosity, sometimes minimal and sometimes spectacular, such as making the difficult trek up to her room to bring down cough drops to a novice who was coughing, or dreaming of a residence for the sisters' elderly parents, or giving up her medical appointments with the pulmonologist to any of her community sisters. Everything seemed small to her when it came to others.

What about her community sisters? She reserved the best part for them. She loved them with endearing love. It was so important to her that they truly loved each other! In 1999, María Ana Aizpúrua, a junior sister, asked her for permission to miss class at the university for the funeral of the father of another religious sister.

> I remember finding her in the hallway and telling her that we had been told about the funeral and asking whether we should go to it or to class. Madre Félix's first reaction was to tell us that it did not seem necessary for us to miss class, that many of our sisters were already going. At her response, tears came to my eyes, and she asked me: "Little daughter, what's wrong?" Crying, I told her something like this: "It's hard for me not to be with her in her father's death." It seemed to me that I had stuck my foot in my mouth because Madre Félix had already told us clearly what she thought we should do, but I could not help it. Much to my surprise she started to get emotional, she embraced me with love, she even started crying with me and said: "Yes, my daughter, that is charity! Of course, you will go to the funeral!"[135]

She was moved to see that her daughters really loved each other. But she was not at all naïve. She knew that natural affection must be lifted up by charity. Faithful to her conviction that holiness in community life requires 90 percent good manners and 10 percent virtue, Madre Félix exercised that virtue and those good manners for a supernatural reason: she wanted to communicate

[135] Testimony of M. Ana de Aizpúrua, September 12, 2001 (AGCS M 503.01,028).

to each of them the love of God, especially to the youngest ones. She did not want them to remain in the materiality of their activities and daily frictions but rather encouraged them to live from the depth of the gift of their vocation:

> When I speak with my young sisters, I should not present life as a repetition of events and experiences. In the human, temporal sphere, it is true. Everything passes by, as the current of a river, as the succession of time: day, night, day, night.... Yes, everything passes by, everything is old, there is no novelty. This truth is a gift from God, my Lord, and it is a glimpse of the marvelous light of your ever new, ever precious, complete TRUTH. But there is a time for everything. The young are thirsty for novelty. This thirst is given by the Lord our God, and the Lord wants those who accompany young women to show them the spring of living water that is my Christ, my God, and my All. They are thirsty, we are thirsty. They seek the Source; we seek the Source. They seek without guidance, with danger of drowning in puddles, in illusions. We look for the Source, who is always present and at the same time always hoped for. One day the Lord opened His Heart to me and I went in. I entered with human, temporal packaging, with lights, with shadows, with divine grace, with the sting of sin. I entered with faith, hope, and charity. Nothing of mine. All Yours. Nothing good of mine, in You, all-loving mercy. My God, my All, open Your Heart to my young sisters, to all the young people of the earth that they may know You, love You, and be Yours. Forgive me my blindness, and allow me to love You without measure and forever. My Mother, Most Holy Virgin, my father St. Ignatius, may I be faithful.[136]

This was what she wanted to give them, but it was her human deeds and words that she could use to transmit those riches of God.

After her sisters, those who knew Madre Félix's immense capacity to love were the priests. She had always had very special veneration and care toward

[136] Personal Journal, January 15, 1996 (AGCS M 202.39,001).

them, into which she poured all her gratitude for their sacred ministry. When she learned of someone's new assignment, she would help him with generous alms and maternal gifts; she tried to give them gifts for their ordination or first Mass; if one came to visit, she made sure they attended to him as best they could and lavished on him all the signs of attention that her natural inventiveness came up with.

With Fr. Mendizábal, her gratitude was overflowing. Every time he came to direct the monthly retreat for the sisters, Madre Félix would notice that his cassock or sweater was too worn, or that it was tight or loose, or she guessed he would be interested in something or knew something he needed, and immediately took the chance to give him a surprise. In 1996, when he was admitted to the Rúber Clinic due to a car accident, she would have liked to have given him a place to stay in El Rosalar, as after his heart surgery in 1987. Since it was not possible, this time she had to be content with visiting him frequently. Since that was not enough, she made sure that his sister, Conchita Mendizábal, ate daily at El Rosalar; she took care of finding someone to pick her up and take her back to the clinic, and she had them take the priest chestnut cake because she knew he liked it.

Her way of acting was not only an expression of a natural gratitude, to which, of course, her temperament was inclined, but of a deep vision of faith. This is how she understood the ordained priesthood:

> Our poor human understanding fails to measure in all its magnitude the great mystery of the High Priesthood of Christ in His Ministers. [...] We respect and venerate even the youngest one because he is CHRIST on earth. Neither can the priest defraud Christ, nor can the simple faithful ignore Christ in the priest. May Christ always be found in you and in your ministry, and may you always give and show Christ. We need Christ in our society; the living Christ in His Christians. We ask for Him and only Him from the priests; in the cloisters, in the cathedrals, in the factories, in the countryside, in the street. Without Christ, we perish.[137]

[137] Letter to D. Ramón Treserra Faja, January 15, 1961 (AGCS E 49,093).

Therefore, she treated God's ministers with veneration, regardless of their age or their position. Fr. Pablo Fernández-Martos, who went to celebrate Mass in El Rosalar a few days after his ordination, was impressed to see it:

> Her veneration left an impression on me because it was not affection but veneration born of faith with which she kissed my priestly hands. Outwardly, the gesture may seem like everyone else's, but a priest, during those days when everyone kisses his hands, knows how to appreciate the difference. After Mass, which she always experienced with contemplative reflection, we were in the visiting room with Madre Lora and some other sisters. I cannot remember well the topic of the conversation, but I do remember that in a few words, she again pointed out that she prayed for us, that she had a great affection for priests. I left there with great gratitude to God because to the gift of my priesthood was added the gift of a holy soul who prayed for me. I left there sure that, leaning on her prayer, I was going to be holy.[138]

That predilection extended to the aspirants to the priesthood as well. Fr. Javier Siegrist recalled:

> Someone introduced me to her saying that I was a future priest. As soon as she heard it, she held my hand tightly and with her other hand she patted mine firmly while repeating a single word: "Holy, holy, holy, holy!" She said it a few times and ended by kissing my hand. I was so shocked that I didn't know how to react, and she continued to greet other people. This image has remained deeply ingrained in my memory, as I was impressed by the composure, conviction, and urgency of her words. She implied that everything else was dispensable and that the only important thing in a priest of Jesus Christ was the holiness of his life. This was something that she radiated with her presence.[139]

[138] Testimony of D. Pablo Fernández-Martos, July of 2005 (M 503.02,018).

[139] Testimony of D. Javier Siegrist Ridruejo, Februrary 6, 2007 (AGCS M 503.02,031).

She also loved the students of their schools like a true mother. She was glad when the younger sisters had activities with them for their apostolates; she prayed and sacrificed for them. Without trying to occupy a place in their hearts, she carried them deep inside her own and wrote down on her agenda the gatherings and formation meetings that were offered to the girls. She also followed with great affection their first steps in university and professional life; she hoped that they would be apostles in their environments and, as far as possible, formators of formators.

However, her love was not restricted to a small group of people. She loved everyone. She loved through deeds, because she carried within her the Ignatian admonition that *love is shown more in deeds than in words.* To anyone who came home in May or June she offered a bouquet of roses from the rose bushes in El Rosalar; she invited the firefighters who one summer put out a fire in the neighborhood to eat at the school; she did the same with the doctors and nurses who cared for her during her last hospitalization, etc. In addition, the sisters who lived with her feared her generosity when she went out to pay for the services of some worker because it was not uncommon for her to offer a considerable amount to workers she was acquainted with when she knew they needed it. On a certain occasion when the superior general and the treasurer wanted to cut their giving a little, Madre Félix replied, in a very serious tone, that she had always been generous and never lacked anything and that she feared the day the Company ceased to be generous. Hers was a love that served, and she met the needs of her neighbors with immense creativity and great care.

The Constitutions

In 2000, Madre Félix experienced an enormous joy: that of accompanying the superior general to Rome to deliver the latest edition of the Constitutions and of receiving Communion from the hands of St. John Paul II at the closing Mass of the International Eucharistic Congress. This journey, like so many beautiful things that God granted her, was accompanied by a certain trepidation. On the eve of Madre Lora-Tamayo's journey to Rome as superior general to deliver the Constitutions, Madre Félix, with simplicity, told her that she would also like to accompany her. With immense surprise, Madre Lora told her that of course, it would be a joy to have her. She had not proposed it before only because lately Madre Félix had not been in great health and strength, and for a long time she had not accompanied her on trips to the houses. But of course, the foundress should be present for this act of such significance in the life of the Company.

Receiving communion from Pope St. John Paul II (Vatican City, 2000).

It was settled, but only for a short time. After a few hours, Madre Félix appeared again, with an apologetic tone, to ask for forgiveness. She had overreached. She didn't have to go. She should not go. It was better for her to disappear. The ensuing struggle between the two was as could be expected. In the end, she went, half reluctantly and forced by obedience, but happy deep down at the insistence of Madre Lora, who forced her to accept that caress from God of seeing the completion of her work.

Sixty years had passed since that first summary of her vocation that Fr. Sola had asked her to write during the Spiritual Exercises of 1940. She had shed so many tears over drafting the Constitutions that she would now deliver! It was the work of her lifetime, in which she had left bits of her life, and in which she had also counted on the help of venerable Jesuits: Fr. Mazón, Fr. Mendizábal, and Fr. Manuel Iglesias. But above all, on this last trip to Rome, she saw the fulfillment of that promise that the Lord had made to her when He gave her the first feeling of her vocation: "That I would also live the Rules and Constitutions of St. Ignatius in the manner of the Society of Jesus and that there would be many young women who would embrace that way of life."[140]

One by one, the different motions she had felt as divine promises had been fulfilled: that of "a Society of Jesus for women," that of their direct connection to the Holy Father, that of contempt and humiliation in order to fulfill God's will in the Company. Now, God was satisfying that desire, expressed in 1944, "to chart the path, firmly and unmistakably, of our vocation so that it never deviates from what we believe to be God's will." It seemed that she could now sing the *Nunc Dimittis*, and the sisters commented with some fear whether the same thing would happen with Madre Félix that the early Jesuits had experienced with St. Ignatius:

> We had heard other priests and I heard our Father Ignatius say that he had wished that God would grant him three blessings before he died: first, that the institute of the Society be confirmed by the Apostolic See; second, that the Spiritual Exercises should also be confirmed; and third, that he could write the Constitutions. Remembering this, and seeing that they had been achieved, I feared that he would be called from among us to a better life.[141]

Indeed, the life of Madre Félix coincided in many aspects with that of the holy founder of the Society of Jesus.

[140] Autobiographical Writings, Notebook C (AGCS M 201,003).

[141] Jerome Nadal, "Preface to the Autobiography of St. Ignatius," in *Monumenta historica Societatis Iesu: Fontes narrativi de S. Ignatio de Loyola* (Rome, 1943–65), 1:357.

Like St. Ignatius

As Fr. Mendizábal once noted:

> As a child, she imitated her earthly father and fluttered around his desk babbling: "I'm like *papá*." In religious life, she had found a new father, a guide who showed her the path of following Jesus Christ in the most loyal service to Him.[142]

In fact, Madre Félix understood that God had raised up the Company "so that its members might follow Christ by living the Gospel with the same loving conviction and apostolic effectiveness with which St. Ignatius of Loyola lived it." And she, personally, lived it in that way.

Divine Providence had allowed surprising similarities between her life and that of her holy father. She had started studying in Lleida during the four-hundredth-year anniversary of Íñigo's conversion after being wounded in Pamplona. She had begun her spiritual life through reading about the lives of the saints and, in particular, those signed by "S.J." priests. She also received her first graces of vocation as a result of some Spiritual Exercises, specifically in 1922, the year in which Pius XI named St. Ignatius the patron saint of those who make the Spiritual Exercises.

But the similarities did not end there. Her first private vow of consecration to God, on August 15, 1934, with Carmen Aige, was on the anniversary of that other vow made in Montmartre. The canonical journey of the Company of the Savior began in 1940, on the four hundredth anniversary of the approval of the Society of Jesus. Even the drafting of the Constitutions, as was the case with St. Ignatius, began the year after this event.

It was not strange that she regarded the life and works of the Society of Jesus as her first reference point. She had received from it the Ignatian formation she valued so much and the example of many of its religious priests, who had been an essential help in her own life and in the entire process of founding the Company. For years, in the absence of a legal connection with

142 Luis M. Mendizábal, S.J., "Búsqueda intrépida de la voluntad de Dios," in *Recuerdos de mi vida* (Madrid 2009), 5.

the Society of Jesus, Madre Félix looked to the Jesuit provincial as a privileged consultor since she could not consider him as a superior. Therefore, during the renewal after the Council, she had had to practice Ignatian discernment with particular intensity. She wanted to fulfill God's will for the Company above all else and not close herself to potentially positive changes, but she saw that the newly founded Company of the Savior did not require an "updating" of stagnant structures or sediments of the past. While she loved the Society of Jesus intensely, she understood then that the Company of the Savior had to be its own entity, and her determination became clearer over the years. God wanted it to be Ignatian, rooted in the Rules and Constitutions of St. Ignatius, but independent in its fidelity to the charism received.

However, beyond the external way of living in adherence to St. Ignatius, the most admirable thing was how grace led her to a spiritual identification with this saint, whom she invoked very often "as my father and heavenly patron."

For Madre Félix, the greater glory of God was central. She knew that this was the great desire that the Lord had placed in her heart, His great gift, the great grace He had granted her. It was a desire that saved her, that drove her to live toward the Lord and toward others and prevented her from retreating into herself. This zeal was what had kept her from taking that step into Protestantism in her younger years, what had moved her to undertake great works when she did not have sufficient economic resources, what had served as the driving force to persevere in the drafting of the Constitutions, what had assured her that she would find peace if the Company of the Savior were dissolved because it would be what God wanted. In this particular way she had been shaped — albeit with a chisel — by the holy indifference and rectitude of intention instilled by St. Ignatius.

The glory of God, which she identified with the fulfillment of His holy will, was indeed the compass by which she navigated. If it were not for the markedly feminine style of its expression, we would doubt whether this annotation by Madre Félix was not from St. Ignatius:

> This is the secret of my spiritual rejoicing: I have surrendered myself to the service of the greater glory of God; nothing can happen that does not result in the benefit of it.[143]

Another thing that was very characteristic of her, as well as the holy founder, was her zeal for the salvation of souls. Her educational vocation had no other origin than the desire to bring many young souls to Jesus Christ. She did whatever she could for those who were or who had been students of their schools. Around the year 2000, when she saw that the students of Venezuela emigrated with their families to Miami due to political tensions in their country, she asked the superior general to open a foundation in Florida. She wanted them to at least have, in their new life, the religious formation and maternal support of their Mater Salvatoris School. Everything seemed small to her, and yet she was not a dreamer who lived outside of reality. She knew that a foundation required thousands of concrete details that she had carefully attended to on many other occasions.

She was profoundly happy when the students of the Marian Congregation went on retreat or had Spiritual Exercises and, above all, if when they returned, she found out that some had had a true encounter with God. On those occasions, she would accompany the sisters who were going to attend the group even to the door and would counsel them to be, with great discretion, true instruments of God. She also suffered if she found out that some university student lost her fervor, distracted by plans or circumstances that did not help her. One time, when the sisters in Madrid told her something about this, she even proposed that a "pious disco" could be set up in El Rosalar, a gathering place to rest where young women could have fun with their friends because young people, she said, need to have fun. Everyone laughed out loud. They were already imagining the sisters working as disc jockeys in Madre Félix's new apostolic invention. As they were dying laughing, they tried to make her see that her idea was a little outlandish. Madre Félix suddenly became serious, and with tears in her eyes she said: "What I

[143] Autobiographical Writings, Notebook D (AGCS M 201,004).

want is to save everyone, and if what's needed is to open discos, then we should open them."

As for choosing one apostolate or another, she wanted to apply the Ignatian criterion of seeking the greater good. That is why from the beginning, she was inclined to form young people, preferably university students — or those who could eventually be university students — because of their impact in the family and social sphere.

Inside their walls, her style of governance was, like that of St. Ignatius, both gentle and demanding, attentive to the virtues and qualities of her subordinates, able to arouse generous collaboration, enthusiasm, and heroism.

> It seems to me that a superior must always be kind, meek, and humble when she counsels and when she gives orders, when she approves and when she corrects; and yet she must always rely on her fortitude to rid her community of the deceits of the enemy, to bring it to its highest perfection without faltering. That hidden strength that, with divine grace, overcomes the enemy and elevates souls, is the one that gives the superior holy authority and that deserves the heroic trust of her subjects; an authority that is loved and that makes itself feel necessary and desired, and a trust that makes us surrender ourselves effectively for what is most risky and arduous.[144]

Madre Félix must have achieved that because even the laity, who did not live with her on a daily basis, appreciated the beneficial influence she had on the community. Santiago Fusté, who began to deal with Madre Félix by giving financial advice to the Company of the Savior, soon developed a true spiritual friendship with her. He commented that it was obvious that she had for all the sisters — and even for him — an immense moral authority, circumstances not because of the office she held but because everything in her was love.

It was something similar to what the contemporaries of St. Ignatius perceived in his way of governing. Fr. González de Cámara said of him:

[144] Letter to M. Carmen Aige, December 4, 1955 (AGCS E 21,073).

> It is thought-provoking how our father uses opposite means for things that seem the same: one is treated with great harshness and another with great gentleness; and after it passes, it is always seen that this was the correct remedy, even though it was not understood beforehand. But he always leans more toward love; even more so, to the point that everything seems to be love; and in this way he is loved by everyone. There is no one who belongs to the Society who does not have great love for him and who does not think that the father loves him very much.[145]

Her style of treating people as St. Ignatius did — which was half learned, half infused directly by God — was shown through hundreds of details. At the end of her life, she experienced *contemplation to reach love* more naturally than in her youth. In all creatures she saw and loved God; as she went down to the garden and saw the light from the sunset seeping through the trees, she whispered: "What a glory of God!," and her eyes teared up. Even with regard to her health, the same thing happened to her in her old age that Pedro de Ribadeneira told us about the saint from Loyola:

> When he was sick in bed, some problem would arise that needed his courage, virtue, and prudence to be overcome; and it seemed that he would gain strength for it, and that his body obeyed his will and reason and was sound and strong enough for it. We had seen this confirmed to the point that when he was seriously ill, we used to say: "Let us pray to God that some arduous business comes up so that our father will rise from his bed and be better."[146]

But this resurgence of her strength, which her vocational sisters had experienced so many times, could not be prolonged eternally. One day, as St. Ignatius had, she would definitively surrender her life to her Creator and Lord.

[145] Benigno Hernández Montes, ed., *Recuerdos Ignacianos: Memorial de Luis Gonçalves da Câmara* (Bilbao1992), 88. Translator's version.

[146] Pedro de Ribadeneira, *Vida de San Ignacio de Loyola, fundador de la Compañía de Jesús* (Madrid 1951), 443. Translator's version.

Chapter 13

Toward the Father's House

January 12, 2001

Madre Félix was waiting for death. She loved life, but eternal life had become more and more important to her, and life down here became smaller. From time to time, she would say we'll see when the Lord remembered her; that if God took her to Heaven, she would do greater good there for the Company; that when God called her, she would be delighted, and so forth.

They were not empty words. What she carried in her heart was springing forth from her lips:

> I feel the love of my God and my Lord; I feel it in the depths of my heart, of my soul, but as if half-asleep. Wake up and leap with love! Leap, my whole being! Because I will soon wake up in Heaven, in Your Divine Heart. It is a mystery: I am a sinner, distracted, but my God, my beloved Jesus Christ, my life, the Holy Spirit: the sweet Most Holy Trinity is in me, in my spirit, my soul, and in my almost asleep heart. Asleep? Near death? In life and in death, I am passing through, at the end of my exile. Soon my soul will be freed from my body, the one that weighs it down, the one that is my cross. On the Cross, crucified with Christ. Crucified with You, my Lord, as long as You want. I want whatever You want. I love You; please forgive me my poverty. I love You in You, and I love You in my sisters, in all humanity, in Your creation. I love You in joy and pain, in the beauty of creation, of art, of science. I love You for all those who do not love

> You. I love You because You give me the love I offer You. Everything is Yours. I am all Yours, My God and my All.[147]

However, although on other occasions her health had given cause for alarm, Madre Félix's death came without warning.

In December 2000 she was fine. She participated with great interest in two meetings of the General Council and in the Christmas Eve Mass at the school; she went several times to Madrid to attend to various matters and even traveled by car to Mota del Marqués accompanying the superior general. She wanted to see the community there and give a definitive push for the construction of the cemetery. It was time for them to finish it!

The first days of January were busy as always: several local superiors, with whom she wanted to talk about the needs of their houses, were in Madrid; she received many visits and had many telephone conversations. Some of those who received a call from her in those days thought later, surprised, that maybe it was because she wanted to say goodbye.

On the 11th, the day before she died, she was talking for a while with the architect who was in charge of the construction of the cemetery in Mota del Marqués to specify the last details and speed up its completion. In the afternoon she received a visit from Santiago Fusté, with whom she spoke for a long time. She said goodbye to him around ten o'clock in the evening with an unusual gesture: "My little child," she called him, as she did with her sisters. As Jesus did with His disciples on the night of His Passion. Then, as if reflecting about it, she said: "Did you notice that? I called you my little child...." After dinner she stayed awake — as at other times when her medication kept her awake — checking their accounts until well into the night.

At around four in the morning on the 12th, while in bed, she began to choke. She did not call anyone. She did not want to disturb anyone. But one of the sisters heard her coughing and went to her room. When she saw her, she told the superior general. This time it wasn't just another asthma attack.

They called an ambulance and, as it arrived, they tried to sit her up. Seeing that she had no strength left, that she was collapsing, they told the entire

[147] Personal Journal, April 19, 2000 (AGCS M 202.40,001).

community. They all went down, although since they did not all fit in the room, some had to stay in the hallway. They also called the sisters of the school and Fr. Pablo Cervera, their chaplain.

Madre Félix looked distressed at the concern of her daughters until she heard the first words of the Hail Mary. In an instant, the expression on her face changed completely, reflecting only peace; the peace of the soul that is ready to go to the definitive encounter with her most beloved Jesus Christ. In a matter of seconds, her breathing began to become more and more subdued, as if she were fading away. The Rosary, the commendation of her soul, and the Litanies of the Saints were the last words she heard in this life.

When he arrived, Fr. Pablo Cervera gave her absolution and a papal blessing with the plenary indulgence *in articulo mortis sub conditione* (under the condition of the point of death).

Madre Félix had died at home, almost without warning, but surrounded by her daughters, just as St. Ignatius had. Through tears, but with an unexpected peace, they dressed her with the habit, the same way she had placed it upon so many others. They experienced an extraordinary serenity, as if a gift from God, and felt as if it was Madre Félix's intercession that softened the pain of that hour. Fr. Pablo immediately celebrated Mass for the eternal repose of Madre Félix and in thanksgiving for her life, "a gift to the Church for her fidelity to the mission entrusted to her."

One of the first to find out the news was Fr. Mendizábal. He arrived at about ten o'clock in the morning from his residence in Toledo and, as soon as he opened the door, he went directly to her room without saying a single word. He fell to his knees at the foot of her bed and, holding her hand, began to pray in silence before the compassionate gaze of the sisters. Afterwards, he prayed a prayer for the deceased, and at the end, he told those who were present:

"I woke up last night at four in the morning ... — the same time Madre Félix died — ..., but I didn't get the whole message. When I woke up, I only exclaimed: 'Madre Félix ... !'" And he added, "She was an exceptional woman; everything about her was exceptional, together with great simplicity. She was very prepared for death; I would like to be as prepared as she was. Now, to follow in her footsteps ...."

Then, Madre Lora-Tamayo gave him a framed picture of the Sacred Heart that Madre Félix had been saving in her desk, waiting for the opportunity to give it to him. Upon receiving it, remembering many things and looking off into the distance, the priest exclaimed: "How beautiful; to the end, to the end … I consider this death as something of mine; I loved her very much, and she also had a lot of affection for me." Madre Lora-Tamayo responded, "Affection, *Padre*? It was veneration … !" The next day, Fr. Mendizábal was heard saying that this only showed that saints make mistakes too.

The account that was written the day after her death tells us how that day was an uninterrupted coming and going of priests, former students, school teachers, workers, relatives of the sisters, young people, and children. When they each arrived in the chapel in which she had been placed, they knelt beside her spontaneously. Others moved their rosaries or medals through her hands. Three novices who were soon going to make their profession and the three postulants who were going to take the habit asked for the crucifix and the medal that they were going to receive to be placed on her body. The silence was absolute and only broken by prayers. Some prayed for her, others

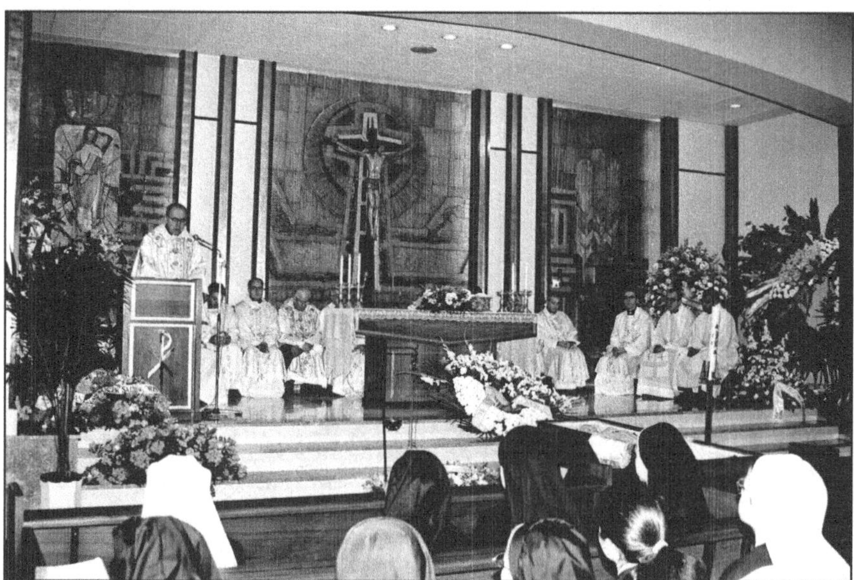

Exequy Mass at Mater Salvatoris School (Madrid, 2001).

said they entrusted themselves to her and expressed their personal conviction of her holiness. There was no shortage of acquaintances who wanted to hold vigil over Madre Félix's body until late into the night.

The next day, Fr. Jesús Higueras celebrated Mass for the community at eight in the morning. In a beautiful homily he said of Madre Félix:

> There are people who die and people who go to Heaven because the spiritual overflows the corporeal. Madre Félix is one of them. Madre Félix was a transparency of the glory of God, she was a transparency of the glory of the Holy Trinity; in her the love of the Father was reflected, although we could also say "of the Mother," because for God there is no distinction between father and mother; she reflected all the power of the Son and the love of the Holy Spirit.... Prepare yourselves for what you are going to see.... As soon as I learned about Madre Félix's death, I entrusted two very difficult cases to her: two agnostic people, who had rejected the Church for years. The insistence and concern of their relatives and acquaintances had not achieved any kind of result. Well, just yesterday, after Mass, these two people approached me and asked me to hear their confessions, after so long, because they wanted to be reconciled with the Church. We are going to see great things.[148]

Indeed, great things began to happen. At the beginning of February 2001, a few days after the archbishop of Madrid, Cardinal Antonio M. Rouco, celebrated the massive funeral in Santa María de Caná, in Pozuelo de Alarcón, the episcopal delegate for the causes of the saints called by phone, saying he wanted to visit the superior general. The reason for the unexpected meeting was a beautiful surprise: the cardinal assumed that the Company of the Savior would intend to introduce the cause for Madre Félix's canonization, and he came to offer the sisters his help and guidance.

[148] Transparency of God: Chronicle Sent from the General Secretariat to the Communities of the Company of the Savior One Month After the Death of its Foundress (AGCS M 501.01,001).

This joyful news was soon followed by more. Along with the notes of condolences, small and large stories of favors attributed to her intercession began to arrive. At first, it was mostly the sisters' relatives and acquaintances who said that they had entrusted themselves to her, but soon letters began to arrive — and they have not stopped — from unknown people from other parts of the world. As a result of the cause of canonization, the declaration of her heroic virtues, and above all the transfer of her body to the Mater Salvatoris Hermitage in Madrid, a continuous stream of people come to

Funerals in Santa María de Caná Parish Church (Madrid, 2001).

pray at her grave and entrust their intentions to her. Each one comes with his personal situation, his age, his history, and so forth, but they all express that in this small hermitage, next to the tomb of Madre Félix, they feel much closer to God and to the Virgin Mary.

Cemetery of the Company of the Savior (Mota del Marqués).

First tomb of M. María Félix in Mota del Marqués.

Many say that what attracted them to her, the reason they began to entrust themselves to her, was her kind and profound expression that gave off a feeling of friendliness from the image on the holy card. Few of them know that this photo was taken of Madre Félix during a eucharistic procession, while she looked at the Blessed Sacrament exposed in the monstrance.

Her devotees also write from different countries to report favors they received and repeat that they always feel her by their side, and that in that proximity they find comfort and relief. Somehow, they experience that God has granted her, for the good of all, what she had written to Fr. Mazón and hoped for with firm faith:

> I long for Heaven because there I will find Jesus Christ and in Him the Father and the Holy Spirit, and I will find Jesus Christ forever, and I will love Him infinitely in a way that I cannot here. I will meet the Blessed Virgin, who has stolen my heart, and my father St. Ignatius — what a pleasure it will be to meet him! And there I will no longer cause Your Reverence headaches with my mischief, and my sisters will no longer have to endure my impatience and bad temper because from all that now comes out of me here, up there the only thing that will endure is my immense love for everyone. Yes, my Heaven will be a perpetual pouring out of my heart, a constant overflowing in the Most Holy Trinity of the immense affective burden that makes my heart tremble on earth. I hope that not a single ounce of this burden will be lost there; instead I hope that it will be increased, perpetuated, and clarified into a living flame of charity.[149]

A.M.D.G.

[149] Letter to Fr. Mazón, November 1, 1960 (AGCS M 301.60,25).

Timeline

1907	August 25: Born in Albelda, Huesca, Spain.
1922	First Spiritual Exercises, in the La Enseñanza School.
	Holy Thursday: Felt the call to consecrated life.
1930	Obtained a degree in chemical sciences (Zaragoza).
1932	Opened Academia Nueva in Lleida.
	July 31: First internal feeling of her Ignatian vocation.
1934	August 15: María Félix and Carmen Aige made a private vow to spend their lives in the service of God according to the spirit of St. Ignatius of Loyola.
1936	Reunited with her family in Barcelona. During the war, risking her life, distributed Communion and helped the Jesuits in their clandestine apostolate.
1939	The Re-Vir-Cien Academy opened in Barcelona.
1940	August 15: After ten days of Spiritual Exercises, in which her vocation was strengthened, she renewed her vows together with eight other companions.
	October 11: The apostolic administrator of Barcelona granted them permission to live in community.
	Opened Bonanova Resident College.

1944 June 12: The bishop of Barcelona erected the Pious Union, Company of the Savior.

July 31: Privately made the temporary profession together with some of her first companions.

1946 Founded a resident college in Madrid.

The Bonanova Residence, in Barcelona, became the university college, with the name of Mater Salvatoris.

1948 Founded the first Mater Salvatoris School, in Lleida.

1952 The Company of the Savior was established as a religious congregation under diocesan law.

She was elected superior general, and reelected until 1971.

February 2: She made her perpetual profession.

1954 Foundation of the Mater Salvatoris School in Madrid.

Foundation of the House in Mota del Marqués, Valladolid.

1957 February 2: Made the promise of special obedience to the Supreme Pontiff.

1958 Founded the Mater Salvatoris School in Caracas (Venezuela).

1961 Founded a Company of the Savior house in Bridgeport, Connecticut, USA.

1965 Suffered a cerebral embolism. Had to learn to speak again.

1966 Founded the Mater Salvatoris School in Maracaibo (Venezuela).

1970 The Generalate moved to Aravaca, Madrid (El Rosalar). Resided there until her death.

1971 Succeeded by Madre Aige in the general government. Remained as vicar general and novice mistress. Suffered intensely due to the postconciliar response.

1975 Foundation of the Mater Salvatoris School in San Juan (Puerto Rico).

1986 May 25: The Company of the Savior was erected as an Institute of Pontifical Right.

1996 The Mater Salvatoris University residence opened in Madrid.

2000 Gave St. John Paul II the definitive version of the Constitutions in the context of the XLVII International Eucharistic Congress in Rome.

2001 January 12: Died a holy death in Madrid. First manifestations of veneration.

2009 January 24: Her cause for canonization was opened in Madrid.

2020 July 10: Pope Francis approved the declaration of her heroic virtues, with which she was proclaimed venerable.

2021 January 12: translation to the Mater Salvatoris chapel in Aravaca, Madrid.

About the Author

Mother Pilar Abraira is a religious member of the Company of the Savior, the religious institute that Mother María Félix Torres founded. After completing studies in Philosophy and ecclesiastical studies in Religion, she has taught for several years at the Mater Salvatoris Schools and collaborates as Postulator in the Cause of Canonization of the Venerable Mother María Félix. Her assignments in Barcelona, Caracas, and the Madrid-General House and Formation House, have allowed her to see first-hand not only the documents, but more importantly, the people and places that witnessed the life of Mother María Félix. Mother Pilar Abraira did not meet the foundress in life, but she is fully convinced that the Mother makes herself known in her writings.

Sophia Institute

Sophia Institute is a nonprofit institution that seeks to nurture the spiritual, moral, and cultural life of souls and to spread the gospel of Christ in conformity with the authentic teachings of the Roman Catholic Church.

Sophia Institute Press fulfills this mission by offering translations, reprints, and new publications that afford readers a rich source of the enduring wisdom of mankind.

Sophia Institute also operates the popular online resource CatholicExchange.com. *Catholic Exchange* provides world news from a Catholic perspective as well as daily devotionals and articles that will help readers to grow in holiness and live a life consistent with the teachings of the Church.

In 2013, Sophia Institute launched Sophia Institute for Teachers to renew and rebuild Catholic culture through service to Catholic education. With the goal of nurturing the spiritual, moral, and cultural life of souls, and an abiding respect for the role and work of teachers, we strive to provide materials and programs that are at once enlightening to the mind and ennobling to the heart; faithful and complete, as well as useful and practical.

Sophia Institute gratefully recognizes the Solidarity Association for preserving and encouraging the growth of our apostolate over the course of many years. Without their generous and timely support, this book would not be in your hands.

www.SophiaInstitute.com
www.CatholicExchange.com
www.SophiaTeachers.org